Ten Fingers for God

The Life and Work of Dr. Paul Brand

TEN FINGERS FOR GOD

DOROTHY CLARKE WILSON

Foreword by
PHILIP YANCEY

Paul Brand Publishing
Distributed by
Dick Sleeper Distribution
18680-B Langensand Road
Sandy, Oregon 97055-9427 USA

Paul Brand Publishing
1026 California Lane
Seattle WA 98116

ISBN 0-9643137-0-7

The author and the publisher wish to acknowledge Servant Publications and Philip Yancey
for their kind permission to use the introductory essay on Dr. Brand. From *Chosen Vessels*
copyright 1985 edited by Charles Turner. Published by Servant Publications, P. O. Box
8617, Ann Arbor MI 4817, Used with permission.

Printed in the United States of America

PAUL BRAND

by Philip Yancey

I FIRST MET Dr. Paul Brand on the grounds of the official U.S. Public Health Service leprosarium in Carville, Louisiana. To get there, I drove from New Orleans for two hours along the leveed banks of the Mississippi River, past crumbling old plantations, crawfish cafés, and gleaming new petrochemical factories. The Catholic sisters who had drained swamps and built the hospital buildings a hundred years before had deliberately located the leprosy center away from major population centers. Laid out in a sprawling, colonial style under huge oak trees, Carville resembled a movie set of a Philippine plantation.

I knew of Dr. Brand's stature in the world medical community: the offers to head up major medical centers, the distinguished lectureships in Great Britain and America, the surgical procedures named in his honor, the prestigious Albert Lasker award, his designation as Commander of the Order of the British Empire. But I waited for him in a cubbyhole of an office hardly suggestive of such renown. Stacks of medical journals, photographic slides, and unanswered correspondence covered every square inch of an ugly government-green metal desk. An antique window air conditioner throbbed at the decibel level of an unmuffled sports car. Charts of the labyrinthine government bureaucracy, not awards and citations, covered his office walls.

Finally, a slight man of less-than-average height entered the room. He had gray hair, bushy eyebrows, and a face that creased deeply when he smiled. In a British accent—a striking contrast to the bayou accents heard in hospital corridors—he apologized for the flecks of blood on his lab coat, explaining that he had just been dissecting rabbit muscles.

That first visit with Dr. Brand lasted a week. We grabbed bits of conversations between management meetings, surgeries, clinical lectures, and animal research. I accompanied him on hospital rounds, leaving a wide berth in the hallways for whirring electric wheelchairs and bicycles jerry-rigged with sidecars and extra wheels. I sat in the examination room as he studied the inflamed, ulcerated feet and hands of patients, trying to coax from them the cause of the injuries.

At night in his home, a rented wooden-frame bungalow on the grounds of the hospital, I would share an Indian-style meal with him and Mrs. Brand (also a doctor). Then Dr. Brand would prop up his bare feet (a trademark with him), and I would turn on the tape recorder for discussions that ranged from leprology and theology to world hunger and soil conservation.

True friendship is measured, over time, by its effect on us. Has the association in some way changed our essential nature? As I compare the person I was on our first meeting in 1975 with the person I am now, I realize that seismic changes have occurred within me, and that Dr. Brand has been responsible for many of those tremors.

I was a college student during the 1960s. That tumultuous era awakened me to the ugly reality of poverty in the third world and here in American ghettos. Everything in America seemed to be cracking apart in those days: the Vietnam war chiseled away at our national ideals (and later, Watergate proved the political cynics correct), revelations about pollution and the environment challenged the industrial ethic that had built our country, and the new counter-culture exposed the hollow, image-conscious materialism that permeated business and the media. The issues are now so familiar that they have become hackneyed. But to those of us who were forming a view of the world in that era, the sixties had a profound and permanent impact.

I now believe that God used Dr. Brand as one of his human agents to bring me out of that period with some stability. I was twenty-five when we first met; he was sixty. We made an odd pair, he with thinning gray hair and I with bushy hair in an Afro style. But somehow our friendship flourished. I look with deep appreciation on the privilege of learning from a great and humble man. I came to know him not through history, but as an actual living model, a man of God I could see in action—at Carville with his patients, in rural villages of India, as a husband and father, as a speaker at both medical and spiritual conferences. He, as much as anyone, has helped set my course in attitude, spirit, and ideals. In this tribute, I hope to identify partially how he has done so.

Dr. Brand achieved fame in the medical world mainly through his pioneering research on the disease of leprosy. He had grown up in southern India, a child of missionary parents, and returned in 1946 after getting an education in England. During eighteen years in India he worked as a surgeon and teacher, directed the large Christian Medical College Hospital in Vellore, and founded a leprosy hospital known as Karigiri. Then, in 1965, he moved to the United States and began research work at the Carville hospital.

I did not expect to find gratitude as the chief characteristic of a man who had spent his life among victims of leprosy. Through the medical ignorance of others, those afflicted by leprosy are often isolated and reviled. In a place such as India, they are the outcasts of society, often doubly so as members of the untouchable caste.

Leprosy disproportionately afflicts the poor. Left untreated, its victims can develop the nerve damage and ulcers that eventually lead to facial disfigurement and loss of limbs. If anyone has a right to bitterness against the way the world is run, it should be someone who works with these unfortunates. And yet the single characteristic that most impressed me about Dr. Brand was his bedrock of gratitude.

For Paul Brand, gratitude began in childhood as simple appreciation of the natural world around him. He grew up in remote hill country, with none of civilization's normal barriers against nature. Snakes lived in the dark corners of the house, and leopards stalked the forests outside, but apart from these dangers nature seemed wholly good. Until the age of nine he did his schoolwork sitting on a branch of a giant tamarind tree, dropping his completed assignments down to his mother on the ground below.

He spent his childhood in a world of tropical fruit trees and of butterflies, insects, birds, and other animals. His artistic mother tried to capture its beauty visually, sometimes calling excitedly to him to come and look at the sunset as she daubed watercolors on a canvas.

His father, a self-taught naturalist, saw nature as an awesome display of the genius of the Creator. He would lead his son to a towering four-foot termite mound and carefully expose the elaborate network of passages and their built-in cooling system, explaining the marvels of cooperative termite society. He would point to the sandy funnel of an ant lion trap, or the nest of a weaver bird, or a swarm of bees hanging from a tree.

The need for education interrupted Paul Brand's paradise, and he was sent to England at the age of nine. Five years later, as a fourteen-year-old student far from his native homeland, he received a cable that his father had died of blackwater fever. Two days after the cable, a letter from his father arrived, mailed by boat before his death. It described the hills around their home:

> God means us to delight in his world. It isn't necessary to know botany or zoology or biology in order to enjoy the manifold life of nature. Just observe. And remember. And compare. And be always looking to God with thankfulness and worship for having placed you in such a delightful corner of the universe as the planet Earth.

Jesse Brand's son kept his advice, and keeps it to this day, whether hiking on the Olympic Peninsula or following birds around the swamps of Louisiana.

Even the most ferocious animals—leopards and grizzlies and rhinoceroses—begin their lives playfully. Paul Brand, too, learned that lesson early. First in the hills of India, and later through a detailed study of the human body, he came to realize that at the heart of the natural world God could be found, and the God that he found was good.

Brand gained a sense of creatureliness, an awareness that he, too, had been willed into existence by a loving Creator and placed on a planet that, despite all its pain and fear, contained much beauty and goodness. He began to develop a consistent outlook of gratitude, undergirded by trust in the One who made the world.

My early conversations with Brand, coming as they did out of a time of personal searching, focused mainly on the dark spots and blemishes on the world. How could a truly good God allow such blemishes to exist? Dr. Brand took them on one by one. Disease? Did I know that 99 percent of all bacteria is healthful, not harmful? Planets could not produce oxygen and animals could not digest food without the assistance of bacteria. Most agents of disease, he explained, diverge from these necessary organisms as only slight mutations.

What about birth defects? He went on to describe in detail the complex chemical changes that must work right to produce one healthy child. The great wonder is not that birth defects exist but that millions more do not occur. Could a mistake-proof world have been created so that DNA spirals would never err in transmission? No scientist could envision such a system without possibility of error in our world of physical laws.

Even at its worst, he continued, our natural world shows evidence of careful design. Imagine a world without tornadoes or hurricanes—calamities that carry the damning label "acts of God." When hurricanes and monsoons do not come, the delicate balance of weather conditions gets upset, and killer droughts inevitably follow. How would you improve upon the world? he asked.

Brand's professional life has centered on perhaps the most problematic aspect of creation, the existence of pain. He emphatically insists on pain's great value, holding up as proof the terrible results of leprosy—damaged faces, blindness, and loss of fingers, toes and limbs—that nearly all occur as side-effects of painlessness. Leprosy destroys nerve endings that carry pain signals. People who do not feel pain almost inevitably damage themselves; infection sets in, and no pain signals alert them to tend to the wounded area.

"Thank God for pain!" Brand declares with the utmost sincerity. "I cannot think of a greater gift I could give my leprosy patients." (Actually, he tried to give them the protective gift, in a three-year research program to manufacture an artificial system.) Even in this instance, so commonly held up as a challenge to a loving God, he sees reason for profound gratitude.

In that spirit, Dr. Brand learned at an early age that God wanted from him gratitude and trust—gratitude for those things he could see and appreciate, and trust regarding those things he could not. To his surprise, that attitude in him deepened even as he worked among people least likely to feel gratitude: the poorest of the poor, leprosy victims in India. In many of them, he saw the transformations that the love of God can produce. The immense human problems he lived among did not dissolve, but his faith supplied a confidence and trust that enabled him to serve God with gratitude and even joy.

In his lifestyle, Dr. Brand has chosen the middle way of balancing off the material and the mystical, the prophetic and the pragmatic. At the hospital he left behind in Vellore, Brand is remembered not only for his spiritual depth and sacrificial service, but also for his practical jokes, love for marmalade and mangoes, and fast driving. As I emerged from the sixties, a decade never accused of possessing balance, I needed an example of someone who lived a well-rounded life in the midst of modern society, not off in a monastery or *ashram*. Dr. Brand had struggled with both extremes of the tensions facing modern civilization, while not giving in to either. On the one hand, he lived a "counterculture" lifestyle long before such a word entered American vocabulary. The Brand family eats simply, relying mainly on homemade breads and vegetables grown in their garden. Dr.

Brand acknowledges a few reasons for discarding clothes—unpatchable rips, for instance—but lack of stylishness is certainly not one of them. Furniture in his home and office is, to put it kindly, unpretentious.

On the other hand, he has learned to use the tools made available by modern technology. Under his leadership, a hospital in the dusty backwater town of Vellore grew into the most modern and sophisticated facility in all of southwest Asia. Later, Brand came to the Carville hospital in the United States because it offered the technological support needed to research treatment procedures that would benefit millions of leprosy patients worldwide. And when personal computers were introduced in the 1980s, he signed up with boyish enthusiasm for one of the first IBMs, to assist his research and writing.

My conversations with Dr. Brand have often strayed to the question of lifestyle, for his experiences in India and America have afforded him a unique perspective on that issue. He has lived in one of the poorest countries and in one of the richest. The enormous gap in economic development can create a moat separating the West from the rest of the world. Wealth can dull us to cries of need and justice, and too much comfort can sap the life from Christian work.

The lifelong tension over lifestyle traces back to Brand's childhood in India. After her husband's death, Paul's mother, Evelyn (Granny) Brand, took on the life of a "saint" in the traditional form. She lived on a pittance, devoting her life to reaching villagers in five mountain ranges. She cared nothing for her personal appearance, not even allowing a mirror in her house. She continued hazardous journeys on her pony even after suffering concussions and fractures from falls. Although tropical diseases ravaged her body, she gave all her energies to treating the diseases and injuries of the people around her.

Sometimes Granny Brand would embarrass Paul with an intemperate outburst; at an official function in Vellore, for example, she might ask in horror, "How could you possibly dine on such fine food when I have people back in the hills starving to death this very night!" She died at age ninety-five among the people she loved, leaving Paul an unforgettable legacy. (The book *Granny Brand* tells her full story.)

From childhood Paul learned that Christian love is best applied person-to-person. His parents traveled from village to village, teaching health, sanitation, farming, and the Christian gospel. They left behind no lasting institutions, only their permanent imprint on thousands of lives. Singlehandedly, Granny Brand rid huge areas of a guinea worm infection that had persisted for centuries. Trusting villagers followed her instructions on building stone walls around their wells; no government program could have been so effective. Yet Paul Brand himself found his most lasting successes through rigid scientific disciplines. At Vellore he fought his wife Margaret for space in the icebox, preserving cadaver hands to study by lamplight and practicing surgical techniques. For years he puzzled over the physiology of leprosy: which cells does it attack, and why?

His most important medical discovery came when he observed that the leprosy bacillus did not destroy hands and feet but only attacked nerve tissue. To prove that theory required years of painstaking research. He had to keep track of patients and their injuries, searching whether all damage could indeed be traced to abuse of tissue, rather than to the disease itself. The results of such research had a dramatic impact on the treatment of leprosy and other anesthetic diseases worldwide. Fifteen million victims of leprosy gained hope that, with proper care, they could preserve their toes and fingers and limbs. Damage was no longer inevitable.

Brand admits he would shed no tears if all advances from the industrial revolution onward suddenly disappeared—he prefers the simple village life in India, close to the outdoors. Still, unlike Gandhi, for example, he does not want to roll back modern civilization. He gratefully uses electron microscopes and thermograms and jet planes.

I sense in him a sort of "holy indifference" to many of the specifics that bother some sensitive Christians. He opposes waste in all forms. If an item is advertised as "disposable," he either refuses to buy it or else enjoys finding ways to make it last and last. He lives a remarkably disciplined and simple life. Yet, he says, "like the Apostle Paul, I have learned to be abased and to abound." To him technology, when used wisely and not destructively, offers a tool that helps advance the goals of the Kingdom.

A similar kind of balance characterizes other areas of Brand's life. His Christian faith developed through a combination of his parents' devout belief and his scientific training in medical school. The church he attended in England, a member of the "Strict and Particular Baptist" denomination, had not adequately equipped him for intellectual challenges to his faith. But his missionary parents had demonstrated love in action, and although he found no quick answers, his faith remained intact as he deferred the questions to a later date, when he could approach them with more wisdom.

Originally, Brand had planned to go to India as a missionary builder, until an unlikely series of circumstances caused by World War II landed him in medical school. He traces much of his spiritual formation to the period of time just before medical school when he signed on for a year with an austere organization called the Missionary Training Colony. The Colony sought to equip missionaries for any rigorous situation they might encounter. It assigned students to live in crude huts, each of which accommodated twelve trainees. Brand's hut had hand-hewn furniture and a tiny charcoal stove that hardly sufficed in the British winter.

The Colony used a simple method of Bible training: each group of twelve trainees would work through the Bible in two years, wrestling with the issues they found there. No classes in theology and homiletics were held—Colony directors believed the Bible alone supplied all that was needed for theology and living. At regular intervals, the trainees would go out into cities and towns to conduct services, open-air meetings, and camp programs. Prewar Britain offered unusual opportunities for confrontational evangelism: sometimes Brand would find his open-air service sandwiched in between a communist rally and a meeting of blackshirt fascists.

Each summer the Colony also sent the groups of twelve "on trek" for a period of ten straight weeks, a program designed to teach teamwork and endurance. Brand's team loaded a two-wheel cart with clothes, tents, and all their necessary belongings. The boys harnessed themselves to the cart with long tow-ropes and marched along the backroads of Britain, singing as they went. When they reached a town in the afternoon, they would check with local church authorities for permission to conduct meetings in the church or in the town square. They slept in tents or on the floors of churches. In ten weeks, Brand's team covered 600 miles along the border of England and Wales.

The Colony had one absolute rule for the trek: it must be conducted on faith. Each team began the trek with the equivalent of $100, sufficient to feed them for two or three days if no money or food came in. Otherwise, they depended entirely on what people gave to them, and were never allowed to ask for gifts or take up a collection. The trek offered a chance for a sincere experiment in faith—for most of the boys at least.

Brand and two others viewed the faith rules of the Colony with considerable skepticism. The forced dependence seemed artificial to them—after all, they had relatives at home who could bail them out if necessary, so why starve for a principle? The three formed a secret club, each hiding away a few shillings. They made plans to sneak away from the group now and then to buy ice cream or a piece of cake.

After two or three such clandestine purchases, Brand and his friends realized they were wrong. The rest of the group was maturing into a deep sense of unity and faith, and the three knew their actions could poison that unity. They stopped their secret activities.

The next weeks offered Brand an unforgettable lesson in faith. After the stores and money supplies had run out, the twelve never knew whether they would have another meal. Yet supplies showed up again and again, offered to them by villagers in astonishingly varied ways. They only missed one meal, a breakfast. Half an hour later a truck driver stopped beside them by the road and asked if they wanted some fresh melons. He had never done such a thing before.

Brand served as treasurer the last week of the trek, and after final expenses were paid, only three shillings and sixpence remained. As he went to the railroad station for final arrangements, one trunk suddenly turned up that had not been paid for. The price? Brand's jaw dropped open as the stationmaster quoted it: exactly three shillings and sixpence. The group of twelve headed back to the Colony, having never missed a meal, with no money but with a permanent lesson in faith.

The Colony taught Brand a lifelong pattern. He would use his own resources and intelligence as fully as possible but freely acknowledge dependence on God for the ultimate result. Later, in India, he had many opportunities to put faith into practice. The massive building plans at the Vellore hospital were all carried out with no sophisticated appeals for funds. Instead, the staff relied on simple prayer and belief. Brand also learned to seek wisdom from God during important research assignments, or in the midst of surgery. For him, faith became a daily habit that affected every part of his life. He no longer felt a dichotomy between the natural and spiritual realms.

Primitive living conditions were not new to Brand. As a child, he had lived in a hand-built cabin with no water or electricity in a disease-infested region known as the "Mountains of Death." He had regularly fought off bouts of malaria. In bed at night he could hear rats crawling overhead. Yet when he arrived in England for schooling, he quickly saw that his childhood had been far more adventurous and thrilling than the middle-class environment around him. Gradually he learned an important part of his life philosophy: that pleasure and pain are not opposites, but rather mutually dependent parts of the richest experiences in life. Most often, the greatest pleasures come after great sacrifice, including considerable pain. The pattern holds true for musicians, who endure tedious hours of practice in order to produce great music, and for athletes, who willingly take on habitual pain in order to condition their bodies. Pleasure derived from producing great music and achieving athletic excellence can come in no other way except through pain.

Brand studied the life of the Apostle Paul, and viewed the sufferings he endured in his attempts to preach the gospel as merely the cost required to fulfill his goals. Brand decided to stop looking at life as a polarity: avoid painful experiences, seek pleasurable ones. Rather, he would first ask, "Is this what God wants me to do?" If so, whatever came along, whether unpleasant or pleasant, provided an opportunity for him to exercise faith. He tried to think of normally unpleasant experiences as something of an adventure.

Brand's family went through trials that would horrify a modern mission executive. His first child was born while he was on wartime duty at a London hospital, fire-watching from the roof in order to dispatch emergency crews to deal with bombing victims. His second came while he was packing for India. He left his wife and children behind in England for six months while he established himself at Vellore (volatile political conditions in India delayed his wife from coming).

Missionary service in India took its own toll. As his body adjusted to a new climate, he broke out in prickly heat in the 110-degree temperatures and suffered through a series of tropical diseases. He practiced surgery under a homemade operating lamp hammered out of a sheet of aluminum.

In India, Dr. Brand insisted that each of his children (eventually six in all) be raised with the same freedom and sense of adventure he had known in childhood. Only half in jest, he calculated that it would be far better to have only four of his children live to adulthood than to have all six survive by living sheltered, overly protected lives. He encouraged them to climb, explore, and enjoy fully the adventures that India offered. As the children reached a certain age, the Brands had the wrenching experience of separation, as they sent each child off to England for high school. Somehow, the family came through beautifully, and all six children survived.

The pattern I observed in Dr. Brand and his family reinforces a trend I have noted among various Christians I have interviewed for magazines. Not everyone fits the pattern, surely. But I have encountered it often enough that I can almost lump these interview subjects into two sets: Christian entertainers and Christian servants. The Christian entertainers—musicians, actors, speakers, comedians—fill our periodicals and television shows. We fawn over them, reward them with extravagant contracts and fan mail. They have everything they want, usually, including luxurious lifestyles. Yet many whom I've interviewed express to me deep longings and self-doubts.

Dr. Brand taught me that self-denial need not be viewed as an affliction, an opportunity for martyrdom. He adamantly refuses to look back on such experiences as sacrifice; they were, rather, challenges, tests of faith. They allowed an opportunity for God to redeem a hopeless situation.

At the hospital in Vellore he encountered seemingly insurmountable problems. Power failures and equipment breakdowns spoiled many of the research projects. He had to train unskilled Indian workers on the job. Attempts to treat leprosy patients ran into brick walls of opposition—initially, no one wanted them admitted to the main hospital.

Brand's theories on treatment and rehabilitation had to overcome centuries-old biases about the disease before they gained a foothold in the world medical community. Eventually, he had to find ways to provide new skills, housing, and employment for those leprosy victims who, even upon successful treatment and release, met hostility and rejection in their home villages. Yet, through it all, God's work was accomplished. Today, the leprosy facility at Karigiri, India, flourishes as a world-recognized training center, and its influence has spread to leprosy treatment centers across the earth.

Dr. Brand expresses the guiding principle of his medical career this way: "The most precious possession any human being has is his spirit, his will to live, his sense of dignity, his personality. Once that has been lost, the opportunity for rehabilitation is lost. Though our profession may be a technical one, concerned with tendons, bones, and nerve endings, we must realize that it is the person behind them who is so important."

Although our conversations together cover a broad range of topics, inevitably they drift back to stories of individual human beings. The essentials of both his medical philosophy and theology had been worked out through constant contact with patients. Most often, these patients are the forgotten people, the poor and lonely who have been ostracized from family and village because of their illness. A medical staff can repair the marred facial features and fingers drawn into a claw-hand. They can provide that most basic human need: touch. But what can they do for the spirit of the patient, the corroded self-image?

It takes a few pennies a day to arrest leprosy's progress with sulfone drugs. But it takes thousands of dollars and the painstaking care of skilled professionals to restore to wholeness a patient in whom the disease has spread unchecked. In India, Dr. Brand began with hands, experimenting with tendon and muscle transfers until he found the very best combination to restore a full range of movement. The surgical procedures and rehabilitation stretched over months and sometimes years. He applied similar procedures to feet, correcting the deformities caused by years of walking without a sense of pain to guide the body in distributing weight and pressure.

New feet and hands gave a leprosy patient the capability to earn a living, but who would hire an employee bearing the scars of the dread disease? Brand's first patients returned to him in tears, asking that the effects of surgery be reversed so that they could get more sympathy as beggars. Then Dr. Brand and his wife saw the need to correct the cosmetic damage as well. They studied well-known techniques of surgery and modified them for the special problems of leprosy.

They learned to remake a human nose by entering it through the space between gum and upper lip (to utilize the moist lining inside) and fashioning a new nasal structure from transplanted bone. They learned to prevent blindness by restoring the possibility of blinking: the paralyzed eyelid was attached to a muscle normally used for chewing. Margaret Brand worked daily with those patients, teaching them to make a chewing motion with their jaw every thirty seconds, in order to operate their eyelids and thus prevent dehydration of the eye.

Finally, they learned to replace lost eyebrows on the faces of their patients by tunneling a piece of scalp, intact with its nerve and blood supply, under the skin of the forehead and sewing it in place above the eyes. The first patients proudly let their new eyebrows grow to absurd lengths.

All this elaborate medical care went to "nobodies"—victims of leprosy who most commonly made their living from begging. Many who arrived at the hospital barely looked human. Their shoulders slumped, they cringed when other people approached. Light had faded from their eyes. But months of compassionate treatment from the staff at Vellore could restore that light. For years people had shrunk away from them in terror; at Vellore, nurses and doctors would hold their hands and talk to them. They became human again.

In his twenty years in India, Dr. Brand operated on perhaps 3,000 hands and did thousands of other surgical procedures. He cannot possibly recall the details of each patient he contacted. But some stand out, such as John Kermagan, an irredeemable social misfit who learned of Jesus Christ through Granny Brand. It was the love shown by members of a local church that brought John back to health. He doubted whether any nonpatients would accept him, but they did, and thus helped transform his life.

Another patient named John showed up, a near-blind old man with severe damage from the disease. When he begged for surgery to free his stiff hands, Dr. Brand hesitated—many younger patients with a full life ahead of them were waiting in line for treatment. But the old man got his surgery. Although blind, he somehow learned to play the organ with insensitive fingers. He spent his last years as official organist at a mission leprosy sanatorium.

There were failures, of course, such as one man who threw himself in a well when he learned two fingers must be amputated. But over time the Brands learned that the human spirit, no matter how battered, can be reawakened and set free. Even in the most ugly, suspicious, hate-filled patients, the image of God began to shine through.

This lesson on the image of God is perhaps the greatest gift Dr. Brand has given me. The great societies of the West have been gradually moving away from an underlying belief in the value of a single human soul. We tend to view history in terms of groups of people: classes, political parties, races, sociological groupings. We apply labels to each other, explain behavior and ascribe worth on the basis of those labels. After prolonged exposure to Dr. Brand, I realized that I had been seeing large human problems in a mathematical model: percentages of Gross National Product, average annual income, mortality rate, doctors-per-thousand of population. I had been wrestling with "issues" facing "humanity." I had not, however, learned to love individuals—people created in the image of God.

I would not predict a leprosarium in India as the most likely place to learn about the infinite worth of human beings, but a visit there makes the lesson unavoidable. The love of God is not mathematical; we cannot precisely calculate the greatest possible good to be applied equally to the world's "poor and needy." We can only seek out a person, and then another, and then another, as objects for Christian love.

Gratitude. Balance. Sacrifice. The Image of God. In no way have I mastered these principles that Dr. Brand has demonstrated for me. I must remind myself of them every day. When I look outside my window in downtown Chicago I ask myself again, How can I achieve a sense of balance in a world tilting toward chaos? Why should I worry about sacrifice or self-denial when my culture offers me an easier, more pleasurable way? And how can one individual matter? I ask these questions, and perhaps I always will.

But as I ask them, I also give thanks that I have had Dr. Brand to help lead me on the way to answers. He would not want me to imply that these qualities have arisen from his own person. The same Holy Spirit that motivated his mother and father in India, and now animates him, is the One who wants to bring adventure and love of life to all who are willing to lose themselves in him. I hope that our collaboration in writing has made it possible for other persons to see those same principles and that same Spirit at work in Paul Brand.

—Philip Yancey

LEPER

His name is Sadagopan, sometimes shortened by his friends to "Sadan." He was born in South India's holy temple city of Kancheepuram, of which it has been said from ancient times, "Blessed are you, even if you happen to be a donkey, to be born in Kancheepuram." But it was not so with Sadan, for it was here that for six long years he lived as an outcast, shunned by society, by friends, even by his own relatives.

He came of a respectable, educated, and artistic family. His father was subeditor on one of the leading Tamil newpapers. His mother, aunts, and two older sisters were musicians. When his father went to work in North India, Sadan went to live with his grandmother. At an earlier age he had also lived for a time in the home of his uncle, from whom he evidently contracted leprosy.

He was eight when the patch on his back was first noticed, too young and happy to realize its significance. Though he went for treatments to the government hospital, he continued at school and enjoyed a normal and happy childhood. The disease gave him little trouble until about his fourteenth year, when his hands began to "claw"; that is, certain muscles showed increasing paralysis, so that the fingers would not bend and straighten normally, and he found it more and more difficult to hold objects. He was puzzled, too, to find that he could not feel things when he touched them, and once he discovered a raw, bleeding place on his foot from a sharp stone which had been in his sandal without his knowing it.

He had completed the sixth class in an elementary school and was hoping to enter a secondary school when the blow came. The headmaster of the new school greeted him with a frown.

"You must bring me a medical certificate of fitness," he told the boy abruptly.

Sadan's grandmother took him to the doctor who had been treating him at the government hospital. The doctor seemed angry at the request.

"And what good," he said to the woman, "do you think an education could possibly do a *leper!*" Without waiting for an answer, he turned his back and left them.

Sadan returned home . . . but it was no longer home. The house had become a prison, its four walls the shrunken confines of all his high hopes and youthful dreams. No education? No fine career? No *friends*? For wherever he ventured from the house now, he was conscious of cold stares or averted eyes, old acquaintances crossing to the other side of the street, faces of strangers filled with horror and revulsion. He left the house as infrequently as possible, usually only to go to the hospital for treatments. Even here he discovered what he had not noticed before, that he was treated not as other patients but in a place apart, shunted through as quickly as possible, handled as if he were a thing unclean.

Once on his way home from the hospital he went into a café and ordered a cup of coffee. The waiter who took his order did not return. Five minutes passed, ten, fifteen. Sensitive and quivering, he thought everyone who passed regarded him with derision and mockery. Though he wanted to run away, he pulled himself together and asked another waiter why he was not served.

"There is no coffee for you," the waiter replied.

Shattered, Sadan stumbled out of the cafe. "No coffee—not even *coffee*—for people like me! No education, no treatment, no friends, no *life! Why!*"

After this for six years he seldom left the house. It became worse than a prison—a dungeon. His mother died, her health broken in part because of her children's suffering. Since she had lived in the north so much of the time, Sadan had difficulty remembering her face. Had it not been for the devotion of his older sister, also a leprosy patient, a woman with strong will power and spiritual strength, he would have found life unbearable. When she died, not from leprosy but from tuberculosis, it was another severe blow. But by now his emotions were becoming deadened to feeling, like his hands and feet.

After six years, when he had long since ceased to be an infective case (if, indeed, he ever had been), there came a ray of hope. A Christian doctor succeeded in getting him admitted to a middle school. He was able after a long and bitter struggle to pass his middle school exams and had great hopes of becoming independent. But he should have known. No one would employ him. It was during the subsequent bleak months of unwantedness, aloneness, that another ray of hope appeared.

In Madras he met Sri T. N. Jagadisan, the secretary of the Indian leprosy relief association. His new friend, himself a sufferer from leprosy, was shocked and distressed by the condition of Sadan's hands, now not only severely clawed but with many of the fingers badly shortened, and of his feet, which for twenty years had seldom been free of ulcers.

"There's a new doctor at a place called Vellore," Jagadisan told him. "He's an English surgeon by the name of Paul Brand. He has been doing some interesting research on reconstructive surgery for hands like yours. You might go to see him."

In February, 1951, Sadan set off for Vellore with a letter to Dr. Brand from Jagadisan. The trip was not a pleasant one. Riding in the bus he was subjected to the usual cruel stares, the insults, the gestures of disgust and revulsion. But he blessed his good fortune for having been allowed to ride at all! More often than not, lepers were put off the public conveyances. When he arrived in Vellore and inquired for Dr. Brand at the Christian Medical College Hospital, he was directed to the Medical College four miles away. He tried to take a bus, but the driver noticed his hands and bandaged feet and ordered him to get off. It was a hot day. Sadan was tired, his clothes rumpled, the dust of the journey ground into his pores. By the time he reached the college grounds the discharge from his ulcerated feet, seeping through the bandages, was leaving wet marks where he walked.

Outside the entrance to the college office building he met a sweet-faced woman who, someone had told him, was Mrs. Paul Brand.

"Pardon me." He approached diffidently, careful from long experience not to step too close. "I am looking for Dr. Brand. I have a letter for him from Sri Jagadisan."

The woman did not draw away, though Sadan was sure she had noticed his hands and feet. She explained that Dr. Brand was away on a trip, but he would be back in a day or two, and if Sadan wanted to find some place to stay in Vellore and return tomorrow—

He tried not to show his overwhelming disappointment. Then, as he turned hopelessly away, she called him back. "You —you can find a place to stay, can't you?"

Turning again, he found she had moved toward him, her blue eyes looking straight into his face. And suddenly Sadan wanted to cry. For years no woman had looked at him like that, not with fear or revulsion or even pity, but with concern, as if she cared about him as another human being. And before he knew it he was telling her about the trip, the bus incident, and how impossible it would be for him to find lodging in the town. He could scarcely believe what followed. She took him home with her. She made him a comfortable bed on the verandah. She brought him food and sat and talked with him. He stayed there for three days, feeling wanted, respected, yes, even *loved* like a human being.

It was late at night when Dr. Brand returned. He had been sick. But he came to Sadan immediately, greeted him kindly, examined his hands and feet. There was a good chance, he told him, that even after all these years the ulcers might be healed because, as he believed, it was not leprosy that caused them, but walking and improper use. And the claw hands, bad though they were, could be made useful again by operations which he had tried and found successful. Sadan would be able once more to bend and straighten his fingers, to hold tools, to write, to convey food to his mouth with a normal gesture. They would start on his rehabilitation tomorrow.

"Sleep well now," the doctor said, and put his arm about the young man's shoulders.

And for the first time in years Sadan did sleep well, not only because in his hopelessness he had found hope but even more because in his friendlessness he had found friends. He had been treated like a man again.

It was over a dozen years later that I met Sadagopan, a tall, attractive, healthy looking man in the full vigor of maturity. Except for the shortening of a few fingers, his appearance was normal. His hands enjoyed a full range of motion. His feet, though encased in unusual shoes, were free from both ulcers and deformity. Beside him was his attractive wife, also an ex-patient. Their healthy young son was being reared like any other normal child. Financially independent, Sadan was supporting his family as an efficient typist and record keeper in a sanatorium in South India. Would he be willing to help me with material for my projected writing project? His eyes lighted with eagerness and gratitude. *Would* he!

This is the story of the man who helped bring new life to Sadagopan and many of his twelve million fellow-sufferers from leprosy throughout the world.

1

Looking back, Paul Brand marvels that the pattern of his life, often carelessly woven, should bear marks of such preconceived design. Certainly some of its strands show the careful intent of a Master Hand. And its warp threads, criss-crossing half a world between England and India, were strung long before his birth.

His great-grandfather, Joseph Brand, was the first to string the threads. There were conflicting stories about him. According to the one which most captured Paul's imagination he enlisted in his teens as a midshipman. En route to India he committed some misdemeanor and was put in chains. When the ship anchored off Bombay he managed to escape, slipped overboard, and swam ashore. There he got himself a job with a rich merchant, worked his way up in the business, and married the boss's daughter. Leaving his money in a Bombay bank, he returned to England with his family and a bag of jewels. The ship was lost in a storm, but both family and jewels were saved. Arriving in Southampton, Joseph put his wife and children in a cab with the bag of jewels, which the cabby proceeded to steal. The bank in Bombay failed, and the family arrived at its destination penniless.

Paul's grandfather, Henry, a boy of less than ten years, wanted to abandon his studies and help recoup the family fortunes, but Joseph refused permission. Henry, however, had inherited a share of the Brand obstinacy along with its penchant for adventure. Not wishing to be a burden, he walked out. He had heard that he had relatives in Haslemere and Cranleigh in Surrey. By walking and hitching a ride with a farmer he traveled there from Southampton and found his relatives, who were in the building and furniture business. He proved his vigor of purpose in his first assignment of sweeping up shavings, and was taken on as a carpenter's apprentice; repeating family history, he worked his way up in the trade to complete the pattern by marrying Lydia Mann, his boss's daughter.

He found that he preferred building to his father-in-law's

occupation of furniture making, so Henry Brand started his own business in Guildford, where he became literally and figuratively one of its constructive citizens. Many town structures attested his craft as a master builder. He served for a dozen years on the town council, became both alderman and mayor, and retired from public office only because his doctor told him he must relinquish either the council or his business.

It might easily have been the latter if five of his seven children had not been daughters, only two of whom ever married; or if either of his two sons had fulfilled his hopes by entering the business. But Sidney, the younger, preferred electrical engineering. And just as Henry was preparing to turn over his business to Jesse, oldest of the seven and a builder by both natural aptitude and training, Jesse heard the call of distant drums and began dreaming of the world's spiritually needy millions.

For the warp threads had been carefully strung, and the shuttle moved inexorably. This time it was not lust for adventure or empire which lured a Brand to the Orient, but a yearning for the souls of men. Jesse prepared for his chosen career by taking a year of tropical medicine at Livingstone Medical School, a small specialized institution for training young missionaries. Then on a foggy November Friday in 1907 the Brand family left Guildford for London to see Jesse off for India, where he was to serve under the auspices of the Strict Baptist Mission.

Henry returned home to Guildford to reassume the responsibilities of his business and family alone, though in time his third daughter Daisy became his very efficient secretary. If he felt twinges of regret over the apparent loss of his brilliant young son he gave no sign. Besides, it was he who had helped kindle the vision of the needy millions and set the distant drums beating. For Henry Brand was a pious man. Though he dealt for six days a week with wood and stone and mortar and cold figures, on the seventh, unlike his maker, he took no rest. Sunday after Sunday he went out preaching in tiny Baptist churches all over Surrey, at his own expense.

If there was regret, perhaps a letter he received twelve years later and carefully treasured may have brought some compensation.

"My dearest father," wrote Jesse from a lonely mission outpost on an Indian mountain top, "I feel I ought to tell you how much I appreciate your having given me up for mission work in India. If I had kept on in the business, your life during the past ten years would have been much easier. I was just taking over from you the 'coolie' work, as we call it here, when the call came to India, and you had to put your shoulder to the wheel again. You did it without a complaint and have borne the burden ever since, and all through the trying war years especially, so that all the sacrifice of my coming here has fallen on you and mother."

Jesse Brand arrived in Madras just before Christmas, 1907. Equipped with vigor, intense zeal, his year's study in tropical medicine, twenty-two years of strict upbringing, and a handsome black mustache, the young missionary plunged into his first year's task of learning the Tamil language. By his second Christmas he was in Sendamangalam, a new mission station one hundred and fifty miles southwest of Madras.

Jesse was a pioneer spirit, and even this outpost of teeming human need and challenge failed to satisfy him. Constantly he lifted his eyes to the nearby mountains rising with sheer abruptness from the plain. Kolli Malai, they were called, Mountains of Death, shunned like the plague by plainsmen because a single night spent there, it was said, would bring on deadly malarial fever. But what of the twenty thousand people who were supposed to live above those dense forests and steep clouded slopes? Months passed, and they remained shrouded in mystery.

Until one day an old and disease-stricken man appeared at the door of the mission house.

"Where did you come from?" asked Jesse, finding the man's dress and appearance unfamiliar.

"Hills," the man replied.

The young missionary's eyes kindled. "Is there no one up there to help you?"

"No one."

After that Jesse knew no rest. "We must go up," he urged Morling, the senior missionary in the station.

They went, starting at three o'clock one morning, traveling by bullock cart to the foot of the hills, then placing their baggage on the heads of coolies and crawling, Indian file, up a steep path through tangled forest and along stony slopes. After traveling five miles they came to a green undulating tableland, with wooded hills, winding valleys, and here and there a village of brown conical thatched huts. All along the way people fled from them in terror, until from one village Jesse's patient emerged and, face alight with recognition, ran toward him crying, "It's the doctor!" Then all gathered around, welcoming the strangers as friends. For a fortnight the missionaries stayed among the hill people, lodging in grain huts and cow sheds, trying to persuade the Tamil-speaking villagers that there was a more loving God than their *swamis* who lived in crude temples and piles of stones. Many seemed to listen eagerly.

After that visit Jesse was never again content with working on the plains. On his furlough in England in 1911 he tried to arouse interest in a hill mission. When he returned, and another missionary, Mr. Booth, went on furlough, Jesse begrudged the time he must spend in Madras taking Mr. Booth's place. But there were compensations. For in Madras he found an enthusiastic listener to his plans.

She was not a complete stranger. He had met Miss Evelyn Constance Harris in England, where her father, a Strict Baptist, had made a practice of bringing home for dinner any returned or prospective missionary who visited his church in St. John's Wood. Now here she was in Madras, a new missionary with a year of medical training to fit her for simple dispensary work—yes, and apparently a strong mind of her own, for Jesse could not imagine the jealously paternal Mr. Harris willingly permitting one of his nine sheltered daughters to battle the rigors of India alone. They had more in common than a smattering of medical knowledge and a zeal for healing, even than a passion for evangelizing India's millions. Jesse could tell by the way her eyes flared when he talked of the Mountains of Death with their lonely paths and isolated villages.

The wheels of administration at last began to turn, and Jesse was appointed to a mission field where no wheel of any kind had ever been seen or heard. He built his house in sections down on the plains, and it was carried up on the heads of coolies. He had to do the major assembling with his own hands, for most of his helpers were so frightened by the hill fever that they ran back to the plains before night fell.

In August, 1913, Jesse Mann Brand and Evelyn Constance Harris were married in Sendamangalam. It was a real *tamasha*, a festive occasion, for Jesse had endeared himself to many by his tireless and fearless service, especially during recent epidemics of bubonic plague and cholera. The couple were so weighted with garlands that more than once they had to take them all off and start over again. After a late wedding breakfast including a cake served by the Morlings, the bride and groom, still in their wedding clothes, set off for their new home in the mountains. The first five miles to the foot of the hills they rode in a *jutka*, a small reed-canopied wagon drawn by a pony.

"I've hired two *dholis*," Jesse told his bride with satisfaction, "so we'll have a real wedding procession."

The *dholis* were there, two rough hammocks of canvas fastened in a rectangle of bamboo poles lashed together with rope. But no coolies to carry them! The men hired, it developed, had all run away to hunt a pig. Leaving his bride to guard the baggage, Jesse ran in one direction, his Indian companion in another, to find coolies. They were able to find only four in addition to those needed for the baggage.

It was nearing four o'clock when they were ready to start. Monsoon clouds were gathering, thunder rumbling. Jesse looked anxiously at his bride. He had made all his arrangements so carefully, had wanted everything just right!

"We could still go back and start up tomorrow."

But the young bride stoutly refused. The *dholi* was placed flat on the ground, and she sat on it, feet firm against the front crosspiece of bamboo, white wedding dress tenting her upraised knees. Grunting, the coolies lifted the unwieldy frame, fitted their shoulders into the angles of the poles, and jogged away, anxious to get as far as possible up the steep path before dark, anticipating also the coolness of the higher elevations. Their smooth brown bodies, clad only in loin cloths, were soon glistening with sweat. Tensed by the unaccustomed rolling motion, hands clutching the bamboo sides for security, the bride felt her white dress wilting, the neatly parted hair under its confining ribbon becoming more and more stringy and sodden. It was a relief to feel the first gentle drops of rain against her hot arms and cheeks.

"We're climbing fast now," Jesse assured her. "You'll soon find it more comfortable."

Comfortable? She clutched the poles harder as the coolies started up a rocky slope, twisting and grinding her between them as they tried to walk tandem on the narrow path; relaxed with relief at the top, then stared aghast at an equally steep path leading down on the other side.

"Isn't it wonderful, darling?" exclaimed the exuberant Jesse, breathing deeply of the rapidly clarifying mountain air.

"Wonderful," she echoed faintly.

Trying hard to relax, she yielded herself to the proven skill of the coolies, tilting forward or backward or to the side with instinctive counter-balance, even becoming indifferent to the thorns clutching at her dress. After all, what possible use for a white wedding dress on the top of a mountain?

Then the heavens opened in a drenching deluge. The *dholi*, laced with stout canvas, became a tub, the torn wedding dress a sodden tangle.

"Are you all right?" Jesse asked anxiously.

"Fine," she replied. "I was needing a bath."

When the rain showed no sign of abating, she left the *dholi* and walked along the path beside Jesse, his hand guiding her firmly over the ups and downs of the narrow path. Sometimes the long rank grass tried to tangle her feet. Thorns pulled at her skirt. The low branches of overhanging trees reached down clammy hands, slapping her cheeks and blinding her eyes. But she pushed on. It was dark long before they reached their destination.

Finally the ups and downs leveled off. There was a smell of green grass and cultivated earth and—could it be fruit blossoms? When she put her foot down, it sank deep into mud and water.

"Almost there," Jesse said. "Here we are at the rice fields."

The caravan stopped, and he shouted. Presently a small light came wavering along a hillside, and after a long time a man appeared with a torch. With her new husband firmly holding her arm, Evelyn Brand followed the thin trickle of light, sloshing at every step. Trying to keep the white wedding dress above the mud, she could feel that it was torn to ribbons. Shivering, wet to the skin, she moved toward the dark rectangle of a doorway.

"Life is not going to be easy," she thought with candid appraisal. "It's good all this happened. I may as well know it now."

But she had not come here for an easy time. She had come for love of God, and of these hill people, and of the man whose strong arms were now lifting her and carrying her across the threshold.

In July of 1914 their first child was born. They named him Paul Wilson Brand.

2

One of the boy's earliest memories was of being left alone with his baby sister Connie on a night when his mother had been called out to tend someone who was sick. He may have been four or five at the time, Connie two years younger. There were only the three of them in the house, for Father was away on one of his frequent camping trips at an outlying mission station.

"You won't really be alone," Mother explained, busily packing medical supplies in her sturdy knitted shoulder bag. "God will be here taking care of you. But he needs you to help him take care of your little sister. I'm sorry, but I have to go. You understand, darling?"

The child nodded. Even at that age he had learned that he and his family were here on the mountain for only one purpose, to help the people who lived in the villages hidden within the surrounding hills. Nothing else, certainly not a small boy's fear of being left alone, was of any real importance.

He stood at the bedroom window watching the two lights bob away along the winding path, the steady glimmer of his mother's lantern illuminating her long white dress, the wavering trail of the firebrand held aloft by the villager, his thin body, naked except for a dingy breech-clout, as black as the night which soon enveloped them both.

The night seemed alive with shapes. That shadow slinking across the stone verandah—could it be the terrible tree dog that was supposed to live in the solitary tree on a neighboring slope? Or a cheetah, like the one which had carried away two of their little buffalo calves? Or even something worse? Shivering, the boy crept back through the lamplit room and into bed, tucking the mosquito netting tightly under his mattress, eyes and ears alert for the zooming speck which, he well knew, could be deadly. He had crawled into that same bed often enough with flesh burning or teeth chattering and waited in agony for the quinine to take effect and the attack of malaria to pass. For in spite of Father's and Mother's vigilance—scrubbing, spraying, even putting the children under the nets at sunset before the deadliest mosquitoes were on the rampage —the curse of these Mountains of Death had visited them all.

The world became filled now with sounds as well as shadows. Rats scuttled in the loft overhead. The pad-pad of feet—a bear, a panther?—seemed to pound in his ears. Then, for it was monsoon season, the rain came, shutting out all other sounds, pounding on the iron roofing and on the stone verandah. He lay and listened to it, wondering how Connie could possibly sleep quietly and if the night would ever end . . . and awoke to find the sun shining, mother singing in the next room, and his world again a happy, friendly place.

To make it complete, Father returned from camping. Hearing the beat of horses' hoofs, the monotonous chanting of the coolies carrying the baggage, the children ran down the path, as always, to meet him, and long before they reached him he was off his horse and holding out his arms.

"Ho, there, my darlings! What's this? Don't tell me you've grown all this much in the five days I've been away! You'll soon be as tall as I am."

Never! thought Paul, hurling himself inside the long arms, inhaling the familiar smell of wood smoke and jungle grass and male vigor until his throat hurt. Never in all this world could he be as tall or as strong or as all-wise as Father! No more than he could be like God!

"What do you suppose I saw as I rode up the path today? A whole long train of foraging ants, marching in twos and threes, and sometimes in single file. And the strangest thing was that a very big light-colored fly was standing solemnly at the very edge of the line of ants, just like a general reviewing his soldiers. So I said to myself, 'I'll just stay and watch to see if I can find out why the big fly waits there.' "

"And did you?" demanded Paul.

"I sure enough did."

It was always this way when Father returned. They would dance along at his side, each holding one of his big hands, and listen to his enthralling adventures, usually about some insect or bird or animal.

"Yes, sir. I went on watching until thousands of ants must have gone past. Suddenly the fly turned quickly round and gave a big spring to where an ant had wandered a little way from the main column, and came down with its feet bang onto the head of the poor ant. Now that ant was carrying a nice leg of mutton, or rather, a nice leg of grasshopper home for dinner. When the fly came down with that awful thump on its head it was terribly scared and put down the leg of grasshopper and opened its strong jaws to bite the fly. But already the fly had picked up the nice leg and flown off laughing to a quiet spot about two feet away . . ."

By this time it would be Mother's turn, both for the smothering arms and the story, only now the questions and answers would be of patients treated, schools started, the possibility of converts, the elimination of guinea worm from village wells. And the children would be off again hunting for adventure.

Their world seemed made for children. The hills with their gentle slopes were for running and rolling, the mountain air for inflating young lungs near to bursting, the high spreading jackfruits and sprawling bamboos for shinnying and climbing. As his legs stretched longer, the boy climbed higher and higher, and Connie, though as chubby as he was lean, was always close behind. Mother was inclined to frown on the climbing, though her objection to the lofty jackfruits was not wholly on account of danger. They ejected a sticky and copious sap which played havoc with legs, arms, and clothes.

"Nonsense!" pooh-poohed Father. "Be thankful they can run wild, like the young animals they are. Better a broken bone than a pair of cowards or weaklings!"

Father got his wish. His children were not cowards. True, they developed a healthy fear of some hazards, like the snakes which lived in a crack between the earthen stove and the wall in a corner of the bathroom. Fortunately they were not cobras, though the family never got close enough to find out if they were poisonous. However, they always treated them with as much respect as if they were. There were frogs which also frequented the bathroom, and once one of the snakes swallowed a frog and found it impossible to escape down his hole. Some of the men rushed in to kill it, but the problem solved itself when the frog jumped out of the snake's mouth. Too, there were huge scorpions inhabiting the rocks down behind the trees, and, after experiencing a painful sting from a small one, Paul learned to eye the ground warily before stepping with his bare feet.

Thanks to his parents' teachings, except for that first night when he was left alone he never was infected with the superstitious fears of his small Indian playmates. They feared everything: queer shaped rocks, dead trees, darkness, caves, the tiny little shrines which were nothing but a few iron spikes stuck in the ground or a lump of stone covered with red stain and oil.

"Silly little things!" Paul scoffed.

Once, finding such a shrine in the woods, he pulled up some of the stakes and began playing with them.

"No," reprimanded Father sternly. "Put them back. To our friends over there in the village they are sacred. Never treat another's religion with disrespect."

But one fear branded itself deeply in the boy's memory. One day three men, strangers, came up the mountain. This in itself was not unusual. Strangers were always coming for Father's medical help, from villages all over the mountains, even from "downstairs" on the plains. But these strangers were different. There was something about them . . . not their clothes, they wore the usual breech-clout and turban, with a length of dingy blanket draped over their shoulders. Perhaps it was their skin, not a deep black or a rich brown like most people's but mottled with queer patches of white. Their hands and feet too were different. They seemed to have stumps instead of fingers, and one of them had no toes at all. There were sores on their feet. Mother took one look, and her face looked suddenly queer and a little pale.

"Run and get Father," she told Paul quickly. "Take Connie with you. And don't come back. Stay in the house."

Paul obeyed—to a point. He called Father, who, in response to the urgency in his voice came running. But when Connie, always more obedient to the letter of the law, ran into the house, he crawled on hands and knees via bushes and rocks until he reached a good vantage point for seeing and hearing.

Then he began to tremble, for Father too had that queer look on his face. He looked uncertain, as if—as if he didn't know what to do!

The three men prostrated themselves on the ground. Nothing unusual in that, Indians were always doing it, but Father didn't like it. He was no god, he said, to be worshiped. He always stooped over and lifted them immediately to their feet. But not this time. He just stood where he was.

"I'm sorry," he said. "There's not much we can do for you. But wait there, right where you are. Don't move. We'll do what we can."

The men waited, squatting in a tight circle where they had knelt. Father rushed to the dispensary and came back with a roll of bandages and a can of the salve he used when people came with cuts and bruises. And something else. Paul stared. How did Father think he could treat them wearing gloves! Mother came also with a basin of water and a cloth.

Still wearing the gloves but working with his usual thoroughness and concern, Father washed the feet of the strangers, put some of the ointment on the sores, and bandaged them. Paul watched, wondering why Father gestured him back when he tried to come closer and why he did not talk and joke as he usually did with patients. Soon Mother came with a basket of food which she set down on the ground near the strangers.

"Basket you may take and keep," she said in her imperfect Tamil, which Paul often had to correct.

He watched, more and more puzzled. Why didn't they invite the guests into the house? And why did Mother give away that perfectly good basket when they had so few? After the men had gone back down the hill, leaving the basket, the boy emerged from his hiding place and went to pick it up.

"No!" Something in Mother's voice compelled instant obedience. "Don't touch it. And don't go near that place where they sat."

The boy watched while Father took the basket and burned it, then scrubbed his hands with hot water and strong soap and changed all his clothes.

"But—why?"

"Because," Father explained, "those men were lepers."

The word sent a chill down the boy's spine. Even that night, lying in bed but unable to sleep, he still felt cold and frightened. *Lepers!* He had heard about them in Bible stories. They were something bad like sin and unclean animals and whited sepulchres. They lived in caves and tombs, and nobody dared go near them—no one, that is, except Jesus, who had healed them.

The incident was not again mentioned. It was something which had briefly entered their lives and been swiftly banished. Yet the memory persisted. After that day the children avoided the small patch of ground the way their dark-skinned playmates avoided the heaps of greasy rocks where their devil-*swamis* were supposed to live.

Like its mountain-girt hilltop, the little house seemed designed for children. Its three rooms, small and snug, were tandem, like a train of cars. You could lie on the big double bed at one end and look straight through the living-dining room into Father's study at the other end. Even their small single beds in two corners, with the huge chest between them (at least twelve feet high!) did not seem isolated. Perhaps that was why they didn't mind crawling under the nets at sunset, for when Mother was not singing or telling them Bible stories the gauze canopies could become *jutkas* or sailing ships or Arab tents or elephant howdahs.

Father was a clever builder. The house sat two feet off the ground on sturdy stone posts, which the white ants could not penetrate. And if they did manage to build their secret tunnels up beside the stone, at the top they would find inverted plates of metal, like frying pans—in fact, they *were* frying pans—which were sure deterrents. The wooden steps too were set away from the doors for the same reason. The space under the house was ideal for playing. It was almost as impenetrable to adults as was the house to white ants.

At first the roof had been of thatch like those of the round mud houses of the villagers. But because many of the patients came at night with flaming torches, holding them dangerously close to the overhanging roof, after their return from the Nilgiris the summer Paul was born, Jesse had had the thatch replaced with corrugated iron roofing.

Father's energy and ingenuity seemed inexhaustible. He was doctor, teacher, preacher, naturalist, agriculturist, industrial promoter, legal intermediary. He taught the people how to build and gave many of them employment as building after building was erected on the hilltop compound. He introduced brick making and tile making. He planted orange trees and sugar cane and helped the villagers market them; raised poultry and sheep, introduced better methods of growing the staple village crops,—rice and ragi and millet and castor oil plants and *kaveri*, a grain which looked like a human hand stretched upward with its fingers folded together. He established outposts in a half dozen centers scattered over the hills, camping out at each one in turn and setting up schools, clinics, agricultural projects, as well as ceaselessly proclaiming the good news of the Gospel. He was a fluent linguist and could speak Tamil like a native. He spent hours reading law so that he might better understand the rights of the hill people who were constantly victimized by the landowners and money lenders down on the plains. Time and again he acted as the people's champion, once even leading a delegation of four hundred hill people down to the plains and through an appeal to the British magistrate helping them win justice.

But it was as healer that he was most beloved. Wherever he went he took his bag of simple medicines and instruments, which were constantly in demand, especially his forceps for extracting teeth. Though his medical knowledge was meager and his remedies simple, to the hill people he seemed a miracle worker. His magic could banish the *naga poochie*, big round worm, and the *kirumi poochie*, small thread worm, which caused such agony in the bowels. His pills eased the tortures of malaria, prime curse of their Mountains of Death. He could wind up a yard-long guinea worm bit by bit, an inch or so each day, so it would not cause an abscess. And if they did what he told them, kept their feet out of water and cleaned up their wells, they could banish guinea worm altogether.

Once Paul was with Father when a villager came with a huge swollen leg, abscessed from a guinea worm. It was far from the dispensary. Father took the man up a grassy bank, stuck a sharp knife into the leg, and out came a whole bucketful of pus. The boy turned his back in disgust.

"Filthy ulcers, pus!" he thought. "That's what doctoring is. Pah! Horrible!"

In spite of his multiple activities Father found time for his children. He was never too busy to stimulate their curosity.

"How do you suppose those white ants build their towers? Let's watch!"

Then he would carefully break open one of the great towers,

some as high as four feet, to reveal the tunnels and runs, the beautiful intricate compartments with doors and passageways. And once they dug clear to the bottom of an ant hill, at least three feet, through combs of eggs and young ants, to find the queen.

"Look at her, see how big she is—at least two inches! She's as much bigger than an ordinary ant as an elephant is bigger than a dog."

Or the object of their nature lesson might be an ant lion, a weaver bird, a swarm of bees in a hollow tree, or a trap-door spider.

Mother was also an ingenious teacher. She even made lessons not too unbearable, and Paul, unlike Connie, was no avid student. Seated at the round table with sums to do or a composition to write, Connie would perform her work diligently while Paul sat staring through the window.

"Come," said Mother one day. "I know where you'd like to be."

After that he did his sums sitting high in a tree in the little copse at the left of the house. When he finished, he would drop them down to Mother, sitting on the ground below. If they were wrong, he had to climb down and get them, reascend, and start over again. For years this was his schoolroom.

Usually they devised their own pastimes, running as wild as their dark-skinned playmates, if not in the same state of undress. Mother insisted that they be at least partially covered, though Paul's one good outfit was kept for photographic purposes. After taking the picture with her big, bellows-like camera sent by her church back home in England, she would disappear with her developing fluids under a big red blanket while the children, forbidden to interrupt, would wait breathlessly for the finished product, which would then be sent to some mysterious relatives in far off England, all with incredibly pale skins like their own.

They seldom saw another white person. Once Mr. Morling, the missionary at Sendamangalam, came up the mountain. Seeing a figure and clothes like Father's, Connie ran to meet him, flinging her arms about his legs, then, looking up, screamed in horror. She thought Father had become a changeling!

Paul took pride in believing himself Connie's protector,

though it was often she, more amenable to rules, who kept him out of mischief. In fact, he sometimes got her into serious trouble. There was an old pram, topless, which he had been wheeled in as a baby. Marvelous, he thought, for the making of a horse and cart! After much maneuvering, he managed to tie it to the rear end of Dobbin, his father's horse. Connie, he decided, should have the honor of the first ride. He set her in the pram, and the horse obediently started. Then, feeling the pull of the cart, he took fright.

"Get out!" the boy yelled.

She did, just in time. Dobbin leaped, overturning the pram, and, wild with panic, tore around the yard. Both horse and appendage disappeared, and Paul had dire visions of their being lost forever. But the horse turned up a few hours later, pramless and, to Father's bewilderment, frothing. The pram was found later far away, a battered wreck.

More often it was Paul himself who suffered the consequences of his experiments. Once he literally hanged himself. While on a preaching tour the family was camping on a hill above a huge hollow banyan tree. The hollows made a wonderful playhouse, and the trailing tendrils of the banyan were ideal for climbing and swinging. Paul called one of his favorite tendrils his horse. To tease him, somebody tied it up out of reach, linking it with another to form a loop. But there were plenty of other tendrils. The children knotted two of them together to make a chair swing, and Paul, pumping and straining, swung himself higher and higher.

"Look at me!" he shouted to Connie far below. "I'm—"

His neck suddenly caught in the loop, which suspended him in mid-air, and with a terrific jolt he blacked out, as neatly suspended in a noose as any lynching victim. He did not even hear Connie screaming for Mother. When he awoke he was lying in bed with no worse consequences than a pain in the neck.

Holidays varied their recreation. They went to the Nilgiris once or twice, traveling across the plains in bullock carts. Fording the Cauvery River, which was wide and shallow, they would sometimes find themselves sitting in the water. The frightened horses had to strain to pull them safely through. Once they crossed the river in *coracles*, the big round tublike boats made of bamboo strips with buffalo hide stretched over them. Arrived at the hill station, they would find other missionary children to play with.

But it was their holidays at Kulivalavu, a camping spot wild and high on their own Kollis, far above the malaria, that they enjoyed most. Here their play became inspired, for they had the full benefit of Mother's creative genius. She was as adept as Father at making something out of nothing.

"Look, children! All these rocks—no, not rocks! Birds, animals, ships, trains!"

Great stones lay all around on top of the hill. With Mother's help they lifted them into standing positions. They ran around to find triangular shaped stones to place on top of the standing rocks to look like great birds' heads. Soon they had a big flock of vultures, storks, prehistoric birds like dodos, looking so real that when a little dog came up one day it rushed around barking at them furiously. They found long rectangular rocks and laid them down; then, chipping off pieces of crumbling stone to form round shapes like wheels, they made engines and carriages.

Mother taught them more than creative play on these holidays. Climbing with her to the mountain top to see the sun rise, watching her joyously splash water colors on art paper and, when that ran out, on the backs of old letters and envelopes, they discovered that food for the spirit could be as satisfying and exciting in flavor as rice and curry or even coconuts and mangoes. To Mother a sunset was a thanksgiving feast.

"Oh!" she would cry out when the gorgeous colors began to unfurl. "Look what it's doing, look what it's doing! Quick, quick!" Then she would rush to get her paints. And over and over, while her swift fingers were trying to capture the glory, she would break out in joyous gratitude, "*Stotherum! Stotherum!* Praise the Lord, praise the Lord!"

Paul was five when the big worldwide epidemic of influenza swept over the Kollis. For six years now Father and Mother had labored among the hill tribes without making a single convert. The people would accept Father's medicines, learn his skills, beg him to settle their disputes, send their children to his schools, even listen eagerly to his preaching, but when it came to breaking caste, giving up their demon-*swamis* to worship the God of love, none had been willing. The priests had seen to that, especially the *pujari*, chief priest, who lived in a village about a mile away. At first, when Father had been building his little house, this *pujari* had been his friend, letting him live for months in his shed, waiting on him, drawing water for him. But when he had found what belief in the Jesus-*swami* would do to his people, demanding their rejection of the old gods and eventually depriving him of his job, he had secretly begun to work against him.

Then came the influenza. Hundreds of people died of it. Father and Mother were away day and night visiting the villages for miles around. They made rice-water soup by the gallon, feeding it to the sufferers whose tortured bodies were shrunken from lack of fluids. *Pujari* gave no help. So frightened was he of the infection that he would not leave his home even to help in the burials. The epidemic had almost passed when the report came, "*Pujari* and his wife are both ill!"

Since Father was ill with fever, Mother went alone to minister to them. Both were dying, their young baby crying to be fed. "You—must bring up my baby," whispered *pujari*. "Please —do not give it to my people."

Mother ran home. "We're going to have another baby," she blurted, breathless with excitement.

Sick though he was, Father rose immediately and went to *pujari's* house. He returned, radiant. "I think you are going to have a new little sister," he told Paul and Connie.

At the *pujari's* request he had signed a paper promising to look after the priest's small son and adopt his baby, but on one condition. Unless the *pujari* sent the baby to him and the son came of his own volition, he could not take her. He wanted to take no chance of being accused later of taking the child against the family's wishes. Father went again to the priest's house to see if he really wished to give up his child and if he would send the baby's brother with her. Paul and Connie stood with Mother at the edge of the garden, watching, hoping, fearing. For even if the priest did not change his mind, would the boy be willing to bring his little sister, after all the stories he had been told about the foreigners?

Then they saw him coming through the gap in the hills, a tiny, forlorn figure with a small bundle in his arms. When he came closer they could see the tears running down his cheeks.

"Don't be afraid," said Mother. "We'll take good care of her. And you can come every day and watch me bathing and feeding her."

Slowly he relinquished the bundle into Mother's arms.

The baby was scarcely more than a little skeleton, racked with dysentery. They washed her, dressed her in one of Connie's baby dresses, and placed her in a little bamboo basket. It was a month before they knew she would live. They named her Ruth, and the children loved and cared for her as if she had been their own sister. Later her brother came too, becoming one of the first pupils in Father's little boarding school. They named him Aaron.

Slowly after the *pujari's* death the Christian community on the Kollis began to grow. In the camps the hill people flocked to watch the baby Ruth being bathed, fed, clothed, and tenderly nursed. A different sort of *swami* it must be, they decided, who told his *pujari* to care for a helpless little orphan instead of leaving it to die!

Paul was acutely conscious of his parents' devotion to their mission. He had shared in the family prayers each night since he could mouth the words "Mummy" and "Daddy." Weeks of his life had been spent in camps, listening to Father preach, handing out tracts and gospels, helping Mother display the big rolls of Bible pictures while she told the familiar stories. The burden of their mission in this strange land was at an early age a weight on his own small shoulders.

"We must go all over the world," he once told Connie earnestly, "in trains and motor cars and *jutkas* and bullock carts and maybe even airplanes, *all* over the world and tell people about Jesus."

"But," inquired Connie anxiously, "won't Father and Mother go too?"

Paul wasn't sure about that. One of the gnawing worries of his childhood was that some member of his family might die before the other. He had expressed the fear once to his parents. "Couldn't we possibly arrange to die all together, just fall down bang flat?" But as on the night when he had been left alone, he tried to remember that no one of them was really important, only the mission they had come to perform on these mountains.

Impossible that their beloved world could come to an end!

But it did. Paul was nearly nine when it happened. Father and Mother had been ten years on the Kollis. They had refused one furlough, unwilling to leave until they could show some fruits of their labors. Now, by 1923 there was a small group of Christians at Valavandi. An Indian teacher was in residence, together with a compounder and a doctor. A small chapel had been built. A half dozen little schools had been established, a girls' home started. Villagers were being taught carpentry and weaving. Guinea worm had been practically abolished. The work could go on without them for a year. And the children were old enough to be left to attend school in England.

It was Paul's duty to lay the mats for the Sunday service in the chapel, a long one on each side, one for the men and one for the women. He performed the task each week with a deep and meticulous devotion.

They were leaving the compound for the last time when he suddenly remembered. "But—who's going to lay the mats for the chapel?" he called out anxiously to Father.

Turning, Father smiled down into the small worried face. "Yes, yes, son, we must arrange that," he agreed reassuringly.

3

It was a new world: trains, cars, boats, food, suits, shoes. Especially shoes. Not mere temporary encumbrances, as on a trip to the mission station in Madras. Permanent, inescapable liabilities.

But the excitement compensated somewhat for the loss of freedom. Debarking at Tilbury in England, they were immediately surrounded by hordes of relatives. Imagine, all these people knowing their parents, and well enough to hug and kiss them! Impressed, bewildered, Paul and Connie drew close together, a small island of security in a chaotic sea.

For weeks names and faces swam in confusion. Brands, Harrises, aunts, uncles, cousins. The Brands weren't so hard to untangle, there weren't so many of them. But the Harrises! Paul and his cousin Peggy, born four days after him, had been the forty-ninth and fiftieth grandchildren. Mother had rushed Paul's photograph to England so that a picture gallery of all fifty could greet her parents on their golden wedding anniversary in the summer of 1914.

Fortunately they need not untangle the snarled skein all at once. A few strands disengaged themselves—a house, two aunts, one grandmother, two cousins—and began weaving the new pattern of Paul's life. The house was called Nethania, a narrow, four-storied rectangle of gray brick with white pillars and cornices, neatly compressed by high walls between two similar structures, as impeccably genteel as the London suburb of St. John's Wood which formed its environs. The name Nethania was taken from the book of Nehemiah, and it meant "Gift of God." There had always been a Nethania in the Harris family.

Aunt Eunice and Aunt Hope resembled the house, this second Nethania in which they had now lived for over thirty years: thin, high-browed, patrician in features, impressively genteel, though Aunt Eunice was more so in all respects than Aunt Hope. Neither of them had wittingly given harbor to an improper thought, much less action, in her whole life . . . with one exception. Aunt Hope loved to run up and down stairs and to whistle. Neither of these unladylike pursuits had been permitted in her childhood. Now that she was grown up she was determined to do both, and did. Tempering the more austere virtues in both sisters was an innate kindliness which transformed gentility into gentleness, what might have been affectation into warm affection.

Aunt Eunice presided over the household at Number 3 Cavendish Road, for it was the custom for the oldest unmarried daughter to stay at home and look after her parents. She was the fifth of the nine Harris daughters. Though she had been rather beautiful in her youth and had had chances to marry, she never wished to. It was her one desire to look after her parents until their death, keep the house and family accounts in the meticulous order compatible with her mathematical brain, cherish the shining mahogany furniture, the cabinets of fragile heirlooms, the priceless specimens of Martinware pottery collected by her father, in the state of perfect preservation in which they had been inherited, and, above all, expend her loving energy on her beloved church and chapel Bible class.

Into this peaceful paradise of upper-middle-class sobriety burst two young savages who had known little inhibition, had never seen a bathtub, a Brussels carpet, or a water tap, whose confining walls had been mountains, schoolrooms the treetops, playthings any object under the sun which their curious fingers could find or make. Yet graciously the aunts welcomed their young charges, Aunt Eunice with genuine, if sometimes concealed, kindliness, Aunt Hope with open arms. With unequivocal and loving acceptance they completely transformed their lives for the sake of the two young interlopers.

The first day was not auspicious. One of Paul's early discoveries was a little chair with casters. Setting Connie on it, he pushed her madly across the room with dire peril to polished furniture, treasured trinkets, and slender pedestals holding priceless pottery. Before many hours passed they were sliding down the long polished balustrade which ran, continuously curving, the full depth of the house. Starting at the top, on the third floor, they could increase momentum to a terrific speed, narrowly missing the alabaster statue standing on its pedestal at the foot. Discreetly hustled out doors, they contented themselves for awhile with sliding down the flat sides of the twelve steps leading to the front door and climbing the high iron gate which opened on the street. But these were tame sports for confirmed tree climbers. The lamp posts lining the street, however, offered temporary substitutes. Hanging from the high crosspieces upside down by their knees, they grinned engagingly into the startled faces of passersby.

Everything strange had to be observed and examined: the brass letter slot, the food lift from the basement, the clock with the angel on top blowing a trumpet, the Martinware statue of three birds whose movable heads were their covers, the huge blue jar covered all over with dragons.

"Look, look!" shouted Paul the first night from his perch on the windowsill, and all rushed to see the marvel at which he was excitedly pointing. It was a horse and cart.

The children were not willfully naughty, merely intensely curious and lively. In fact, they tried hard to please. They could not understand why anyone should object to their sitting on tin trays and sliding down the stair carpets. Silly, they thought, to care about such things as carpets and furniture! And even on their first Sunday with their father's relatives in Guildford when they preceded their horrified aunts down the aisle of the church carrying their shoes in their hands, they were merely following acceptable and devout Indian custom.

Time effected moderate adjustments, and life resolved itself into a fairly civilized routine. Paul and Connie were enrolled in Miss Chattaway's school, a small private institution dominated by its strongminded mistress. Cousins Annette and Norman, who was a year older than Paul, assisted greatly in the adjustment. Their father, Uncle Bertie, was the youngest of Mother's ten brothers and sisters. Aunt Rose, his second wife, had married him when he was a widower with seven children, one of them, Wendy, a mere baby; then proceeded in time to have six children of her own. In spite of this obvious hardihood Aunt Rose was at first reluctant to entertain the uninhibited newcomers for meals, but they were gradually integrated into proper customs.

Of course Mother's and Father's presence for the first few months also made adjustment easier, though Father was away much of the time speaking to church groups about his beloved Kollis. And the complex relationship of four females, with Mother the youngest, did not always produce unanimity in matters of conduct and discipline.

Life in Nethania was really dominated by Grandma, who was an invalid of over eighty and confined to her room on the third floor. Every evening after tea there was a ritual of going up and sitting with her, a not unpleasant duty, for Grandma was gentle and kindly and loved children. Seated in her arm chair, usually in a purple velvet gown, snow-white ringlets framing her little lace cap, face shining, she would talk to them always of religious matters, sometimes telling them stories of her Huguenot ancestors, one of whom had been tortured to death for his faith by being forced to drink powdered glass.

In spite of her infirmities there was nothing senile about Grandma. Her pink cheeks were unshriveled, her voice strong and coherent. Her children both adored and respected her. Even Uncle Bertie, the most strongminded and dominant, came to her with his problems. Gentle though she was, her views were always positive, for, like all the Harrises, she saw life never in shades of gray, always in blacks or whites.

Though the children were constantly aware of Grandma, an all pervading presence, a little like God, high over all, it was a kindly, uninhibiting presence, and fortunately their playroom, the basement breakfast room, was far enough removed from the celestial stratum to keep noise from penetrating. Here, except for the two maids and the cook Cissie, who presided over adjoining kitchen, pantry, larder, and cellars, they enjoyed comparative freedom. And the maids Dora and Caroline, although they strongly disapproved of certain activities, like swinging on the curtains, were remarkably lenient and understanding.

In lieu of trees to climb, the children devised other sports. One was to get completely around the room, filled with old polished mahogany furniture, without once touching the floor, effecting the circuit via bureau tops, picture rails, window cornices, and other projections. Another diversion was playing in the food lift. They would take out the shelves, squeeze themselves in, and pull themselves up and down by the ropes and pulleys.

Usually only on Sundays were the children allowed in the drawing room, and then activity was strictly supervised. The mahogany cabinet was opened and its treasures carefully exhibited: an opal from Australia; shells with wonderful iridescent hues; an ivory crab; a china Neptune; a tiny condiment set and egg cups carved from ivory; circles made with beetles' wings and gold thread; a tiny table made of peach stones, not more than two inches high, eight sided with a star in its center; and, most marvelous of all, a glass tumbler cut spirally, so that if you picked it up by its top, the spirals sprang open, but when you set it down it would hold water!

Certain toys were allowed on Sundays, but only those designed for religious purposes: Bible puzzles, books, picture cards. They were permitted to use building blocks provided they made religious objects, such as models of the Hebrew temple or of the tabernacle. But, since Aunt Eunice was an avid student of archaeology and took them to the British Museum to see such marvels as the Rosetta Stone and Egyptian mummies, they became rather interested in reconstructing these ancient wonders. In spite of the long church services and lack of physical activity, the day was not unpleasant. And besides, there was Sunday tea. Though afternoon tea included jam on most days and plum cake on Wednesdays, on Sundays there were always jam *and* cake.

As the time drew near for her return to India Evelyn Brand said to Jesse, "It's no use. I can't bear it, to leave them both. Of course Paul has to stay, even though it tears my heart out. But Connie—she's such a baby, only six and a half! I must take her with me, Jesse!"

Her husband shook his head. "It would be cruel to separate them." Then, seeing her ravaged eyes, he relented. "Very well. Why not take Connie apart and ask her if she would rather go back with us?"

Evelyn did so. Connie regarded her gravely. "Can Paul come too, Mummy?"

"No, darling. Paul must stay here and go to school."

The child shook her head. "Oh, not without Paul, Mummy. Not without my Paul!"

They were leaving early in the morning, about the time the children started for school. The family knelt and prayed together for the last time. It was all both parents could do to keep their voices steady. Then Paul and Connie hugged them tightly, seized their school satchels, ran down the steps, and turned once to wave goodbye before they disappeared.

"As I stood watching them," Evelyn Brand confessed later, "something just died in me."

Paul missed his parents, but the routine of his new life was well established. Under the aunts' careful tutelage he repeated each Sunday morning the five Tamil texts which he had learned, and each night the English ones which his mother had painted and hung on his bedroom wall. "I will be a father unto you." . . . "As one whom a mother comforteth, so will I comfort you." . . .

After attending the little private school for a year, he entered the junior branch of the University College School, located nearby in Hampstead. But he disliked both study and the school routine and stubbornly refused—or neglected—to conform.

"Dear Miss Harris," the headmaster wrote Aunt Eunice on July 24, 1925, close to Paul's eleventh birthday, "We have not

been too satisfied with young Brand of late. He is really a boy
of good ability and I feel that if he will wake up, he will do
very well indeed. No doubt he is not yet used to our English
climate. But he is often late and reads on the way to school
and misses the prize giving owing to forgetfulness about his
collar. He ought to have a good talking to, both now and just
before the beginning of the new term. Yours truly, Lake."

The aunts, feeling their duty keenly, talked, even attempted
a show of sterner discipline, buying a little whacking stick
from the shop on the corner and hanging it in a conspicuous
place. Aunt Eunice used it perhaps twice. Her approach to
problems of naughtiness was characteristic: precise, logical,
businesslike. Paul should be taught proper conduct with the
same meticulous patience with which she taught him to manage his allowance of two, and later four, pence a week.

Aunt Hope, who felt things intensely and showed it, often
burst with impatience. "Always dreaming! I declare, child, you
don't listen to a thing we say. We might as well be a cat
meowing. Come on, boy, wake up!"

Even Connie, who started studying the moment she arrived
home from school, did her share of reproving. "Paul, you'll
never pass," she worried.

But somehow he did, and felt small for having done it with
so little effort. In fact, he was painfully conscious of his inade-
quacies. Everybody else in the family was gifted with artistic
or literary talent. Mother painted pictures. Connie could draw
well and write poetry. Grandfather's pictures, superb in detail
even to each blade of grass, were all about the house, and at
least one of them had been hung in the Royal Academy. Many
of his aunts were poets. Only he seemed to have no talent
except for getting into mischief.

His school work continued to elicit disapproval. While Con-
nie's report cards consistently bore such comments as "Good,"
"Excellent," "Bien," "Tres bien!," "is artistic," "most original,"
Paul's were equally consistent.

"Michaelmas term, 1925–26. Fair, poor, poor, fair, fair, poor.
Next term we shall hope for better things. Headmaster Lake."

"Lent Term, 1926. House Rose, Form 4-B. Poor, fair, poor,
fair, weak. Rather disappointing. Lake."

It wasn't books that Paul disliked, merely school books. He
read avidly, often on the way to school, with such eagerness

that he often ran into people. His taste in literature was respectable if not highbrow, tending largely toward adventure tales such as *The Coral Islands* and *Westward Ho!*. He liked Dickens but abhorred Scott. In fact, English, next to the sciences, was his favorite subject. Encouraged by two unusual teachers, he came to enjoy composition and speaking, especially the latter. Using material from his father's weekly letters, he shone at public speaking, giving little lectures on animals, insects, and birds.

But he shone more in less admirable activities. In geography, for example, his teacher was conspicuous for his red head and laxity of discipline. The class was held in a big sloping classroom on the third floor. Sitting in the rear, Paul frequently managed to climb out the back window, let himself down on the roof of the cycle sheds, thence to the ground; whereupon he would reenter the building by the front door and proceed once more to the classroom.

"Good morning," he would greet the teacher cheerfully for the second time, deriving great amusement from his look of baffled puzzlement.

In fact, climbing continued to be one of his prime interests. During holidays he would walk nonchalantly along the edge of sheer cliffs, petrifying all his companions except Connie. After he had moved on to the senior branch of University College School, he distinguished himself by climbing one of the square corner posts of the main building, clinging catlike to its alternating layers of brick and cement, and scratching his initials with his locker key on the second stratum from the top, perhaps 40 feet above the ground. Only one past hero had gone higher, and his scrawl on the top stratum was illegible. The aunts never hindered the children's climbing or taking physical risks, probably because they did not know of these adventures.

The poor maids were not always blessed with the aunts' ignorance when Paul conducted his scientific experiments. Once he built a generator for making cooking gas out of boiling methyl spirits. Putting a candle under an alcohol can, he got a fine flame, and all went well until the tube melted and burst away from the can. Instantly the liquid boiling spirits shot up to the playroom ceiling, which became a mass of dripping flames. For once the maids were really disturbed and administered stern reproof.

The playroom contained a carpenter's bench and tools, and Paul loved to build. At one time he built a full sized aviary in which they kept birds, at another a house for their white mice, with two stories joined by little staircases. He made himself a pair of stilts and learned to walk on them, finally building a set so tall that he could get on them only from a first floor window. Together the two children constructed a canvas canoe, Paul furnishing the ideas and Connie most of the labor.

Their interests were not all scientific or mechanical. With Cousins Norman and Annette they wrote a monthly magazine called "The Superior," with poems and stories, puzzles, jokes, riddles, and a section called "Tips and Gadgets." They wrote its sixteen pages with special ink, then duplicated copies on a jelligraph, and sold them to members of the family and church friends. There was always a missionary page containing anecdotes from Father's letters, and all the profits were devoted to his mission work.

Norman shared Paul's antipathy to school sports. They would often march to the playing field, then sneak away to Hampstead Heath, where they would climb trees and come home with their clothes stained black with smoke. Aunt Rose, who was rearing a family of thirteen, could take this accumulation of dirt in her stride, but the fastidious aunts must have been sorely tried.

"They were saints to stand us," Paul remarked fervently long afterward.

But he was not so appreciative at the time. He welcomed the occasional visits to Belgaum, the Brands' home in Guildford, where the atmosphere was less rigid. Here on Sunday he was allowed to read the "Boys' Own Paper," with stories about Tiger Tim. Dice were not a forbidden evil, but useful accessories for playing "Ludo" and "Snakes and Ladders." With the Brands, religion was wholesome and genuine but not so much a full-time business as with the Harrises.

Not all the Harrises, however. There was Uncle Charlie, who had deeply shocked the aunts by turning Presbyterian. "How could you, Charles!"

Paul and Connie enjoyed visiting Uncle Charlie's family in Northwood. The freer, more tolerant atmosphere infected them the moment they left the train, and they started running so fast that Cousin Peggy, who came to meet them, never did catch up with them until they reached the house. Vivacious, mischievous, only four days younger than Paul, she was for years the children's companion during the six-week summer vacation they spent at West Runton on the east coast of England. Cousin Nancy Robbins, Aunt Stella's daughter, who was a year older, was also in the family party on these holidays, and if Peggy was Paul's play companion, Nancy, deeply thoughtful and religious, was his "soul" companion.

These holidays, almost as free and wild as life on the Kollis, were the petcock which kept his pent-up energies from bursting. Here he could discard shoes, routine, conventions, and climb to his heart's content. After a summer at West Runton Paul could return almost cheerfully to the concrete prison of London and University College School.

After one such summer, in fact, he made a sudden spurt of academic progress. It was his last year in the junior branch, and he made such an excellent record that he received a double promotion. Father's letters, usually reflecting disappointment, were exuberant.

"If only you could know, dear boy," he wrote in July, 1927, "how much joy the news of your success has given us both! To hear that you have passed, not only well, but VERY well, and that you are to be promoted over two or three classes, is indeed a delightful surprise."

But the burst of brilliance was only a flash. Less than a year later Father's letters were echoing the old refrain. "May 14, 1928. The report that came this week was certainly a disappointment. I don't mind low marks in some subjects, because you were away from school on account of sickness. But what I object to is a remark like 'could do better if he tried', or 'lazy'!"

But, Jesse Brand's weekly letters, far from being all critical, were a delightful miscellany of animal stories, parental advice, mechanical wisdom, and news of the Kollis.

"Congratulations on your promotion to trousers! I hope they will fortify you to maintain a dignified 'superior person' attitude in face of Connie's jokes at your expense." . . . "We sympathize ever so much with your disappointment in the marring of your grand plans for the holiday owing to sickness. But I hope you took the blow like a man, without whining."

(Paul hadn't. It was enough to make any boy whine, coming down with chicken pox the day before Christmas holidays began and getting over it one day after the next term started! He was infuriated.)

"I wonder if you know the principle of the force pump. Our well near the Girls' Home is 50 feet deep and yesterday we had to pull the pump up and repair it. We let a young man down into the well, sitting on a stick with a rope between his legs, lowered him into the black hole and plump into the water at the bottom." . . .

"Ruth is standing at my elbow watching the typewriter. She is a dainty, pretty girl, but she does not grow very big. Aaron was with us for Christmas. He has grown into a fine tall boy." . . .

"We are disappointed to give up our furlough this year, but there is another man in the mission who needs it more than we do. Looking forward to next year, we think that the first week in March will be the probable time of our setting sail. That will land us home in time for your Easter holidays."

March! That meant almost a whole year to wait. Paul's disappointment at the postponement of his parents' furlough was keen. He was nearly fifteen years old, and it was six years since he had seen his father and mother. Together he and Connie tried to think of some way they could make the time pass more swiftly.

"We have started a hobby," he wrote Mother. "Today we took out all your weekly letters and have started putting them in order. Then we bought a loose-leaf notebook to hold them, so when you come to write your book about work on the Kollis, you will have them to use."

On May 13, 1929 Father wrote Paul one of his most beautiful letters.

"I was glad to hear of your long walk with Norman to Northwood, when you did twenty miles or more. Yesterday when I was riding over the windswept hilltops around Kulivalavu, I could not help thinking of an old hymn that begins, 'Heaven above is deeper blue; flowers with purer beauty glow.' When I am alone on these long rides, I just love the sweet smelling wood, the dear brown earth, the lichen on the rocks, the heaps of dead brown leaves drifted like snow in the hollows. God means us to delight in his world. It isn't necessary to know botany or zoology or biology in order to enjoy the manifold life of nature. Just observe. And remember. And compare.

And be always looking to God with thankfulness and worship for having placed you in such a delightful corner of the universe as the planet Earth."

It was Jesse Brand's last will and testament to his son.

4

The cable reached England before the letter. It read: *Jesse taken to be with the Lord after blackwater fever for two days. Break news gently to the children. The Lord reigneth.*

Paul was out on a long walk with Norman when it came. It was mid-June, and school was over. Tired from hours of romping on the heath, soaked with sunshine, black and scratched from tree-climbing, he returned home happier than he had been in months. He felt light and heady, the air filling his lungs almost as clean and fresh as that on the Kollis.

"Come into the dining room, Paul," said Aunt Eunice. Her face looked old and pinched under the neatly parted hair with its circle of velvet ribbon.

Aunt Hope was in the dining room, and Uncle Bertie. Both looked very stern and sober. Paul's heart fell. What had he done now? It must be very bad indeed for Uncle Bertie to be called in. He braced himself.

Aunt Eunice had a piece of yellow paper in her hand. She looked at Uncle Bertie, who cleared his throat as if about to speak, but nothing came out. Never before had Paul seen Uncle Bertie at a loss for words.

"We're sorry to have to break the news so suddenly," said Aunt Eunice with abrupt gentleness. "But your dear daddy has gone to be with Jesus."

She may have said more words. Paul did not hear them. *No!* He gave a small hoarse cry. Everything seemed suddenly to have stopped moving. He saw the aunts' faces, and Uncle Bertie's, as solid and motionless as the alabaster statue on the pedestal. He tried to move and couldn't. It was like the story of the sleeping beauty, with everything frozen solid. Then, after what seemed a hundred years, Uncle Bertie broke the spell. He went to the center table and picked up his hat.

"I must go to Guildford," he said, "and break the news there."

Connie was visiting the Brands at Belgaum. A few hours later Uncle Bertie returned to Nethania, bringing her with him. Her lips were bravely smiling, but her eyes had a queer, frightened look, so Paul knew she had been told. *It isn't real,* he wanted to cry out to her. *It's just a bad dream or something.* But he didn't. They just stared at each other.

"You children will want to be alone," said Aunt Eunice. "You'll have things to say to each other."

She led them upstairs to Paul's room on the third floor, gently pushed Connie in after Paul, and shut the door. It was a grownup kind of idea, and both of them felt embarrassed and awkward.

"It's—dreadful, isn't it?" ventured Connie at last in a high, unnatural voice.

"Yes, isn't it?" replied Paul. "I—I just can't believe it."

Unable to think of anything more to say, they just stood uncomfortably silent.

Paul's sense of unreality persisted during the days and weeks which followed. It was impossible to think of Father—big, strong, all-wise, tender, jolly—as *no longer there!* But he went through the motions of dutiful grief and acceptance.

One factor that contributed to this sense of unreality was the increasing vagueness of Father's physical substance during the six years of his absence. Without his picture Paul would almost have forgotten how he looked. He had remained real, but almost in the sense that God was real, a somewhat distant living entity. Paul had gotten used to doing without him in the flesh. It was his weekly letters that had been the potent reality and—since sea mail was many weeks in transit—*the letters continued to come!* Father was riding his horse to Kulivalavu, smelling the woods and earth, listening to the wind stirring in dead leaves, reveling in the pinks and purples of the lichen and lantana.

"I wonder if you remember," he was still asking in a letter written on June 3rd, "the double line of Silver Oak trees planted by the path as you approach the house here? They were quite small shrubs when you left, but have grown to great trees now." And in the same letter: "We have been talking over the date of our departure from India next year, and we think that the first week in March will be the probable time of our setting sail."

But there was no use pretending. Father would not be coming home in March or any other time. At first Mother refused to leave India. Then Cousin Ruth, oldest daughter of Uncle Bertie, though she was just about to take her medical exams and it meant interrupting her studies for a full year, offered to go out to India to help Mother and try to persuade her to come home. All the family was relieved when she left almost immediately. Then when they received letters with Indian postmarks announcing plans for sailing home to England, Paul knew that a new pattern of life had really begun.

Riding down on the boat train from London to Tilbury to meet them, he was almost sick with excitement. He tried to picture Mother as he had last seen her, tall, graceful, full of fun and laughter, vibrant as the bits of quicksilver he had once spilled from a broken thermometer. Thanks more to her pictures than to his memory, he knew that her smooth brown hair was parted in the middle and tied with a velvet ribbon, like Aunt Eunice's, but that the features beneath were much younger and more beautiful. Would he know her? Would she look the same?

The ship was in, the gangplank down, the passengers poured off. Paul stood on the dock amid a swarm of relatives, his heart pounding.

"There they are!" someone shouted.

Then here came Ruth bustling off the boat, down the plank, cheerfully competent as always, coming toward them, being enveloped in the swarm, shaking hands with everybody, and trailing along behind her—Paul's heart almost stopped beating—behind her . . . a little, incredibly little, shrunken old lady.

It was a shock far worse than the cable, for this was reality, stark, inescapable. He stood motionless, wooden, while she came toward him, arms outstretched, tears running down her cheeks. She had to reach up to kiss him, for his body was too rigid to bend, but he must have kissed her back, for he could taste salt on his lips.

"Mother!" he heard Connie sob, over and over. "Mother, darling!"

But he could not bring himself to speak the word, and he felt no tears, just a queer hardness. Fortunately there were others to do the talking. Even later, in the boat train, when she sat between him and Connie and sounded a bit more natural and animated as she plied them with questions, he answered dutifully, but still the important word would not come.

This is Mother, he told himself over and over, trying to make himself believe it. This is my beautiful, tall, graceful, sparkling Mother!

It did not occur to him that at least part of the change was in himself, and that his mother was finding it even more difficult to convince herself that "this is my son." No, it must be his father's death which had made all the change. And his mother's words and actions made him surer of it, for, like all the Harrises, she kept few thoughts and emotions to herself. All the light had gone out of her life, she kept asserting, wiping her eyes. She could never be the same again. She and Daddy had been absolutely one, and now she was worth nothing by herself. Paul listened, becoming more and more miserable and rebellious.

No! he thought. *No, it's not right!* Then came decision, so subconscious that it found no words but so fierce that it was to recur again and again: It was wrong for anyone to love another so much, to be so dependent on any one person. *He would never, never let this happen to him!*

But time was the servant as well as the master of change, and he slowly adjusted himself to this new concept of "mother." Evelyn Brand was also in a period of profound adjustment, and it was not an easy time for either of them. Her presence during his last year at University College School was a delight and a stimulus, but also, in some indescribable way, an irritant. She saw to it that he did his studying. She inspired him anew with the needs of "India's millions", especially those tens of thousands on the Kollis and other neighboring ranges.

"A few months before he died," she told Paul, the old sparkle in her eyes turned now into a fever of purpose, "we sat on that high crest at Puliampetty, Jesse and I, where we could look out over all the five ranges, the Kollis, the Pachas, the Kolaryans, the Bothai malai, the Chitterais. And we said to each other, 'All of them, we must win all of them for Christ.'"

It was understood, of course, that Paul would try to fill his father's place (As if he could!). Though he had never made any actual decision to become a missionary, it had been one of those remote developments rather taken for granted, like growing up to be a man. Now suddenly, with the end of school only months away, he was faced with the necessity of making decisions. Though his mother tried hard not to dictate, she was not the sort of person who could keep silent.

"You can stay on at school, you know, dear, and take your higher certificate, then go on to college. You have the offer . . ."

No, Paul didn't want that. He had had enough school.

"Your father, dear, always wanted to be a doctor. Did you know that he started a course in medicine at Madras University, even after he went to India? I know he would be pleased if you—"

No, *no!* The memory of his father's medical work roused images of ulcers, pus, and blood which still filled him with revulsion. If there was one thing he was sure of, it was that he did not want to be a doctor.

A lay preacher came one Sunday to the church in St. John's Wood. Though a builder by trade, he was known all around London as Pastor Warwick. He was a gifted and practical speaker, using homely illustrations from his own experience. When at one point in his sermon he drew a carpenter's rule from his pocket, Paul felt a quickening of emotion which almost brought tears to his eyes. Just so, with the same gesture of a loving craftsman, his father had pulled out a similar rule, and with the same pithy homilies.

"See this line, son? Looks straight, doesn't it? But let's put the rule to it. Ah, see how crooked it really was? Like us. We always need to keep the Golden Rule handy, and apply it to everything we do."

As when Grandfather was alive, the visiting preacher came to dinner at the Harrises. Paul liked Mr. Warwick better and better. He was more like his father than any other man he had ever met.

"Like tools, boy?"

"Yes, sir, I—I have a small bench in the basement."

"Use it?"

"I've made a few things."

"Let's see them."

Heart beating hard, Paul exhibited the canoe, the elaborate apartments of the white mice, the stilts, the aviary, and Mr.

Warwick nodded approvingly. "Good. Like your father. He had a feeling for wood and tools."

Paul was becoming more and more excited. It was as if the maze in which he had been wandering had suddenly opened. He saw his way out. During the afternoon he managed to take his mother aside. "I like that man," he confided, then, trying to sound casual, "You know, I wouldn't mind learning to be a builder myself."

Evelyn Brand's eyes lighted, almost with the old sparkle. Before the day was over she cornered Pastor Warwick. "My son wants to be a missionary like his father," she explained with her usual directness, "but if he does he must learn to be a builder, since in the mountains of India we have to build our own houses. Would you take him into your business and teach him?"

In December, 1930, Paul left University College School to become a building apprentice. Already his mother had returned to India to join another missionary couple assigned to work on the Kollis, making his break with the past even more complete. It was more than a transition from student to laborer, from one social stratum to another. He moved abruptly from boyhood into manhood.

Mr. Warwick was thorough in his training, starting his new apprentice in the general offices, where he learned first the routine of costing and contract, of entering all materials. Then he was transferred to the surveyor's department, where he was trained to estimate the costs of each contract. Only then, after all this preliminary training, was he set to work at actual building, first in the shops, later on the building setups. His pay was eight and sixpence a week, about a dollar.

At first Paul lived at home. In order to get to work at seven-thirty, an hour's ride across London by train, he had to get up at five-thirty. It wasn't easy. Connie, feeling keenly responsible, would herself rise at five, then come into his room and shake him every five minutes. Still he found it almost impossible to waken.

"This isn't right," he finally decided. "It's my problem. Let me solve it."

He purchased a huge two-bell alarm clock and set it beside his bed on a tin tray. It was Connie who had to turn it off. He slept through its tintinnabulations like a baby.

"It's because you don't really want to get up," a helpful

friend told him. "Even when asleep you know what you're doing, and anything you really want to do you can do."

That night he set the alarm and ordered Connie not to wake him up under any circumstances. The second it started to ring he jumped up. The next night he reduced the amount of winding, and kept reducing it. He removed the tin tray. Then he removed one bell, after that the second bell, so the alarm went off with a mere rattling sound. Finally he wound it and turned it off, finding he could waken at the sound of its click. It was one of the most triumphant moments of his young life. He had proved he could master something.

After he had taken his preliminary training in office work and indoor carpentering, Paul entered a new world, as different from the snobbishly genteel little orb of St. John's Wood as that was from the savage simplicity of the Kollis. For a time he felt himself an outcast from both worlds. He was ashamed to go home with his broken nails, his dirty work clothes, his muddy boots. Pushing a wheel barrow through the streets, he would cast furtive glances to make sure none of his former associates was watching. Connie, insisting on getting up in the dark winter mornings to serve his breakfast, then watching by the window for hours at night, worrying about accidents, would sneak him upstairs or to the basement to discard his filthy work clothes and make himself presentable to the aunts' fastidious society.

But Paul was more disturbed to find himself a misfit in his new world than in his old one. His rough, profane, unlettered daily companions were partners in the most exciting adventure he had ever undertaken, and he wanted to be one of them. He spent hours learning to speak Cockney, practicing gutturals, using glottis rather than lips in forming words, sloughing h's. And in time, except for the profanity, he became indistinguishable in speech and appearance from a laborer hailing from Billingsgate instead of the chastely respectable St. John's Wood.

His first outdoor work was mainly on roofs, in bitter cold weather, with both ladders and tiles often coated thick with ice. Then, leaving the housetops, he plunged into cellars to serve his apprenticeship there. Helping to alter one huge basement, he worked for days peering through glasses into a red haze, choked with dust and deafened by frequent blasts and the ear-shattering rasp of pneumatic drills. His head seemed to be splitting open. Rinsing his mouth before eating lunch, he spat red dust. But he liked it. Most of the time he was living in the "digs" with the other men, sharing their food, their dirt, their simple speech, their crude but canny philosophy of living.

He was almost sorry to move on into the joiner's shop, learning the finer techniques of doors, windows, and other finish work. He spent his days in practical labor, and then on most evenings he attended classes in surveying and architectural drawing. From carpentry he moved into plumbing.

"Plumbing on the Kollis?" he questioned sometimes skeptically. Of what earthly use would such knowledge be to him! Only long afterward could he see that it was all a part of the pattern. "It takes a lot more skill making a watertight joint 'wiping' lead to lead," he was to tell his surgical trainees, "than making a watertight joint in the intestines!"

But of all his five years in learning the building trade he liked best the year in masonry. Now for the first time in his life since leaving the Kollis he was *really* happy. Though he liked wood and his hands seemed shaped for carpenter's tools, he was fascinated by stone. He reveled in learning which kinds were best for different kinds of work and was exultant when he could move from the soft Bath stone to the harder marbles and granites. He took almost as much pride in chiseling and filing a perfectly curved window sill as if he had sculptured a Pietà or a Venus de Milo. Even his final promotion to foreman, "cock of the works," where he had to oversee all phases of work on a building site, did not give him greater satisfaction.

For five years he lived in two worlds, linked only by the London underground. Most of his daily companions would not have known him on evenings and weekends. Crossing from east side to west, he divested himself of dirt, boots, coarse clothes, cockney accent. He played furious competitive tennis and badminton, often on the winning teams. He even attended cricket matches at Lord's, just around the corner from Nethania, becoming genuinely excited over some contests. But most of his extra-work activities centered around his major interests, religion and the church. Throughout the five years he taught a Sunday school class of small boys. And at an early age he started preaching. He was perhaps eighteen when he went one Sunday to preach at Guildford Chapel. The Brand aunts attended with great trepidation. Not Connie, however, for she had absolute confidence in Paul's ability.

"People will expect so much," said Aunt Minnie, "remembering his father."

They need not have worried. Paul held his audience spellbound. He preached on the text, "My grace is sufficient for thee." A certain man had had a dream, he told them, in which he had seen these words written on a long wall. The MY, being nearest, had loomed large; the *thee* in the distance much smaller. The words "My grace" had grown larger and larger in the dream until they had filled the whole wall, crowding the diminishing "thee" into the far corner. This was perhaps Paul's first expression of what was to become a focal point of his philosophy: God big, self very small and unimportant.

"Well!" exclaimed Aunt Minnie with mingled amazement and satisfaction.

But youth work was Paul's greatest concern. Soon after coming to England he had visited a mission camp and liked it. Why not a similar project for young people? He succeeded in helping to start a "Fellowship of Youth," which included young people of his denomination from all over London and southern counties. A committee was formed to promote a religious camp, or house party, and Paul was chosen the adjutant, or organizer, for the boys' camp. A girl, Molly Chilvers, became secretary for the girls' house party.

The project grew year after year, and as it grew Paul's responsibilities increased. Sometimes they involved him in real difficulties, but they also provided him with a wealth of new friends. One of the most congenial of these was an adventurous boy named Laurie Kurht.

From at least one of Paul's adventures with Laurie he managed to escape death merely by the skin of his teeth. At one of their seaside camps a man was giving short rides around the bay in an airplane. Laurie, who was trying to decide whether to join the air force, seized on the opportunity.

"Come with me," he urged Paul.

It was a tiny, old-fashioned plane with three open cockpits, one behind the other, equipped with no canopy, only little windshields. It took off from an ordinary farm field. Paul got into the back cockpit, Laurie in the one just ahead. Without telling Paul, Laurie had asked the pilot to put the plane through every stunt possible, so that he could find out if he had enough nerve to become a flier.

The engine turned, began to roar. In sudden panic Paul stood up.

"Hey!" he shouted. "Not yet! I'm not strapped in!"

Nobody heard him. The plane taxied along the field, picked up speed. Still his shouts brought no response. The roar of the engine and the wind sweeping over the open cockpits drowned out all other sounds. As the plane left the ground, he sat down, fumbling for the straps. But while he was feeling around for them, the plane began to turn into its first loop the loop. All he could do was grab the sides of the seat with his fingertips and hang on tight.

"Hey!" he yelled again. "Help!"

He might have been Canute shouting above these same winds and waves. The plane veered and careened, executed turns, loops, barrel rolls, falling leaf, and every other conceivable stunt. Bracing his feet, clutching desperately at the sides of the little barrel seat, he faced dizzying alternating glimpses of clouds, tossing waves, blue sky, rocky headlands, clouds, treetops, blue sky, tossing waves. He had brought a little camera with him, hoping to get some views of the camp as they passed over. Hung around his neck, the case swung out over his head, round and round, with the centrifugal force of the barrel rolls. Hands aching, shins throbbing, rigid fingers slowly turning to clamps of ice, he hung on for what seemed an eternity. Then, just when he was sure he must let go, the plane dived, swooped in a long curve toward the field, and came gently to rest.

Laurie unbuckled his belt and turned around. "Hey, Paul! What say? Are you still there?"

Paul slowly unclamped his hands. He was glad to see that they weren't trembling. "Still here," he replied cheerfully.

There were more girls than men in the camping groups, and Paul was one of their more popular male members. Though by no means indifferent to feminine charms, he kept remarkably free of romantic entanglements. Even Molly Chilvers, who lived near his building work on the east side of London and with whose name his was most often paired, never became more than a very good friend. However, when she married an architect and Paul acted as best man at her wedding, he made a gallant admission in his speech.

"An architect not only plans things," he said pointedly, "but he sees that they get done. This one did, leaving all his rivals behind him as best men."

5

Paul was twenty-one years old. As he neared the end of his fifth year in the building trade he was conscious that people were raising their eyebrows. "Are you going to spend your whole life training?" The unspoken question further churned his own seething unrest and indecision.

Grandmother had died and the aunts had moved into a new Nethania. Connie was studying in Ridgelands Bible College, preparing to be a missionary. Evelyn Brand had come home on furlough, frustrated, convinced that she could not return alone to her beloved Kollis. There had been inevitable personality clashes between the wife of Jesse Brand, herself not the meekest of souls, and the couple assigned by the mission board to fill his shoes. The latter would have proved a difficult task for any mere human aspirant, like trying to walk in the steps of a giant.

Paul knew that he was expected to do this same almost impossible task. Already he had applied to the mission board and, to his consternation, been rejected. "You are not ready," he was told. Not ready! With a public school diploma, a lifetime of active church work including preaching, a fervent religious experience, and all his years of building training? He had assumed they would snap him up. It was missionaries the board wanted, they told him kindly, not technicians.

Two avenues of training through his church were open to him: Bible School, and a brief course in tropical medicine such as his father had taken. He rebelled against both. More required study? Heaven forbid! Medicine? Memories of his father's loathsome duties still made him shudder.

Once more he was deeply troubled and confused. He believed firmly in divine guidance. A person was "called" to be a preacher or a missionary. But—what constituted a "call"? He had never heard a voice, seen a vision, at least since childhood. In the end it was not the assurance of guidance which prompted his decision. It was the memory of his father. Jesse Brand had left the building trade for what he considered a nobler calling. He had prepared for his work by taking a short course in tropical medicine. His son would do the same.

Livingstone Medical School conducted its classes in a big old house in Leyton, near where Paul had worked. It offered a year's compressed medical course, with emphasis on tropical diseases. The pupils, numbering about twenty-five, were taught basic principles of physiology, first aid, diagnosis, and simple surgery. In addition to the two full-time teachers, Dr. Jays and Dr. Wigram, there were visiting lecturers. Two of the leading authorities in the world on leprosy, Dr. Cochrane and Dr. Muir, came here to lecture.

There was field work also. The students went regularly to a mission hospital in Bethnal Green and, under the supervision of their doctors, assisted in the casualty department of Poplar Accident Hospital, attending clinics, examining patients, doing dressings.

To Paul's utter amazement he loved both the work and the study. Always before, his school work had been purposeless. Here everything was linked with reality. It was as challenging as learning how to shape blocks of stone by wielding the heavy mason's hammer without undue tension on the arm muscles; as practical as building a soundproof office in an underground in City Road.

"Yesterday," he wrote his mother in October of 1935, "I spent most of the evening pulling teeth. I rather enjoyed it after the first one. I had one beast to do, an upper right canine, the roots must have been up in the forehead somewhere."

But a month later he wrote with even greater enthusiasm: "Already my whole attitude toward medical work has changed. I used to think diseased people would be rather repulsive en masse and that it would be an effort to spend a whole day in hospital with blood and pus and sickness around. But as we begin to understand more of the causes and cures of these things and are able to help people in pain, the whole thing is taking on a new aspect."

He was making other discoveries. For the first time in his life he was coming into contact with diverse nationalities, philosophies, and creeds. In the group were two Scandinavians, three South Africans. There were Father Kroll and Father Longdon, High Churchmen. One belonged to a holy order and wore a long black habit. There was a Moravian named Marks, going out to Central America. One of the students was a Friend, several were humanists, some seemed to Paul to have no religion at all. Yet all felt "called" to become missionaries. And all were mature people, with well formulated philosophies which they were able and anxious to defend. Paul discovered somewhat to his shocked surprise that sincerity of faith and missionary zeal were not confined to those of his narrowly orthodox upbringing. It was an illuminating and sobering experience.

Paul's closest friend was a young student named David Wilmshurst, his opposite in many ways, quiet, shy, solid, studious, sometimes a little slow but always thoroughly honest and kindly. Though there was healthy competition between them, it was not in the area of theology, for both were keen Baptists. Rather, they were academic rivals, taking turns being at the top of the class.

At the end of the year's course, both of them did exceptionally well in their examinations. Dr. Wigram called Paul into his office.

"You like medicine, don't you?"

"Like isn't the word," replied Paul. "I love it."

"Yes. I can see you do. We had a student who led his class last year," the doctor continued, "a lad named Ben Walkey. We advised him to take up medicine as a profession. I'm happy to say he has done so. And—I most earnestly advise you to do the same."

Paul's throat felt dry. "But I—I'm planning to be a missionary."

"And why not? Didn't you ever hear of a missionary doctor?"

"But—it would take years—"

"At least five. All worthwhile things take time."

"—and money—" Paul floundered.

"It's a pity for you to stop with this one year." Dr. Wigram raced on, in the same manner that he lectured. "I've felt about this so strongly that I've approached your family about it. I've even written to your mother."

Paul gulped. "You—you have?"

"She wrote back that one of your uncles once promised to assist financially if you ever decided to take up medicine."

"Uncle Dick," murmured Paul. Richard Robbins, Nancy's father, husband first of Aunt Rosa, who had died, then of Aunt Stella, had started life very poor. A brilliant student, he had lived on bread and cheese in order to buy books. He had become a successful market gardener, had been president of the Farmers' Union for all of England, had served the government under both Asquith and Lloyd George, and had been offered a knighthood. Uncle Dick had refused the honor.

"I have also been in contact with Mr. Robbins," continued the doctor, "and he is willing to renew his offer."

Paul was shaken. Never had he been so sorely tempted. Already his plans were made to enter a missionary training colony, insuring almost certain acceptance by his mission board after two years' time. If only this opportunity had come five years ago! Then he remembered to his bitter dismay that it had. His mother had suggested medicine. But—was it too late now? Five years more studying medicine, then another two years in missionary training . . . Many men started their careers at thirty.

No. He had already spent too many years marking time. And, after all, it was men's souls that needed to be saved, not their bodies. A man, if he had any guts, couldn't be always preparing, never acting. He would proceed as he had planned. He entered the missionary training colony in the summer of 1936.

The Colony was a small institution in Norwood, Surrey, designed to give missionary trainees not only intensive Bible study and practice in preaching, but also practical experience in the crude Spartan life they might be expected to encounter in the jungles of Asia or Africa or South America. The wooden huts, all built by Colony boys, were, to Paul's disappointment, finished before he arrived. There were four huts, each large enough to accommodate twelve trainees, and appropriately named Asia, Africa, South America, and India. Paul was assigned to Africa. Its furnishings were crude, a small charcoal stove, which in winter failed to give proper heat, and for each trainee a bed, a table, and one straight chair. Life was intended to be crude and stark and tough. The chief business of the Colony was Bible study and preaching. In their Bible study the trainees would study verses as they came, covering the whole Bible in two years. If a passage in Corinthians mentioned church order, then the group would discuss church order. There were no classes in theology or homiletics. The whole Colony was based on the premise that the scriptures were a sufficient basis for all of theology and living.

There was plenty of practice in preaching, however. The trainees went regularly on deputation assignments, holding preaching missions, open air meetings, youth camp programs. Paul's activities, some of them related in letters to his mother, were typical.

"August 27, 1936. Cycled to Big Ben late Saturday night. Met group of boys and had prayer meeting on a side street. All split up into two parties, ten in each. Divided our food and cocoa, mapped out London into districts, and cycled off. Frank was my partner. We went first to the 'Hot Plates,' a wee turning behind the Savoy Hotel where hot smells ooze through gratings at pavement level. About a dozen men were huddled about those warm spots. They were glad to see us and more glad to have the hot cocoa and sandwiches. Then we went to Fleet Street and combed the alleyways. Found men more keen on sandwiches than on the bread of life. Cycled back to Colony uphill, against a strong wind and soaking wet, but had enough breath left to sing. Arrived home about 5:30, made tea."

"September 20. Had a big open air meeting. There was a noisy Communist meeting on our left and a black shirt meeting opposite. They had bigger crowds than we did, but we had the loudest speakers."

David Wilmshurst was Paul's closest friend at the Colony, also, and frequently Paul took him home for a weekend holiday. Connie was usually home at the time of these visits, and jolly parties were often arranged. Connie was now taking a year's course at the Missionary School of Medicine, a rival institution to Livingstone, specializing in a homeopathic type of medicine. It was here that Evelyn Brand had taken her brief medical training, and Connie, in beauty as well as spirit, was following in her mother's footsteps. Even the distress of a recently broken engagement to a fellow student could not quell her lighthearted radiance. But if David Wilmshurst, shy, close-mouthed, reserved, succumbed even slightly to the spell of her charms, he gave no sign.

"David is the kind of person who could fall deeply in love," Paul once remarked of his friend, "but he's also the kind who would sit down with pencil and paper to list the qualifications of the girl he wanted to marry."

Paul enjoyed the missionary training colony, yet at the same time he often suffered a feeling of isolation from the others. It was not that he found himself in rebellion against the life of the Colony. He enjoyed its rigor and fellowship, its spiritual discipline. The variety of its membership was mentally stimulating. There were trainees from France, Germany, Jamaica, North India, Ireland, New Zealand. One of the men had been a communist agitator. Many different religious denominations were represented. Yet all seemed in perfect harmony with the colony and its aims. They had no religious doubts, no questions about their divine commission to help save the world. Why could he not share their certainty, their sublime self-confidence?

Then suddenly he was stricken with influenza, and in his weakness and isolation the conflict within him became panic. Had he really been "called" like these others to be a missionary? Did he have the white-hot zeal of absolute conviction, so that he could preach year after year as his father had done, without making a single convert?

In the semi-delusion of fever he seemed to lose his own identity. Books he had read, like Honoré Morrow's *The Splendor of God*, letters his mother had written, came alive. He was Adoniram Judson toiling a lifetime in Burma with few converts to show for his labor, pitting the tenets of his faith against the strong and intelligent opposition of a Buddhist priest, shrewd champion of a religion far older and more deeply established than Christianity. He was Evelyn Brand as she had looked on her return from India the first time after her husband's death, a pitiable ruin with the foundation of her whole life collapsed. Yes, and he was himself, Paul Brand, as he might be years hence, having toiled all his life in the heat and dust of India, preaching in endless encounter with an intelligent and aggressive Hinduism, then confronted suddenly with doubt and failure. Am I right? And even if I am, what profit if no one believes me! He felt no such doubt now, could not really conceive of himself as feeling it, but—suppose he should!

"No, no, it's not for me!" he cried out in sudden revulsion.

He couldn't do it. Life was too precious a gift to risk even the possibility of failure. Being a missionary like these others, just preaching and trying to convert people, wasn't enough. Perhaps it wasn't really missionary zeal which had brought him here to the colony. It was love for his father.

"I must have something else that I can do," he decided with that clarity of vision which comes often in moments of deepest despair. "I must be able to know that, whatever happens, I have at least helped people."

Following Dr. Wigram's urgent advice, he wrote to Uncle Dick, telling him that he had decided to study medicine. Richard Robbins generously renewed his offer to be financially responsible for Paul's medical education. Together they applied for help to the Missionary Medical Association, which agreed to assist with the hostel living expenses. That fall of 1937 Paul left the colony and entered the University College Medical School.

6

It was as if he had been floating for months on some quiet backwater and was now suddenly plunged into the mainstream. The Medical School on Gower Street and the hostel at 49 Highbury Park, where he lived with twenty or so other students, were in the heart of London. His new zest and awareness were spiritual as well as physical. At last he was acting in harmony with his own deepest desires and instincts. People, things, events, all sprang into new and sharp focus. Every person passed in the streets was a marvelous human body, a miracle to be explored. He felt his fingers on the pulse of the world.

But it was a nervous pulse, for war was already in the air. Although Chamberlain, recently become prime minister, was carefully constructing a policy of "peace in our time," his voice was drowned out by other sounds, sabers rattling in Germany, marching feet thudding in Ethiopia, even British planes droning with increasing stridor over London. And in one of them was Paul's old friend Laurie Kurht, now a qualified instructor in the air force. All of young England, it seemed, wanted to take to the air, and Paul, entering his new life with zest, was no exception. He would have joined the University Air Squadron and been initiated into flying along with medicine, but medical students were not included in the program. Very well, he decided. He would learn, anyway.

"Teach me to fly," he begged Laurie, and his friend cheerfully agreed.

It was necessary to hire a plane by the hour. All they could afford was a tiny Aeronca with a single two-cylinder engine, much like that of a motorcycle, a little dual control machine with a single high wing. Its rental was small, perhaps ten shillings an hour. Paul's first lessons coincided with his first classes in medical school, and he found them equally challenging.

One day they took off from Northolt Airdrome in a particularly gay mood, for they were meeting Laurie's fiancée, Pat, and another girl for dinner. Scarcely were they in the air, however, when Laurie's face turned grim.

"This is a faulty plane," he said. "I think I'll take it back."

"What's wrong?" Paul asked.

"The instruments aren't working. We can't tell our air speed, and the throttle is completely loose and uncertain."

Paul refused to panic. "Is it going to be dangerous while we're flying," he asked, "or only when we're coming in?"

"Mostly when we're coming in," replied Laurie, "because we shan't know our air speed."

Paul relaxed. "Well, we've got to land anyway," he reminded Laurie cheerfully, "whether we go in now or later, and if we're going to crash, let's at least enjoy our hour first—besides getting our money's worth."

Laurie grinned. They had always seen eye to eye about things. The plane soared upward. When they were well in the air, he turned over the controls to Paul. "It's yours," he said. "You fly it."

Though he had had only a few lessons, Paul could manage ordinary maneuvering. He enjoyed every minute of the flight. Never had the English countryside looked so beautiful. If this was to be the last hour of his life, what a marvelous way to spend it! When the hour was nearly up, he handed back the controls to Laurie.

The plane descended, circled around the airdrome waiting for its turn to come in. What happened then neither of them ever quite knew. Unable to read his air speed, Laurie was judging it by the ground speed and, flying with the wind with a two-cylinder engine, of course had no spare power. The plane stalled, then suddenly faltered and nose-dived. Instantly Laurie leaned forward, jerking back the joystick, and pulled up the throttle. The engine had just started roaring again when the plane hit the ground.

Seeing the crash coming, Paul instinctively leaned back and braced his feet. It came with a blinding jolt, forcing him through his seat belt, smashing his feet against the instrument panel, and hurling him straight through the nose of the plane. He found himself sitting on the grass outside, staring at the jagged hole his body had come through.

"Laurie—" one thought penetrated his numbness—"fire—must get him out—"

Somehow he crawled to the plane, inched himself halfway back through the hole, reached for Laurie's inert figure, put his hand to his face and drew it away covered with blood—No, not his, Laurie's, from the big wound on his head—jerked away the seat belt to drag him out, then saw that the door was jammed shut because both wings had broken off. No use. The door wouldn't open. Helpless, he fought desperately to remain conscious; then, seeing help coming in the shape of a fire engine, gratefully passed out.

After riding with Laurie in the ambulance to the hospital, Paul remembered the girls they were to meet. He thought, "It will frighten Pat if we don't turn up." His coat was covered with blood and his shoes had been torn off, yet his feet didn't seem to be damaged. He picked up Laurie's shoes at the hospital and put them on; then he went back to the drome, found Laurie's coat, left there before the flight, and donned that. He went by underground to meet the girls. Seeing him in Laurie's clothes, Pat went white. "Is he dead?" "No," Paul replied. He went back with her to the hospital, where Laurie was still unconscious, and where he was to remain for the next two years.

Paul returned to the hostel and walked into the big drawing

room. He was still a stranger there, having been only a short time in medical school. He must have looked queer, for the students all crowded around. "Brand! Where on earth have you been?"

Paul's feet were beginning to hurt. He sat down on the sofa and threw his overcoat open, revealing the bloody clothes underneath. "I've just—crashed—an airplane," he announced; then, before he could enjoy the sensation he, one of the "new boys," had created, he again passed out.

The next day his feet were the size of balloons, and he could not walk a step. But astonishingly they were not broken, and he was soon able to get around with the aid of canes. Not so Laurie, who, after two years in the hospital, recovered sufficiently to marry Pat and return to his post in the air force, only to crash again during the war, this time with no reprieve.

Soon after the accident Paul hobbled into the big chemistry laboratory and was assigned to a bench with another student whose name began with "B." Always alert for new and interesting acquaintances, especially female, his eyes turned with interest on the girl already working at the bench, her blonde head bent with absorption.

"Very young, pretty, a little too sober," his mind registered automatically. "Wonder what she looks like when she smiles."

He took his place opposite her. "Hello. Paul Brand." He introduced himself with pleasant informality.

The smile left nothing to be desired. Springing from an overly-generous mouth, it brightened the young face into piquant liveliness, kindled sparks in the tranquil blue eyes.

"Hello. I'm Margaret Berry."

During the laboratory period they compared notes on personal data as well as chemistry. Paul discovered that she was the daughter of a doctor living in Northwood Hills, that she also had thought sometimes of taking up mission work, and that she had taken this chemistry course once before at a polytechnic, but had not been allowed to take the examination because she was too young.

"If I don't make it this time," she smiled again before returning to her work with the same absorption, "I shall take up washing dishes."

As the period drew to a close Paul remembered that the Christian Union of the Medical School was holding a prayer meeting shortly. A girl even slightly interested in missions was a likely patron of such an organization.

"Are you coming along to the p.m.?" he inquired.

Her face lighted. "The p.m.? That sounds interesting. I'd like to come."

They walked along together. At the door of the meeting room she turned, puzzled. "Didn't you say a—p.m.?"

"Sure. What's the matter? Doesn't this look like a prayer meeting?"

"A—" She laughed, both amused and embarrassed. "Oh! I thought you meant a post mortem!"

In spite of this difference in their backgrounds they had interests in common during that first year in medical school, including both the Christian Union and the chemistry bench, where they laughed over each other's mistakes and compared the results of their various experiments. But if Margaret Berry permitted herself brief romantic dreams, she was soon disillusioned. For Paul Brand, mature, cleancut, keenly interested in people, was a common object of romantic dreams among the freshman girls, many of them extremely attractive, and he was by no means exclusive in his attentions.

But during his first term he had little time for social activities. Nearly eight years out of school, he was struggling desperately to bridge the deep gap in his studies. His year at Livingstone was of no help, for it had included no basic sciences. He approached his first exams with deep self-distrust and trepidation. However, he was able to write his mother on December 12th, "Praises be! I'm thankful to say that in no exam was I lower than 10th place, out of a total group of 75 or 80! But I've had to work jolly hard so far."

Now he could afford to relax and really enjoy himself. For the present, at least, he had given up all idea of missionary work and, though he continued to be active in such organizations as the Christian Union, most of his friends had little interest in religion. Here at "49," in a row of three old houses joined by connecting doors, twenty or so medical students lived together in a sort of men's club, presided over by Dr. Bradley, an ex-medico with a passion for yachts and big old American cars, and his wife, an exceedingly tolerant house mother. It was a cosmopolitan group, juniors rubbing shoulders with seniors, the moderately religious atmosphere conducive to hard study yet not inhibitive to more lighthearted pursuits. Paul's favorite among the inmates was Ben Walkey, who had preceded him by a year at Livingstone, a small, very clever lad with a vast fund of humor and musical ability. Severe mental activity alternated with physical. The boys would study hard for a few days, then explode into a tremendous fight. Any excuse would suffice. Ben Walkey might play his violin. Somebody would shout, "Shut up, Ben." "No," Ben would refuse firmly. Somebody else would throw something, and the battle would be on. Weapons of every variety were employed, one favorite being "jerries," chamber vessels, used freely for flinging water down the stair wells at each other. During these forays some part of the house was sure to be wrecked, and here Paul, the carpenter-mason, was in great demand, his stock of popularity rising to excessive highs.

Once even his skill was challenged, however. Finding himself the object of attack, he retreated to his room, slammed the door, and leaned on it. But the whole house was against him. The door, frame and all, burst inward, together with a large section of adjoining wall, burying him in fragments of splintered wood and broken plaster. As usual, at the first signs of demolition all enmity vanished. Emissaries were hastily despatched to buy bricks, plaster, finish boards, cans of paint. But the case looked hopeless. Door frame and plastered wall could be restored, but not the battered wall paper. Paul and his team worked for hours, hammering, plastering, painting. Around midnight someone let out a triumphant whoop. He had discovered a small cupboard lined with matching wall paper. They spent the rest of the night peeling it off, piecing, repasting it on the newly-plastered wall. By morning the place looked like new.

To Paul's utter amazement he finished his first term second in his class. Margaret Berry was first. Visiting her home in Northwood Hills several times, Paul thought he knew the reason why. Dr. Berry, her father, had set high standards for his children. The son of a poor draper, he had pinched every penny to become a chemist, saved his chemist's earnings to get a doctor's training, his doctor's earnings to become a specialist. In World War I he had served in German East Africa, and he had visited South African ports a few times. After the war, he had been moved to return there, and in 1921 had become medical officer of health in the Orange Free State. He had remained there until his three daughters were ready for higher education in England. Though a rebel against the rigid Presbyterian group in which he had been reared, he set for himself moral standards as difficult as the intellectual ones so painfully achieved. In fact, in South Africa he had almost lost his job because of his scrupulous honesty in publicizing a breach in sanitation laws. And he demanded of his children equally high standards. No penny, no moment of time should be wasted. If there were gold medals to be won, they were just naturally expected to win them.

Paul liked Margaret, but as yet he had neither time nor inclination for romance. And in their second year their intimate relationship as classmates was abruptly severed. Chamberlain's brief and uneasy peace secured so dearly at Munich burst like a bubble when on September 1, 1939, the Nazis marched into Poland. Five days later Paul wrote his mother from the new Nethania at 7 Carlton Hill:

"We've been at war now for about four days, and everything in London seems fairly normal, very calm and cheerful. The only strange things are the *pitch* black nights and to see everybody carrying their gas mask boxes around with them. We've had three air raid warnings so far but no air raids. We've a lovely safe shelter at the college. A coal cellar strengthened and furnished like a drawing room, electric lights and carpets and chairs, etc. But in a fortnight I've got to go to Cardiff and stay there to go on studying. I don't like leaving the aunties, but it can't be helped."

The whole medical school was evacuated, the girls to Sheffield, the men to Cardiff. Here, during the first year of the "phony war," Paul continued his studies without interruption, delving deeply into anatomy and physiology and, in a world gone suddenly berserk, taking a fierce delight in the orderly wonders of the human body.

"It's just terribly fascinating!" he told young John Harris, Uncle Bertie's son and ten years Paul's junior. "Look at the marvelous hand of yours, boy. You should just see the wonderful way the superficial tendon divides in two, allowing the deep tendon to pass through the tunnel formed by it! I tell you, it's a miracle!"

The boy stared at him, making little sense out of the words

but so profoundly stirred by the shining gray eyes, the soaring enthusiasm, that a quarter century later, himself a doctor in India, he was to give them credit for changing his whole life.

"We're dissecting again," Paul wrote his mother from Cardiff. "My same dissecting team is here—all, that is, except the women. They, poor dears, have been sent to Sheffield, a dreadful place and only a very meager staff to teach them. This place where I'm staying is just splendid. Mrs. Morgan is a charming old lady, very Welsh, very Christian, very deaf, very Baptist. She has an ear trumpet at least 18 inches long, which seems to wind away from her forehead, and she thrusts it into your face when you speak."

Mrs. Morgan, in fact, *was* that year in Cardiff. A wealthy grandmother who before the war would never have thought of taking paying guests, she absorbed Paul and several other students into her motherly menage, bestowing on each the largess of generous concern with which she promptly gave away all her new clothes to the first shabbily dressed person she encountered. When she discovered that Paul's mother was a missionary, she refused to take a penny for his lodging until, at his insistence, she finally compromised reluctantly on half the thirty shillings a week he had been paying. She would have been equally generous, however, had he been a worthless tramp.

Fearful of bombings and of the possibility of ejection at night in nothing but a nightdress, Mrs. Morgan wore all her clothes all the time. In addition, she made a voluminous pocket in one of her underskirts which would accommodate all her valuables: big family Bible, spare ear trumpet, spare glasses, all her keys, ration books, and ready cash. When she went to the butcher's, she would often have to delve for ration books at the very bottom, pulling all the other objects out and laying them on the counter while a long line of customers queued up behind.

But with all her eccentricities Mrs. Morgan was one of the truly formative influences in Paul's life. Because of his missionary connections, Paul became her special protegé. He was also her special worry, for this was his most lighthearted, least religious year in his whole medical course, and he had several girl friends in Cardiff.

"He's a shade too beautiful," Granny Morgan complained

dubiously to Margaret the following year, when the girls had taken the men's place at Cardiff and Margaret, on Paul's recommendation, had secured lodging in the Morgan domicile. "I'm afraid he's going to have a lot of trouble with girls in his life."

Margaret laughed. "Maybe. I know all the girls in my year were crazy about him."

Mrs. Morgan's little robin-bright eyes turned to her shrewdly. She thrust her long ear trumpet into the girl's face. "You aren't by any chance in love with him yourself, are you, dearie?"

Margaret's laugh this time was a bit strained. "Well, I thought I was once, but I'm thankful that's over now. We're just good friends."

"Hm!" was Mrs. Morgan's only comment.

It was not her fault if during this year in Cardiff Paul's interest in religion was at a slightly lower ebb than formerly. She insisted each morning on holding family prayers in her drawing room and would expect each member of the group to take voluble participation. Then, not wanting to miss a word, she would travel on her knees around the room, thrusting her long ear trumpet into the face of whoever was speaking. A bit disconcerting, Paul found, tilting his head to avoid hitting the trumpet with his chin, until finally he was almost leaning over backward to avoid it, and extremely difficult to concentrate on God and the trumpet at the same time!

Back in London in June of 1940, Paul started his clinical work in a surgical firm. But it proved to be no mere training period. The "phony" war had ended. France had fallen, to be followed by the grueling siege of the Battle of Britain. They had barely returned when the blitz started. The east end of London went up in flames. The docks were completely demolished. There was bombing around the hospital section almost every night.

Swiftly the hospital was organized into a casualty clearing station, its main departments evacuated, operating rooms transferred to the basement. Each day buses would move the previous day's casualties into the country to make room for those of the next night. The medical students were soon on full duty basis. Until a rota was organized Paul and his classmates were on call every single night. After their regular daytime work in the wards and surgery, they would try to sleep between tea and supper, then begin to sort out the casualties, set bones, give transfusions. Sometimes before midnight they would start assisting at operations, four tables continuing constantly in use by relays of surgeons, often until the small hours of the morning. Then they would get an hour's rest before breakfast. After a system of rotation was established, each surgical student was supposed to be on duty only on alternate nights, but on the nights when crowds of casualties came in, all got up, whoever was on duty.

Much of the work was on bodies crushed by falling buildings or injured by broken glass. Hour after hour Paul spent picking little bits of glass out of chests, intestines, arms, legs, feet, hands. It was while doing this patient, microscopic salvaging that Paul began to feel special interest in the human hand. Such a thing of beauty, such a perfect, exquisite tool, yet so terribly vulnerable!

The hospital was not spared. One night the University College library, third best in all England, was burned out. On another the great hall was destroyed. A bomb fell outside the resident doctors' quarters and made that uninhabitable.

"It's strange," Paul wrote his mother soon after that Christmas of 1940, "how one gets used to all this. It really does not worry us, and conversation is hardly interrupted by the roar of the planes or the gun crashes that set furniture rattling."

But finally, after an especially heavy bombing of the hospital, the whole medical school was again evacuated, Paul being among those students sent to Stanborough Hospital in Watford. Here he remained for nearly two years, doing his clinical and surgical training. Though the staff was reduced and library facilities meager, the war encroached little on their training, except to bring occasional casualty cases from the continental coast towns.

It was a period of intense stimulation and challenge. Sir Thomas Lewis, the great physiologist and heart specialist, and Dr. Kellgrin, later to become famous for his studies in pair, were doing research there, and it was through them that Paul's imagination was first stirred by a subject which was later to become of enthralling interest: the physiology and mechanics, the nature and control, of pain.

Life was not all academic work. Paul sometimes distinguished himself as a cook. One of his great war privations was marmalade, of which rationing allowed only one pot a month. He would save orange peels, sliver them, combine them with apples, and use all his sugar ration to boil a passable concoction, which he jealously parceled out to his friends in their "digs."

In spite of such talents Paul had few really close friends. It was easy for him, it seemed, to be two or three persons at once. Though he felt no conflict within himself, he could be equally at home with deeply religious people in the Christian Union and with others of secular viewpoints who would have been extremely embarrassed in the company of his religious acquaintances. To only a few had he found it possible to reveal every facet of his personality. Nancy Robbins, his cousin, had been one. Laurie Kurht had been another. And it would be many years before he would meet a third, John Webb.

Perhaps this sense of isolation was one reason for shying from romance—that and the memory of what total involvement had done to his mother. But now he felt a growing need for such involvement. It was a part of living, inescapable. And he was well on the road to thirty.

He wrote to his mother: "The family all seem to want me to get married, but they must provide a girl, mustn't they, if they are so keen! There are a couple of charming lassies about, but I seem to be too busy to get to know them nowadays. One, Margaret Berry, is very nice indeed."

Margaret's path and his had become diverted. First she had been at Sheffield, afterward at Cardiff. Then, activated by her father's driving ambition, she had taken six months to prepare for the primary exam toward the F.R.C.S. (Fellow of the Royal College of Surgeons) degree. Failing that, she had rejoined the clinical course, so their paths had seldom crossed.

Mrs. Morgan furnished the strongest link between them, and determined she was to weld it even stronger. Even loyalty to her own son, who was fond of Margaret, could not alter her conviction that Margaret and Paul were made for each other.

"He needs looking after, dearie," she would say pointedly to Margaret, "and you're just the one to do it."

"She's the right girl for you," she would say *very* pointedly to Paul on his occasional visits. "You ought to marry her."

Both would merely laugh. But Mrs. Morgan kept the link from breaking.

Now again their paths converged. It was the beginning of 1942. Both were in residence, Paul doing his obstetrical appointment, Margaret on the casualty intake. One night she was conducting a meeting of the Christian Medical Students' Association, and during the discussion she impulsively called on Paul to speak. After the meeting he walked home with her. It was a journey of discovery. Not only were they in remarkable agreement on a variety of subjects, but Paul was suddenly intensely aware of her as a woman and a most desirable one. London in blackout, in a night of cold winter fog, enclosed them in a new warmth of intimacy.

But for a long time he did not commit himself. And his approach to marriage continued to be objective. He sat down and tried to figure out what he wanted in life, whom he would want in his home, particularly whom he wanted as the mother of his children. The possibilities increasingly boiled down to one person: Margaret. She also was wary. Having cured herself once of too serious involvement of her emotions, she refused to take the same risk again. But in the following weeks they seized every opportunity to be together.

It was May, hottest of all months in India, when a letter made its way up the steep slopes of the Kolaryans, a neighboring range to the Kollis, where Evelyn Brand was spending her vacation in a tiny mosquito-net shelter, ministering to tribes among whom no missionary had ever before labored.

"The one thing that is different," wrote Paul with the exuberance of the small boy who had once raced and rolled and climbed on another nearby mountain, "is that I've got Margaret! It all happened one day when I went over to Northwood to spend an evening with the Berrys. Margaret and I went for a walk and sat on a stile and talked and talked. And then I said, 'Will you?' and she said, 'Yes!' Well, I never have been so really happy before as I was from then on, and still am."

Sitting by a little hurricane lantern in her lonely shelter, Evelyn Brand read and reread, and tried to picture a beloved face she had not seen for seven years, and another, blue-eyed and young and sweet which she had never seen, and wept a little even while she uttered prayers of thanksgiving.

7

Strange that such serenity could exist in a world gone mad! In the peaceful Wye Valley even the drone of planes portended soaring wings of adventure, not instruments of death. London with its nights of horror, its rubble of gaping walls and mutilated bodies, seemed a whole world, rather than a hundred-odd miles away. For eight glorious days in June 1943 Paul and Margaret spent their honeymoon roaming through sun and fog and rain, mostly the latter, exploring the wonderful world of Wye and the equally wonderful but infinitely more complex world of two suddenly merged personalities.

They considered plans for the future, doing much praying as well as discussing. Both had now been qualified, and they had received their university degree results just a week before the wedding. Should they look forward to missionary service, and, if so, where? But this decision was for the far future. Meanwhile Paul was faced with more pressing problems. His military call was coming up. Should he apply for foreign service in the air force? Should he accept a medical post in England which would mean temporary exemption? And what should Margaret do? After she finished her present job at Hemel Hempstead at the end of July she must take some medical position or be called up for military service. And—how should they run their family finances, which at the moment consisted of about ten shillings?

They were discussing the latter problem when Margaret discovered some of her husband's less endearing propensities. They had been walking along a railroad line for a long time and came suddenly to its end.

"I know a lovely short cut back to our lodging," Paul told her. "Come on. I'll show you the way."

Dutifully Margaret followed him along a circuitous path, the beauties of which would have been more apparent if she had not been wearing her best "going away" clothes and it had not been raining. Finally they came to a spot on the edge of the river which offered two alternatives: one must either swim or climb a tree.

"Come on," encouraged Paul without concern. "It's easy."

He started swinging across, monkey-like, from branch to branch, only looking around occasionally to see if she was following. And after the first startled gasp she was, although expecting momentarily to take a dip. It was her first of many such experiences taking Paul's beloved "short cuts."

They had reason to treasure the few days of peace and privacy. It would be years later, and in another country, that they would have a home of their own. Paul continued his war casualty work as house surgeon in London, while Margaret went into general practice with her father in Northwood. They were able to spend a weekend together only once a fortnight.

Dr. Berry urged Paul to work toward his F.R.C.S. "All right," Paul agreed. "I'll have a stab at it." The examinations were in two parts, primary and finals. The primary over basic subjects—anatomy and physiology—presented the first big hurdle. Usually attempts ended there. "If I *should* get through primary," he thought, "then I'll go on."

His teaching and casualty work left him little time for study. When the time for the examination drew near, he took two weeks' holiday. A week of it he spent at the medical school, which had now been evacuated to a new site in the south of London, and asked some of his old teachers to give him special tutoring. He also hired a physiology lecturer to give him private lessons and for a week dissected bodies, worked in special seminars and classes, and studied all night. Then he went home for a week and studied morning, afternoon, and evening, reading, reading, reading, filling himself with facts. Normally he despised "swats," those eggheads who stuck to books and got by on concentrated memorizing, but for a primary it was legitimate to swat, since one needed to retain the information only long enough to pass. At the end of the two weeks he walked to the exam, head steady, careful not to stumble, sure that if he took one erratic step, jarring his brain, most of the accumulated knowledge would spill out. He sat down at the desk, opened the paper, and let it spill. Since it was a war year, an even higher standard had been set than usual. Only eleven out of the more than one hundred aspirants passed. By a miracle Paul was one of them. Now he knew he must go on to the finals.

But in the following year there was even less time for study.

Early in 1944 he became surgical officer at the Hospital for Sick Children in Great Ormond Street, the old Foundling Hospital of London, one of the foremost children's hospitals in the world. In peacetime it would have been difficult for such a raw recruit to receive an appointment on its staff, but his experience in the casualty department of University College Hospital was a deciding factor, for the basement of Great Ormond Street's new building, still uncompleted, formed an ideal casualty center for that part of London. As Resident Surgical Officer Paul was organizationally in charge of this center. Living in quarters there with the other young doctors, he was often on duty around the clock. With bombings recurring almost every night, the operating schedule was exhausting but intensely challenging. Most of his work was in children's surgery under two famous specialists, Denis Browne and Sir Lancelot Barrington-Ward, and his year's experience there was worth ten in a normal peacetime situation. While most of the days were concerned with routine work, particularly orthopedic surgery with cases like club feet and congenital dislocation of the hip, nights were grim successions of patient reconstruction of small mangled bodies, interludes of horror when the whole city seemed one vast holocaust.

It was on one of these worst nights that his son Christopher was born. Margaret was in the Royal Northern Hospital, a couple of miles away from Great Ormond Street. Paul had tea with her in the afternoon, then returned to work knowing that, although labor had already started, birth was not likely to occur for many hours. Meanwhile there was a night of casualty work ahead. Part of his duty was firewatching on top of the eight-story hospital. Never had the bombing seemed so heavy. And the most tremendous crashes, the worst blazing explosions, were just where Royal Northern seemed to be. But there was no time to worry about his own. The crushed bones and torn flesh of a hundred other children soon demanded his full attention.

He dropped into exhausted sleep just before dawn. Starting to dress later in the morning, he noticed a little scrap of paper on his table. "Haven't seen that before," he thought. He picked it up. *To inform you that you are the father of a bonny, bouncing boy.* The sister in charge had received the message but, seeing him asleep, hadn't had the heart to wake him. Paul covered the two miles in record time. Bombs had come very close to Royal Northern, but the hospital had escaped damage. Rejoicing with his wife, inspecting his new son, whole, perfect as God intended, he felt profound awe, humility, and thanksgiving.

The coming of Christopher did little to disturb his parents' schedule. With a mother who had had some experience in pediatrics, he was reared with a minimum of fussing. Mother Berry helped with his care so that Margaret could continue her medical practice. On the weekends when Paul was able to visit his family he also assisted with his father-in-law's practice.

There was little family living until the autumn of 1944, when they took Christopher on a brief holiday to a little house in Bromley loaned them by Aunt Lillie. It was a reprieve of near-peace, for the bombing in London had almost stopped. But only a reprieve. One evening as they were sitting in the little garden they suddenly heard a great rattle in the sky. Then to their mystified horror they saw what looked like tiny planes with flaming tails passing low over the house.

"Machine guns!" yelled Paul, the only explanation he could think of.

Grabbing up the baby, they rushed inside. But it was not machine guns. Even at that distance from London, they soon heard tremendous crashes, saw the sky toward the city burst into geysers of flame as the first of the deadly new flying bombs reaped their harvest of destruction. The brief reprieve was ended. Quickly packing, they sped back to London.

So began an era of death and terror worse than any yet encountered or conceived. Casualties began to pour into Great Ormond Street Hospital, for the flying bombs came thick and fast, and in the beginning there was no defense against them. To compound the horror, if you were on watch on the hospital roof, you could see the bombs coming miles away, and, since they always traveled in a straight direction, you could tell where they were headed. If you saw one coming to one side, you just watched and waited; if straight, you rang the bell. When the warning bell rang, meaning that a bomb was headed for the hospital, all those who could ducked for cover. Nurses rushed to pull into the corridors the babies who had to be kept isolated in the glass cubicles until the very last moment, then when the bomb had passed over took them back in again. This went on, night after night after night—the air raid alarms, the moving of child patients away from the glass walls, the watchings, the warning bells, the listening for the sound of the thing rattling, the tension when the sound came, the worse tension if it suddenly stopped, which meant the fuel of the missile had been exhausted, and everybody, including the watchman on the roof, would duck for cover . . . then dead silence and more waiting, for after cutting out, the thing would hover for awhile before falling. More than once they heard it swish softly over the roof on its way down. Everything around was hit, but not the hospital. It was a world gone berserk.

Yet in some respects life remained surprisingly normal. The aunts pursued their quiet pattern of living a few miles away in Carlton Hill. Christopher grew two teeth, then two more, learned to wave bye-bye and night-night, and, with someone holding his hand, to walk steadily with long steps and a great deal of laughter. And Connie . . .

She was surprised when David Wilmshurst wrote her a letter from his new mission post in Nigeria. So was Paul. His friend had certainly evinced no romantic interest on his visits to Nethania. Connie, believing David to be merely lonely, responded with impersonal courtesy. The letters increased in frequency, became more and more personal. David, it seemed, had been by no means indifferent to Connie's charms, merely too shy to express his real feelings. They had much in common, religious zeal, dedication to missionary service. The result: they fell deeply in love by letter, and Connie, radiant, tearful, hopeful, took ship for marriage and mission in Africa, there to send back highly colored word pictures which brought back vivid memories to the African-reared Margaret and gave keen delight to her parents.

The Berrys were less enamored, however, of the idea of mission service for Paul and Margaret. While generally approving Paul as a son-in-law, Dr. Berry undoubtedly charged to his debit his daughter's obsession with religion. Certainly he had not encouraged it in her, nor could her mother's gentle tutelage or the High Church of England convent she had attended be wholly responsible. (He did not know about Mrs. Morgan!)

Paul wished his own future could be as easily determined as Connie's. As the end of his year at Great Ormond Street drew near, he was faced with more torture of indecision. Only casualty work had kept him from military service. In spite of its importance many, including Margaret's two brothers-in-law, looked at him askance because he wore a surgeon's mask and gown, not a uniform. He was inevitably faced with military call-up. The R.A.F. was building up a big force in India and would be needing doctors. Should he apply for a post there? Or should he stay on another year at Great Ormond Street, as the doctors there requested?

It was a period of depression as well as uncertainty. On the advice of one of his chiefs, also an examiner, he had gone up for his finals only a year after passing his primary, an unwise decision, for, though passing the clinical, he had failed in one of the practical exams. It might be years before he could accumulate enough experience to try again. His whole life seemed a muddle, continually shooting off on a tangent. He settled the matter temporarily by applying to the R.A.F. and continuing at Great Ormond Street on a month-to-month basis.

Then came an amazing offer, the job of assistant on the surgical unit at his old University College Hospital. What an opportunity! Invaluable experience under Professor Pilcher, one of London's finest surgeons, a chance to try again for his F.R.C.S., another year with the family! But it would be impossible, of course. The Central Medical War Committee would not sanction a change of senior post from one hospital to another. He made application for the post and then promptly forgot it.

But the unexpected happened. Possibly the job at University College Hospital was considered a priority, and his experience in the casualty clearing stations had made him more useful in a civilian than in a military capacity. "They've released me!" Paul reported, almost with awe, by phone to Margaret. "The Committee has told U.C.H. they can have me for a year. I still can't believe it."

The year at University College Hospital under Professor Pilcher was invaluable in its teaching experience and surgical training. The noted surgeon's techniques were outstanding, some of them brilliant. Paul took his finals again, a long tough examination, and passed, qualifying for his F.R.C.S. As second assistant in the surgical unit, with a shortage of staff because of the war, he was operating almost constantly, many of the cases casualties coming over the channel from Dunkirk and Bordeaux. Though acute surgery, such as repairs of cuts, gun wounds, ruptures, was his special area, he became profoundly interested in the mending of severed nerves and divided tendons, of which there were many cases, especially in hands and feet.

However, the months at University College Hospital were postponement, not substitute, for military service, and the end of the European phase of the war merely hastened this obligation. By the beginning of 1946 all the young doctors involved in casualty work expected to be called up. Paul applied for a commission in the army and knew that it was being processed. Though continuing with his work at the hospital, he expected to be called at any time and sent to the Far East.

The end of the war, however, brought fewer problems than blessings, one of them the return of Paul's mother to England. She had been in India for nearly ten years. Paul thought he had prepared himself this time for the changes which the years would have effected, but Evelyn Brand was to be always unpredictable. The ten years had not aged her. They had made her ageless. She had looked the same at fifty-five—wispy body, features pared almost to the bone, short straight gray hair tied back for utility's sake by a ribbon, young probing eyes—and she would look almost the same at eighty-five.

Her agelessness created problems for her mission board. Having reached the age of retirement, she was naturally expected to retire gracefully. But, no; instead she proposed not only to return to her mission work on the plains, but to use it as a jumping-off point for a mission project of her own, on—of all places—the top of an uncivilized mountain!

"Just send me back for a year," she begged. "I promise not to make any further claim on the board."

And, since for some years she had been returning her pittance of a salary, using her small inheritance from her father to finance her work, the board found its usual arguments of "precedent," "rules," "never been done," not quite adequate to meet the situation. For Evelyn Brand *was* precedent. She had been breaking rules, doing things which had never been done, all her life. Reluctantly the board acquiesced.

"Your father and I," she explained to Paul, "set out to take the Gospel of Christ to the people on five mountain ranges.

The Kollis were the first. The Kolaryans came next. After that the Pachas. If God gives me time, I shall go to all of them. And don't try to stop me."

Paul did not try. Unlike the aunts, the uncles, some of the cousins, and most of the members of the board, he knew exactly how she felt. For he had been there on the Kollis, shared his father's dream as he had looked out over the five mountain ranges. In fact, he envied his mother, who knew exactly what she wanted to do and where she was going. He only wished his own purpose in life was as clearly indicated.

And then suddenly out of the blue came a telegram.

"There is urgent need for a surgeon to teach at Vellore. Can you come immediately on short term contract? (Signed) Cochrane."

Too surprised even to comment, Paul handed it to Margaret.

"Cochrane?" she repeated, knitting her brows.

Paul searched his brain. "The name sounds familiar. I know. Livingstone. Dr. Robert Cochrane, one of our lecturers. Expert on some kind of tropical disease. But he didn't know me from Adam."

"Vellore?" prompted Margaret.

Paul was still vague. "I believe it's a big medical college and hospital in South India, supported by a lot of different missions. But—how did he happen to pick *me?*"

He would have understood better if he could have heard a conversation which had taken place some months earlier in India between his mother and Dr. Cochrane.

"Would you be interested in having my son come to Vellore?"

"Certainly not," Cochrane had replied, "if he hasn't an F.R.C.S."

"But," Mrs. Brand had shot back triumphantly, "my son has his F.R.C.S."

"I suppose—India's changing so fast," Paul continued, "getting ready for independence—with medical standards being stepped up, mission medical colleges must be in a bad way. They probably need doctors, terribly."

Margaret watched him as he walked back and forth, punctuating his somewhat jerky speech with jabs of his fists into his coat pockets.

"*Terribly,*" he repeated with even greater emphasis.

As he turned toward her, she saw his eyes, not their usual warm twinkling gray, but darker, remote, as if focused on spaces deep within or far away.

"You want to go, don't you?" she asked gently.

His eyes refocused. He laughed almost shamefacedly. "It's impossible."

"Why?"

"Dozens of reasons. For one thing, we're going to have a baby."

"*I'm* going to have a baby," she corrected. "And I'll probably have it just the same whether you're in London or the Far East or India."

"It's out of the question, anyway," Paul said abruptly. "There's no possibility of its working out."

"Unless God wants it to," returned Margaret quietly.

Paul wrote Dr. Cochrane that he was going into the army, that he was in no position to take a teaching post, and that he was expecting a second child. He thought the matter ended. But he did not know Robert Cochrane. Presently he received a letter which said in substance, "I will meet you under the clock at Victoria Station at such and such a time."

Paul was there, out of courtesy. A young medico with the ink not yet dry on his diplomas, even on his F.R.C.S., did not keep doctors of Robert Cochrane's reputation waiting under clocks.

"Must be a determined sort of person," Paul thought, remembering him only vaguely.

He was more than determined. He was forceful, aggressive, dynamic. And, with the job he had undertaken, the upgrading of the Vellore Christian Medical College and Hospital to meet the new medical standards prescribed by the Indian government, he needed to be all of these. It had taken an excess of these same qualities in its founder, Dr. Ida Scudder, to build the institution from a little ten by twelve dispensary in 1900 to its present capacity of over two hundred students and some three hundred teaching beds, plus schools of nursing, pharmacy, midwifery, and roadside dispensaries which ministered annually to a hundred thousand people. Now, explained Cochrane with the vigor which characterized both words and gestures, the school was being raised to graduate level in the face of staggering difficulties. Both college and hospital were being opened to men. Nearly a million dollars worth of new buildings must be erected. The number of teaching beds must be doubled. At least four new departments must be introduced. And, his special problem as principal, at least twelve qualified teaching professors must be added to the staff. He had temporarily given up his own work as head of a great leprosy sanatorium to assume this important task.

"That's it." Paul suddenly remembered. "Leprosy! Of course. Dr. Robert Cochrane, foremost leprosy specialist in the world!"

"And we must have you there," continued Cochrane brusquely. "Immediately. Macpherson, one of our two surgeons, has just been invalided home. We need you."

Patiently Paul recounted the reasons why he could not possibly go. First, of course, there was the matter of the army.

"Leave that to me." Cochrane brushed off the argument as lightly as if it had been a fly.

Paul stared at him. The cheek of the man, thinking he could pit his puny strength against the massive officialism of John Bull, and win! Yet, looking at him, you actually believed he could.

"Do you realize," Paul brought up the second argument, "that you are offering a responsible teaching post, which should have at least six or eight years' experience after the F.R.C.S., to a young whippersnapper who's had only two?"

"Let me be the judge of that," barked Cochrane. "I know your record."

"And my wife is having her second child—"

"Wonderful place, Vellore," countered the other blandly, "for women and children. But you needn't bring your family at first. You'd be away from them at least two years in the army. Come to us for one. Then if you like the work, send for them. If not, we'll release you. This is a crisis. We're trying to save from annihilation the biggest Christian medical institution in all of Asia. And we need *you*."

The war department bowed to the persuasion of a stronger will, whether of God (as Margaret devoutly believed) or of Robert Cochrane (as Paul secretly suspected) or of both, which was more likely, since the two were presumably working in cooperation. Margaret carefully kept her parents' disapproval from Paul's ears and tried to guard him from the raised eyebrows and slightly acid comments of her brothers-in-law. She entered the Royal Northern on schedule for her confinement, this time without the accompaniment of fireworks, and their second child, Jean, was born.while Paul was in the very act of packing his bags for India. Bidding goodby to his small family, he remembered his own bleak boyhood loneliness and vowed that such separation must not happen again.

And so once more the shuttle moved.

8

It was a voyage into the past as well as the future. Breathing the air of his native country for the first time in twenty-three years, Paul found it amazingly, excitingly familiar. For the smell of India, that rich composite of dust, cow dung smoke, human sweat, sandalwood, jasmine blossoms, hot spices, poverty, people, changes little with millennia, much less a quarter century. His mouth watered and his throat stung to the delightful aromas of curry. The rhythm of a *tabla* set his pulses racing. The clatter of bullock carts, the nasal wails of hawkers, the color and noise of bazaars, the honking of cars boring seemingly impossible tunnels through choked lanes of handcarts, *rickshas*, lorries, loaded donkeys, bicycles, buses, pedestrians, ambling cows; the grays of loincloths, the shining whites of *dhotis*, the reds and greens and yellows of *saris* and blouses and turbans—all were as much a part of his heritage as London bobbies and rumbling trams and the lights of Piccadilly. And when he awoke the first morning to the raucous cacophany of crows, then he knew that he was completely, absolutely at home.

He reveled in the long train journey across southern India, enjoying even the discomforts. He begrudged the hours of darkness, and with the first light his face was glued to the window, watching tiny fires spring alive, meager warmth for gray-white huddled figures with outstretched hands; shadowy masses resolve themselves into clusters of village huts. The creaking of a windlass turned by a pair of bullocks, the sloshing of water from a full goatskin into an irrigation ditch, were music to his ears. How could he have forgotten the dazzling greens of sunlit rice fields, running the whole gamut from pale lime to jade to deep emerald? or the incredible grace of a procession of ragged village women with tiers of brass pots poised on their heads? or—yes—even the ugly and immense dignity of a slowly plodding water buffalo?

He knew when they came into Tamil country, for the cries of the peddlers at stations became less jargon and partly intelligible. He felt an inordinate triumph when he could distinguish a few words.

"Varaiparam, plantains!"

"Chai, tea! *Chai-ai!"*

"Thanni, water!"

And, to his delight and amazement, when he arrived at the Baptist bungalow in Madras, where he was to be entertained for a few days, and the servant came to his room, the correct Tamil expressions came instinctively from his lips. *"Thanni kondu va,* bring the water." *"Pothum,* enough!" *"Ammam,* yes." *"Illai,* no."

But he had not come to India to relive the past. He was glad when James MacGilvray, one of the staff members at Vellore, picked him up at the mission bungalow and drove him the last eighty-five miles to his destination.

India in December, 1946, was a world in transition; in trouble and turbulence also, for, though Britain had agreed unequivocally to Indian independence, conflict between the Congress Party and the Muslim League had erupted into bitter violence. On August 16 the Muslims had observed "Direct Action Day," calling a general strike against both Britain and the Congress Party, and bloody riots had broken out in Calcutta, spreading swiftly to other areas of North India. On December 9th the constituent assembly opened in New Delhi to form a new constitutional government, but no Muslim League representatives attended. When Paul Brand arrived in India the country was on the threshold of independence, yet also on the brink of civil war.

But in South India there were few signs of turbulence. The unsettled skies of the fall monsoons had cleared, leaving the

earth's long thirst quenched, parched skin freshened, naked-
ness lavishly clothed in greens and golds. True, there were a
few evidences of the social and political struggle, such as an
inflammatory slogan scrawled on a crumbling cement wall:

DOWN WITH **B**RITISH
BANIAS
BRAHMINS

But whatever of violence they portended was belied by the
overwhelming mass of patient plodding figures, intent on the
day's business, of curious but friendly faces.

And though in New Delhi, December 9 was a harbinger of
tragic conflict, a thousand miles south in Vellore it was a day
of rejoicing and high hope. For it was the birthday of Dr. Ida
Scudder, founder and guiding spirit of the Christian Medical
College and Hospital. Though officially retired four months
earlier, Dr. Ida was still linked body and soul with the institution she had labored nearly fifty years to build. Paul gazed with
appreciative amazement at the blue-eyed, white-haired woman
seated in the gaily decorated birthday chair. Hard to believe
that this dynamo of radiant energy was 76 years old!

The success of her life's effort still hung in the balance, for
Vellore also was a world in transition. Founded as a women's
college in 1918 and equipped to give only the licensed medical
practitioner's certificate, it must now step up its program to
meet the requirements of university affiliation or close its
doors. Though in October of 1945 the college had been pro-
visionally qualified by the inspection commission, and the first
M.B.B.S. (Bachelor of Medicine, Bachelor of Surgery) students were now receiving clinical training, the goal was far
from attainment. In spite of the unflagging energy of Dr.
Cochrane, the principal, and "Mac" MacGilvray, the manager-
bursar, the staff was still pitifully small, the buildings painfully
inadequate, and the budget in constant deficit. But the goal
was in sight.

No sooner had Paul arrived in Vellore than he was plunged
into work. The hospital, a big cluster of yellow-washed buildings wedged into the teeming bazaar section of the sprawling
town, was a huge heart of pulsing activity. Each day hundreds

poured through the arteries of its gates, swarmed into the out-patient dispensary behind the wrought-iron silver-painted gateway, clogged verandahs, anterooms, and corridors, queued in patient, squatting masses outside the doors of every department.

At first Paul marveled not only at their numbers but at their incredible diversity: men in tailored suits, flowing robes, white *dhotis*, smart uniforms, single dirty loincloths; women with soft skins and silk *saris* and jewels, dark hair smooth and glistening and braided with flowers; women in scraps of dirty cotton, hair sun-bleached and unkempt, work-hardened flesh ingrained with dust and tough as animal hide; children . . . everywhere children. Scampering, crawling, inertly squatting, riding the overburdened hips of other children. Bright-eyed and smiling, teeth white and knobs of marigolds clinging to their neat oily little scalps; crying; too weak to cry. Skirted, bloused, girt with nothing but a waist-band, naked. Paul couldn't decide which tore most at his heartstrings, the plump smiling tots who reminded him of Christopher and Jean, or the rickety scraps of misery, with their bloated little bellies, their scabby scalps and gummed eyes, their terrible mute patience.

But there was little time for reflection, even for pity. He was too busy. Obliged to make his rounds of the wards with English speaking doctors, he devoted much of his scant leisure to studying Tamil, but with little success. Instead of building on his boyhood knowledge of common Tamil, the pandit chosen for his lessons insisted that he learn the language from the roots up, starting with pages and pages of grammar, which Paul had always detested, drilling him in the endings of nouns and verbs and stressing the written rather than the spoken word. The lessons were a complete fiasco, and he never did fully overcome the handicap. Since, as in many institutions of higher education in India, the academic work at Vellore was entirely in English, it was knowledge of colloquial Tamil that he needed for conversing with patients. He acquired it the hard way, by painful necessity, through trial and ridiculous error.

The scope of his work in surgery was staggering. The head surgeon—in fact, the only other one—was Dr. John Carman, an American Baptist missionary of nearly twenty years of experience in India, who had come to Vellore in 1945 to organize the department. Tall, spare, tireless, a bit taciturn, a man in his vigorous prime, he was as skillful an administrator as he was a surgeon.

"We must have some specialization," he told Paul at the outset of their work together. "We're both general surgeons, but I understand you've done orthopedic work in London. If you'll take all the orthopedic cases, I'll take all the urinary."

Paul's surgical knowledge and skill were taxed to the limit. As second in command of all surgery in a hospital of nearly four hundred beds, with a limited staff and, at that stage, limited facilities, he was faced with medical problems which would have challenged the skill of a doctor with twice his experience. Many major forms of surgery had never been done before at Vellore; yet in his very first days a whole succession of such cases came along, demanding far more experience than he possessed. Not even in the terrible days of the blitz had he worked longer hours or dealt with more baffling cases.

But life at Vellore was not all work. The same driving intensity which kept most staff members at their posts for ten or twelve hours each day activated their hard-won leisure. Dr. Ida's was one of at least three birthday celebrations which Paul attended in December. The collector invited all the resident foreigners to a big Christmas party, complete with banquet and an excess of British formality. There were almost daily opportunities for vigorous tennis. Though Paul lived with the Carmans in a big rambling mission bungalow at Viruthampet, two miles from the hospital and six from the college, he was soon absorbed into the congenial and closeknit fellowship which included all staff members.

"Never," he wrote Margaret with a burst of boyish enthusiasm, "have I seen a more wonderful place with such marvelous people, so utterly dedicated and warmly friendly."

His descriptions were all in superlatives. He loved the college, located in a most beautiful valley outside the town. The buildings were all of stone built in an immense rectangle about the most lovely sunken garden with a lily pool in the center. His class in surgery of seven fifth year students was *very* intelligent and *tremendously* challenging. And as for his work in the hospital, it was a joy to feel oneself so *terribly* needed. Two years would be all too short to contribute to a work like this, so she had better plan to come as soon as possible.

Margaret read his letters with sympathy and elation. Not so her parents.

"What's the boy trying to do?" fumed Dr. Berry. "Make us think India is a Utopia when every paper we pick up fairly screams that it's nothing but a blood bath? Listen to this! 'RIOTS SPREAD TO PUNJAB. The last encounter between Hindus and Muslims saw the slaughter in cold blood of 300 men, women, and children.' "

Troubled, her gentle nature always susceptible to the moods of those she loved, Margaret reread the letters. "He doesn't seem to mention any kind of conflict. I wonder why."

Her father snorted. "He wants you to come, that's why!"

"Oh, but Paul isn't like that!" Margaret rose loyally to his defense. Surely you don't think he'd want to take his wife and children into danger!"

"Then tell him to explain these." Testily Dr. Berry thrust into her hands a half dozen papers with black headlines. "Ask him what he means by suggesting that a woman with two babies go to a place like this!"

Answering Paul's letters, the dutiful daughter quoted the headlines, posed the questions, while at the same time the loyal wife made plans for sailing, as Paul had urged, at the earliest possible date.

In India Paul continued to write with exuberant enthusiasm blithely ignoring both questions and quotations. For, tragic though the birth pangs of the new nation must be for any lover of India, to his and Margaret's personal life they seemed relatively unimportant. The riots a thousand miles away in the north seemed as remote from Vellore as from England, more so, for the Indian press, anxious to keep emotions from flaming, was far more restrained than the English. Besides, plunged into an exacting daily schedule of surgery, medicine, and teaching, he was an infrequent and haphazard letter writer.

His class in surgery was a constant delight, and the seven girls, vanguard of the candidates for the new M.B.B.S. degree, found him a unique and exciting teacher. Not only did his flair for humor, pith, and drama make learning fun, but he expressed facts so simply and graphically that they never forgot them.

"What's the trouble with me?" he would demand, entering the classroom waddling with a ducklike gait.

"Dislocation of the hip?" someone would venture.

"R-r-right."

They were not at all afraid of him. His relationship with them was like Dr. Ida's with her first class of fourteen girls back in 1918, a little like that of a *guru* with his followers. They went on picnics, climbed Kailas, the mountain near the college, went to the canteen together for their coffee break. So lacking were the girls in awe that they insisted the "W" of his middle name stood for "Wicked".

"How are you?" they would greet him with mock solicitude.

"Terrible," he would reply, listing all sorts of symptoms which they would be expected to diagnose.

The atmosphere of informal levity followed them into the operating room, where Paul insisted that his students be given every possible chance to operate. In spite of his obvious skill and exactness with the scalpel, he seemed never harassed, never tense or hurried. Surgery became for his students no grim business, but a relaxed and fascinating adventure.

"Ramabai," he would order cheerfully, "your job is to hold on to this clamp from morning till evening." Or—"What's this?" he would inquire in lieu of sharp criticism when one of the students was giving a patient too much anaesthesia. "Am I seeing everything blue, including our patient?"

But when they accompanied him into the wards, there was no levity. Always in his bedside lectures he was perfectly serious. And they learned far more from his bedside manner than from his lectures. It was obvious that he actually cared, was deeply concerned, about every one of his patients. His students also. For when Rose, one of the seven, had to miss three months of lectures on account of typhoid, he repeated all the lectures just for her in his leisure hour, between one and two in the afternoon.

Paul was as popular a speaker as he was teacher. Whenever he preached, whether at the college or the hospital chapel, the mats spread on the polished stone floor were crowded with students. His gift for pith and pungency, for the aptly turned phrase, for metaphor and drama was the least important reason for their rapt attention. He talked the language of medical students, used their textbooks as his texts, his sermons often dealing with the commonplaces of anatomy and physics: fat cells, nerves, the reproductive system, bones, muscles. His first sermon at Vellore was about blood, its functions of cleansing, of supplying energy, of protecting against disease, of giving the power to overcome.

"Last week," he reminded the students, "a patient was dying of measles. The call went out for a person convalescing from measles to give blood. Why? Because such a person has suffered and overcome. Just so Christ suffered that he might be effective in helping others overcome."

They listened spellbound while he turned the human body into a universe of wonder, an operating table into an altar, the pursuit of the mysteries of a test tube into an act of holy communion.

In April Paul was able to escape from the mounting heat to Kodaikanal, a mountain paradise some three hundred miles to the south where since the turn of the century, missionaries, including Dr. Ida, had been going for the holidays. His first whiff of the bracing air was like a breath of heaven. Now, he knew, he had spanned the final arc in the cycle of his homecoming.

Though he lived most of the time with the Carman family, Naomi and the children, he was a frequent visitor at Hill Top, Dr. Ida's stone eyrie on the edge of a seven-thousand foot spur overlooking a hundred miles of glorious sky and plain. He had more in common, he discovered, with this indefatigable veteran than abundant energy, intense love of God, and a deep concern for people. They shared a passion for clocks. "Aunt Ida" had a surplus of them at Hill Top, most of them out of order. There was a tall grandfather's clock which would not run, a lovely little French clock which refused to chime. Paul fixed them all, and Aunt Ida was delighted.

Due to his penchant for short cuts he was frequently getting lost on the network of roads and paths leading from the missionary colony into the surrounding hills. Once, leaving the main road and attempting to climb to Hill Top straight up the steep wooded incline, he arrived back home without having reached his goal.

"They've moved Dr. Ida's!" he complained with mock dismay.

He tramped miles over the hills with the Carman children, Bob, Eleanor, and the twins. He felt constantly as if he must take long deep breaths to store up fresh air against the heat of the plains. And with his return to Vellore he was to need all its bracing pungency.

May, climax of India's hot season, saw both her temperatures and her emotions rising. With the appointment of Lord Mountbatten as Viceroy, commissioned to implement the speedy liquidation of British rule, the tense political struggle was moving rapidly toward its crisis. Conflict between religious factions became increasingly explosive. But in Vellore Hindus and Muslims continued to live in harmony, as they had done for generations. Working in an environment largely unaffected by the political situation, Paul continued to disregard Margaret's frequent allusions to the newspaper headlines and her parents' worries. Newspapers were always exaggerating, and her parents were naturally looking for an excuse to keep her at home. It never occurred to him that she might be taking their concern seriously. Fortunately she was planning to sail in June, and his letters, still bursting with enthusiasm, were now overflowing also with anticipation.

Even the appalling heat failed to dampen his ardor. Though Dr. Carman was now on vacation in the hills, Paul had a fine group of Indian assistants, among them Dr. Venkatachalam, a talented young Brahmin, skilled at diagnosing, and the competent doctors Roy and Chatterji. Even so, Paul's days were overwhelmingly full. Almost every day, and sometimes all day, he would remain at work in the scorchingly hot operating rooms, soaking gown after gown after gown, able often to wring water out of them when he took them off. Drinking water copiously to compensate for the loss, he discovered two startling results. First he found himself covered from head to foot with prickly heat. Then one day after an operation he was suddenly so doubled up with cramps that he could not walk. Immediately he recognized the cause. As soon as he could move, he struggled to the hospital pharmacy.

"Salt—give me—salt," he croaked to the man in charge.

"Salt? What kind of salt?"

"Any kind. Tablet—cooking—just *salt!*"

The attendant dumped a big handful in a tumbler of water, and Paul poured it down his throat. It was one of the sweetest drinks he had ever tasted. His problem was to find a happy medium between drinking too much and getting prickly heat, or too little and acquiring kidney stones. It would be at least a year before his body became fully adjusted to the scorching hundred to a hundred and ten degree temperatures.

Both heat and activity had risen to new crescendos when Margaret's letter arrived. Paul waited until he was alone in his room at the bungalow to read it. The last one, probably, before she left England! Tearing it open with a tingle of anticipation, he read with cold dismay. For it was a despairing letter. What should she do? Everybody assured her that, with conditions as they were in India, she was insane to come, Paul worse than insane to let her. She didn't mind for herself, but to imperil the safety of their two babies! And Paul had written nothing to quiet her fears, had not even answered her questions! What was she supposed to think? If he thought after reading this that she should not come, would he please cable her immediately?

Mechanically Paul refolded the letter, creasing it hard between his fingers. The wind clattered in the tufts of the palmyras, sounding like rain. But it was not rain. There had been scarcely a drop since December. He was conscious of hot dry dust parching his lips, stinging his eyes.

He was first stunned, incredulous, then filled with cold, self-castigating dismay. What had he done? Or, rather, what hadn't he? Just a few words of explanation would probably have been sufficient. He had trusted so implicitly in Margaret's clearheadedness, forgotten her gentle susceptibility. But it was too late now. He couldn't take the risk of trying to persuade her.

He was not one to hesitate. As he drove to the post office, all of India unfolded itself. Trumpet vines and bougainvillea flamed. Brown children romped in the dust. A farmer cycled past with a huge basket of golden mangoes poised on his head. Paul had been looking forward to giving Margaret her first taste of mangoes. And showing her jacarandas in bloom. Yes, and children with gummed eyes and spindle legs and bloated little bellies crying out for the skill of her gentle sensitive fingers.

He sent the cable.

For months Margaret had tried valiantly to fight them: the headlines, the gossip, the constant pressures of cautious loving parents.

"INDIA ON THE BRINK OF CIVIL WAR . . . COMMUNAL CONFLICT SPREADS . . ."

"Wait till the British leave. There'll be anarchy, bloodshed, famine!"

"My dear, I can't bear to think of it." This refrain from her mother. "Those two dear little babies! What is Paul thinking of?"

"Utterly foolish!" This testily from her father. "To get into that bloodbath with two children—just looking for trouble!"

She resisted the flood of tirades, persuasion, advice, warnings, stoutly defending Paul against all criticism. Ruth and Monica Harris, Paul's cousins, helped. One a doctor, the other a nurse, they were returning to India in June for another term as missionaries, and Margaret was sailing with them. Their calmness and assurance quieted her fears, added fuel to her missionary fervor, which during the last few years had been far more ardent than Paul's.

But as time went on her resistance broke down. Paul was far away, her parents close at hand, and what they said made sense. As sailing time approached, she felt torn in two. How could Paul do this to her! She wept, prayed, agonized. Finally, just a week before the time of sailing, she wrote a frantic letter. "If you think on reading this that there's any reason why I shouldn't come, then please cable . . ."

The cable came. *Consider it better that you do not come now. I will return in March.*

But it still resolved nothing. Her father, feeling perhaps a little guilty, did no gloating, exerted no further pressure.

"We know it's a terrible decision for you to have to make, my dear. You have Paul's opinion, you know ours. The last decision must be your own."

Margaret was in London at the home of Paul's aunts when she made it. "Let's ask God about it," Aunt Hope suggested simply. But even as they knelt to pray, Margaret rose from her knees.

"Auntie, it's all right," she said with sudden confidence.

From that moment she had no further doubts. Her assurance was as strong as if she had actually seen a vision of the Christ pointing his finger toward the east. It was then nine o'clock in the morning. Purposefully she made final preparations for sailing the next day. That evening, June 3, came Lord Mountbatten's announcement that terms for independence, accompanied by partition, had been agreed upon by both conflicting factions. Instantly the British press changed its tone. As Margaret sailed the following day the headlines were already heralding what promised to be the peaceful and orderly emergence of India into the family of the Commonwealth.

Her journey on the *Strathmore* was not easy. The ship, used for troop transportation during the war, was still crowded beyond capacity, and Margaret's cabin, designed for two berths, held eight, all occupied. Heat was glaring and oppressive. As they steamed through the Indian Ocean in the path of the monsoon the children developed prickly heat and painful boils. But Margaret had not a moment's regret. The vision was still with her.

"Be thankful for it," Ruth Harris told her, "for there will be times when you will wonder whether it was God's will for you to go to India or not. Now when the hard things come, you will always meet them in the strength of this experience."

It was Paul's emotions which worried Margaret now. There was no message waiting for her in Aden, but she cabled Paul from there. She discovered later that it was the first word he had received since the ship sailed. All those days he had not known whether she was coming or not. Now that she understood the Indian situation her lack of trust seemed incomprehensible. The nearer she got to Bombay the more guilty and ashamed she felt. How could she possibly explain to him such a foolish lapse of trust and loyalty!

But there was no need to explain. When Paul came on board the ship at Bombay one look at his face assured her that he completely understood. As so often, when they were together, he seemed to know exactly what she was thinking. The intervening months of separation might never have been, and there they were, one person again.

"What's this? A band of refugees?"

Paul gathered the sorry looking brood into his arms, prickly heat, boils, dirt, whimpers, and all, and miraculously the bad memories of the journey disappeared. "I know," he comforted. "It's been a *terrible* trip, and you're beastly hot and uncomfortable. We must get you away to the hills."

But with all his tender understanding, he could still be remarkably obtuse. A short time later Margaret found herself sitting on a station platform at Arkonum Junction, near Vellore, a mountain of baggage piled around her and Jean, smothered with flies, crying lustily from her pram. Though it was early morning, the summer heat, humid and blistering, was already climbing to near a hundred degrees. Interested spectators soon clustered around, and Margaret, tired and hot, felt trapped and terribly deserted. Paul, trying to keep Christopher happy, had wandered off with him to explore the intricacies of the engine, blithely leaving her to cope alone with heat, baggage, crowds, crying baby, flies, and tightening coils of nausea. Expecting any moment to be violently sick, she tried desperately to fan the flies from Jean's sticky, sweaty little body and, without knowing a word of their language, to fend off the horde of curious, sympathetic spectators, all anxious to inspect or help pacify the small white visitor. Then to her great relief and joy, Monica Harris got off the train and came toward her. Serene, competent, neat braids circling her sweet face like an angel's halo, Monica calmly assumed control of the situation.

"*Daya vu say thu,* please, dear friends," she addressed the crowd in her beautiful Tamil. "This lady is a stranger. She doesn't understand the ways of our country. She's not feeling well, and neither is the baby. She appreciates your kindness and likes you, but please stand back a little. That's fine. *Salaam,* thank you so much."

Magically the tightening coils loosened. Monica gently bathed Jean's face with her handkerchief moistened from the thermos, and the baby stopped crying. Paul appeared with Christopher, crowing on his shoulder. And Margaret smiled into the circle of dark friendly faces. Not even the Carmans' warm welcome and the comfort of their cool screened bungalow made her feel more at home in India.

9

It was one day early in 1947 that Paul Brand took a short journey which was to change his life.

"Come over to Chingleput," said Dr. Robert Cochrane, his habitual bluntness mellowed into affability, "and have a meal with me."

Ha! Trying to make up for his bullying methods in bringing me to India, thought Paul. With equal affability he replied, "I'll be glad to come."

Dr. Cochrane had accepted the principalship of the Christian Medical College only temporarily to guide the institution through its critical task of upgrading, but he had never entirely relinquished his responsibility as superintendent of the Lady Willingdon Leprosy Sanatorium at Chingleput, a government institution but under church management and financially assisted by the British Mission to Lepers. One of the foremost authorities on leprosy, he had done more than any other man not only to alleviate the condition of the leprosy victims in Madras State, but by constant education to change the popular image of the disease, insisting that it *was* a disease, caused like many others by a bacillus, and not the mysterious curse, with vague connotations of sin and divine punishment, which since ancient times had doomed its victims to social stigma and ostracism.

Thanks to his efforts Vellore had become a center of research in the development of the new sulfone drugs which had already showed amazing results in the treatment of leprosy. Heretofore the only means of combating the disease had been the awkward, painful, and not too successful chaulmoogra oil injections. Now with the discovery of the sulfones—promin, diasone, and sulphetrone—which could be given by mouth, dramatic progress had been made. But these drugs were too expensive for India. Only in the preceding year, 1946, the Christian Medical College, in cooperation with other Indian agencies, had embarked on an intensive research program to discover a cheaper drug which could be made available not only to India's two million leprosy sufferers but to the more than ten million victims of the disease throughout the world.

Paul knew all this vaguely, but on the day he first visited Chingleput his interest in leprosy was superficial. There were no leprosy patients in the Vellore hospital or in any other hospital in India except those designated as leprosaria, and his work as surgeon never took him to the isolation clinics or the roadside dispensaries where for many years doctors at Vellore had been treating the disease. He arrived at the sanatorium in Chingleput, a few miles south of Madras, somewhat in advance of the time set for the meal.

"Come for a walk," Cochrane suggested. "You've been in India for some time, but I doubt if you've seen many cases of leprosy. Come and have a look around our hospital sanatorium."

Paul agreed, but with no great enthusiasm. He observed with casual interest the grounds, gardens, shops, hospital buildings, and admired the cooperative set-up in which the inmates practically ran their own hospital, gave each other a good share of the 100,000 injections administered each year, grew all their own fresh food, wove their own cloth and bandages, and even bound their schoolbooks.

"I like the approach, Bob," he observed once. "It's wholesome, human, not at all the way I imagined a lepers' asylum would be."

Dr. Cochrane turned on him fiercely. "Hospital, not asylum," he barked. "And don't say 'lepers.' We never use the word here. Tell me, what do you think of when you hear the word 'leper'?"

Paul flinched. Suddenly all the years of his scientific training became nil. He was a boy again, pulling the sheet over his prickling scalp while his mother intoned from the Holy Book, "Unclean, unclean!"; dragging Connie back in horror from the forbidden spot where the three strangers had squatted . . .

"Exactly," Cochrane said grimly. "Don't answer. I can tell by your face."

The hospital inmates were everywhere, strolling around the grounds, squatting, stumping awkwardly on bandaged feet, staring with empty blind eyes, lifting ravaged faces which turned their friendly smiles into grotesque leers, or, often, displaying no marks of the disease except perhaps a small area of baldness or a whitish patch of skin. Paul's first natural shock and repugnance gave way to deep pity and concern, those in turn to professional curiosity. He knew that the ancient fear of contracting the disease from casual contact was unfounded. Leprosy, though mildly infectious, especially for children exposed to close association with the disease for long periods, was less contagious than tuberculosis, and adults were relatively nonsusceptible. At least ninety percent of adults were completely immune. Moreover, the victims who displayed the most obvious stigmata—hairless brows, clawed hands, depressed noses, stumps of fingers and toes—were often "burned-out" cases and not even mildly infectious.

"Look at this," Dr. Cochrane kept pointing out one feature after another which, as a dermatologist, he found of special interest, a patch of skin, a nodule, a plaque, a peculiar discoloration.

Paul was not interested in skins, and he found his attention wandering, but not indiscriminately. For there was something which did interest him tremendously. *Hands.* Always his eyes were drawn to them, as were those of a portrait artist to faces. For he loved human hands, had always loved them but especially since he had come to understand their incredible, beautiful mechanism, making them the most skillful and exquisite tool, except perhaps the brain, which God had ever devised. Now he became suddenly conscious of them all about him. Folded before smiling faces in the Indian manner of greeting. Held up in waving salutation. Outstretched in western style. Hiding mutilated faces. Empty. Clutching tools or bits of food or cigarettes. Everywhere hands. But not human hands. Some of them were more like claws, fingers stiffly flexed, unable to close palm to palm in the gesture of greeting. Some had the fingers shortened or one or more of them missing; others were just a bunch of stumps. Some did not even have stumps. Finally Paul could stand it no longer.

"Look here, Bob," he broke into the smooth discourse on patches and nodules and plaques, "I don't care about skins. Tell me about these hands. What's the matter with them? How do they get this way? What do you do about them?"

He may have asked all three questions at once, or one at a time. It did not matter. The answer to all three was the same.

"Sorry, Paul. I can't tell you. I don't know."

"Don't know!" Paul was almost inarticulate in his shock and amazement. "Here you've been a leprosy specialist all these years, and yet you say you—you don't know! Surely something can be done for these hands!"

Dr. Cochrane turned on him almost fiercely. "And whose fault is it, I ask you, that I don't know! Mine or yours? I'm a skin man. I can tell you all about these skins. I know the correct way to treat leprosy. But it's you, not I, who are the bone man, the orthopedic surgeon!"

He continued more quietly. "I wonder if you can explain to me why, when there are more than ten million leprosy patients in the world—maybe as high as fifteen and a good percentage of them with deformed hands—not one, I repeat, *not one* orthopedic surgeon has ever really studied the deformities of leprosy."

Paul stared at him. His first impulse was to say, "I don't believe you." Impossible on more than one count: First, that there could be so many deformed hands in the world, more than all those caused by polio, far more than those resulting from nerve injuries through automobile and other accidents! Second, that with the thousands of orthopedic surgeons working to repair hands injured by other causes, not one should have concerned himself with injuries affecting up to fifteen million people!

"You see," explained the older man, his voice weary now, for he had been fighting a long battle against the very ignorance and incredulity Paul was now displaying, "people, even doctors, have never really considered leprosy a disease. They've put it in a different category. In one part of their brains they think about influenza and tuberculosis and all the other ailments commonly dealt with, but leprosy is something different. It carries an aura of the supernatural, as though its victims were no longer people but somehow accursed, outcasts from the human race. Priests and missionaries may concern themselves with them, crackpot idealists like Damien, very nice and kind of them, but it's not a job for doctors."

They strolled on in silence, while Paul continued to study the multiple deformities around him. Suddenly he stopped and looked hard at a young patient sitting on the ground trying to take off his sandal. He kept trying to hold the leather strap of the sandal and jerk it free of the buckle, holding it between the side of his thumb and the side of his palm, but it kept slipping out of his hands. Dr. Cochrane's gaze followed Paul's.

"Nerve damage," he commented, "and muscular paralysis, the intrinsic muscles. Also complete anaesthesia. There is absolutely no feeling, as you probably know, after this type of leprosy has reached this particular stage, in either the hands or the feet."

No. Paul did not know. Or if he ever had, the fact had made no impression. Now suddenly its implication struck him like a blow. To hold the hands of another human being, to touch an object and feel nothing! To walk along the ground unconscious of the softness of grass or the hardness of clay or the sharpness of stones! He moved toward the young man.

"Please," he blundered in Tamil, "may I look at your hands?"

With that sideward motion of the head which means "yes", the young man rose from the ground and, smiling, thrust his hands forward. Paul took them in his own, gently tracing the misshapen contours with his sensitive supple fingers. After studying them intently for some moments, he pried open the stiff fingers and placed his own right hand in the right hand of the patient. "Squeeze my hand, please," he directed. "Press as hard as you can."

To his amazement, a sharp, intense pain shot through his palm. The man's grip was like iron! It was not a normal handclasp, of course, because of the curled fingers, whose nail tips dug so hard into Paul's flesh that it seemed skin must be broken, but no normal hand could have exhibited greater strength. Paul winced and almost cried out. But even sharper than the physical pain was the sudden thrill which coursed through him.

"That hand isn't all paralyzed!" he exclaimed, nursing his bruised fingers. "He still has some good muscles, some mighty good ones!"

As they walked back to the bungalow, Paul kept firing questions at the older doctor. Why did fingers and toes of leprosy patients wear off? Was paralysis in the disease haphazard, or did there seem to be a pattern? Was there a possibility that surgery might be effective in making a claw hand usable, and if so why had it never been attempted?

Dr. Cochrane's reply was virtually identical to all these questions.

"You tell me!" he challenged.

And that was exactly what Paul Brand intended to do.

For it was that night that the seed was sown. Like most seeds, there was nothing sudden or sensational about its growth. It did not come to him in a blinding flash, "This is my divine call. This is why I was brought to India. This is the road to which all these devious paths I have been following through the years have been leading me." He knew only that he was terribly concerned about these people he had just seen, their bodies as well as their souls, because the two were inseparable. And if caring tremendously constituted a divine call, then he received one that night, standing there on the grounds at Chingleput with pain flowing through his hand and nail prints gouged deep in his palm, received it as surely as had his namesake long ago on the road to Damascus.

But when he started his research in leprosy in 1947, it was with no sense of embarking on a crusade. He had just one goal in view, to answer some of his own persistent questions.

His study had to be done at odd hours and on weekends. For, though Dr. Norman Macpherson had returned from furlough, raising the number of qualified surgeons to three, Paul was often on duty eight, ten, twelve hours a day, in addition to which one of them must be on call each night. If a night call came, a messenger would usually come from the hospital on a bicycle. They had one car at the Carmans' bungalow, ancient and temperamental, so that the person not on call usually must get up and push it to get it started. But Paul found time for research, largely because of the loyal cooperation of colleagues like Jack Carman, who often sacrificed the leisure of his own weekends to give Paul extra freedom from surgical duties.

First he searched the hospital libraries for books and magazine articles on reconstructive surgery and paralysis. He combed page after page of titles for some chapter or article dealing with the subjects in relation to leprosy, but never once was the disease mentioned. After weeks of research he had not found a single refutation of Dr. Cochrane's claim, that with thousands of orthopedic surgeons working to repair disabled hands, not one had even speculated, much less experimented, on the possibility of repairing disabilities from a disease which threatened to cripple the hands and feet of ten to fifteen million victims! Incredible in this age of scientific specialization, but true. A Dr. Milroy Paul in Ceylon had used plaster casts on trophic ulcers. Many amputations had been done. A few doctors had done nerve stripping in an attempt to prevent the paralysis, and Dr. Cochrane himself had tried taking out diseased metatarsal bones, but that was about all. Nor could Paul find anything much under pathology on the actual nature of the disease in its relation to deformity. Little had been discovered since the late 1800's when Woit and Dehio had attempted some constructive descriptions of the way paralysis progressed. No, unbelievable as it seemed, there were no reliable data on record to answer his most pertinent questions: Was the progression of paralysis in leprosy as haphazard as it seemed, or did it follow a predictable pattern? Was the flesh of a leprosy patient "bad flesh," as everybody maintained, or would it respond like normal tissues to operative procedures? Most pertinent of all, did those fingers and toes actually rot away and fall off? And, if so—why?

Very well. If he must find the answers himself, where could there be a better place than at Vellore, center of the world's highest leprosy incidence, with two or three persons in each hundred victims of the disease; Vellore, with its concentration of specialist physicians, surgeons, and scientists, each one equipped to make his own contribution to the problem's solution?

"Give me just a few beds," he begged Dr. Norman Macpherson, the medical superintendent, "five or six, even as few as four, where I can bring in a few of these patients, study them, and perhaps try some operations?"

Dr. Macpherson knit his brows. An extremely gifted, dedicated doctor, he usually kept his innate kindliness concealed under an exterior of austerity, even of sternness. "I'll take it up with the administrative committee and the senior doctors, Paul, but—I'm afraid—"

When he rendered their verdict, the kindliness was for once uncamouflaged. "I'm sorry, Paul. I hope I can make you understand why it's impossible."

Paul did understand, and he sympathized with the authorities' position. In its fight for survival the college was still woefully deficient in teaching beds, and every one available must be used for the training program. It would also be an additional financial burden, for nearly all leprosy patients were destitute, most of them beggars, unable to pay anything for their treatment, and heaven knew the institution was in financial straits enough already! There were other equally potent objections.

"Admit leprosy patients to the main hospital," some of the authorities argued, "and all the other patients would run away in fright. Why not go out and treat leprosy in the leprosy centers where it belongs?"

"Because," Paul reasoned, "that's the real source of the trouble, keeping the patients away from the medical specialists who might help with the problem."

But to the fourth and final objection he had no answer.

"Everybody knows that leprosy patients have bad flesh. You're suggesting operating on these hands, reconstructing them, but if the flesh rots away, the incisions wouldn't even heal. You should know that. I ask, what's the *use*?"

Given time and effort, the first three objections were not insurmountable. But if it was true that the patients really had bad flesh, causing the fingers to rot away, then his colleagues were right. He might as well stop the whole experiment before it started. Not until he was sure, however, that they were right.

He began more months of slow and painstaking research. The staff was not indifferent or unconcerned, merely skeptical. He gathered about him a little interested team of helpers. Visiting the village leprosy sanatoria within traveling distance of Vellore, he made careful surveys and examinations of patients. He began making weekly visits to the sanatorium at Chingleput, leaving after tea on Friday, traveling by train and *jutka*, spending the weekend holding hand clinics, consulting with the specialists, making test after test, list after list.

Colleagues in other departments made their invaluable contributions to his research: pathology, dermatology, radiology. Dr. Ida B. Scudder, niece of Dr. Ida and head of the radiology department, though often working singlehanded and always with deficient staff, put the facilities of her department at Paul's service, making hundreds of X rays as his studies involved increasing investigation of the bone changes taking place in leprous hands and fingers. When, a little later, Dr. Donald Paterson arrived to augment the radiology staff, Dr. Ida B. often spared him for Paul's special research projects, though it usually meant taking on extra work herself.

With his small core of helpers Paul practiced an assembly line technique, examining every patient possible, in all about two thousand. A social worker would accompany the team on its trips, taking a quick history. They would test the patient's sensation with a pin, with a feather; measure the movements of thumbs, of fingers, of feet; make further tests to discover which muscles had become paralyzed, which fingers absorbed, which nerves thickened, and listing every one.

And as the survey continued Paul became more and more excited, for a striking phenomenon was revealed. The paralysis was absolutely uniform and conformed to a precise pattern. Although many patients had different degrees of paralysis, the order in which muscles were paralyzed seemed always the same. And the muscles that remained strong were always the same. That first thrill of discovery when the paralyzed fingers had exerted such surprising pressure on his hand was now reinforced. However haphazard the paralysis in leprosy appeared in some respects, with periods of rapid progress or of complete arrest, one could say with confidence that at any stage of the disease the paralysis was predictable, and, what was more important, you could predict which muscles would never be paralyzed even if the disease progressed. It was a major breakthrough, for it brought the possibility of surgery one step nearer. He knew now that there were "good" muscles available to take the place of those paralyzed.

But was there "good" flesh? He was no nearer solving the main problem: why did those fingers rot away? He became a sleuth, always on track of the cause, the deadly villain.

"Have you ever seen a finger falling off?" he kept asking one leprosy specialist after another, more or less in teasing fashion.

Well—no. Of course they hadn't actually seen one falling off, but they had definitely disappeared. Otherwise they would not be missing.

And there were plenty missing! It was like leaves falling in autumn, thought Paul. If you went along a road in the fall, you saw some leaves on the ground, some on the trees. And if you waited long enough, you would see one actually fall. Surely one should be able to catch one of these missing fingers in the act of disappearance!

He and the team made more experiments, kept a number of patients under strict observation, inspecting their hands every day at the same time. They gave them work to do, carpentry, gardening, farming, and examined their fingers at the end of the day, measuring their length, photographing them, putting the hand on paper and drawing around the fingers to see whether they could catch the hand at the period when the finger was shortening. But to no avail.

Paul also began opening up some of the hands and taking tiny specimens. Here was a patient who said a certain finger had been full length two years ago, and it was now only half as long. Very well. He took a tiny piece of its tissue, with a bit of skin and fascia, and sent it to Dr. Edward Gault, the Australian head of Pathology.

"Now, Ted, I want to know what's wrong with these tissues. Are they bad? Are they going gangrenous?"

Ted Gault put them under his microscope. "There's no disease in these tissues," he reported, "no inflammation."

"All right," said Paul. "We'll fetch you some more."

After the same thing had occurred five or six times, Paul challenged him, "Now listen, Ted, there's something wrong here. I'm sending you fingers that are presumably rotting away! You know very well normal fingers don't do that. Go and have another look at those tissues."

Dr. Gault, a meticulous scientist, returned to his microscopes. He came back scratching his head. "You know, Paul, those tissues look and act like normal tissues. Aside from the slight excess of fibrous tissue and less than normal blood vessels and, of course, no nerve endings, they're like any others. I can't even find any sign of leprosy in them."

His findings seemed to corroborate Dr. Cochrane's repeated contentions that, in spite of the destructive action of leprosy, the tissues of leprosy patients had the capacity to heal normally, as he himself had proven through amputations and the removal of metatarsal bones. Paul accepted the pathologist's reports with mingled bafflement and satisfaction. Even though he had not succeeded in tracking down the villain, he at least knew some of its limitations. He felt that he was now almost ready for the next step, a long one—an experiment in surgery.

Meanwhile Margaret was also asking questions and finding answers. How to adjust more quickly and easily, a mother with two tiny children, to this superabundance of heat, people, and germs? How to discover the ways in which she could serve best as a doctor? She saw so much need that she felt guilty going away to the mountains, but Paul insisted, and she yielded for the children's sake.

They had a wonderful week together in the cool paradise of Kotagiri. Then Paul returned to Vellore. Margaret spent the next three months vacationing and working in the Kotagiri Medical Fellowship, a mission station with clinics, dispensaries, and a small hospital, ministering to a large area of summer colonies, tea plantations, and mountain villages. But, ignorant of the language and bewildered by the multiplicity of strange diseases which she hadn't known existed, she was more student than doctor.

It was the work of Dr. Pauline Jeffery, an American missionary who specialized in eyes, which most fascinated Margaret. Since she had taken her training during the war when the choice of specialization had been necessary, with two types of study often running concurrently in different parts of the country, she had had only the barest minimum of training in opththalmology. Now, watching Pauline Jeffery skillfully cope with India's multiple eye afflictions, marveling at her ability even to make a diagnosis, much less perform the delicate operation or prescribe the correct treatment, Margaret was conscious of her own abysmal ignorance. Yet, useless though she often felt, the summer was an ideal introduction to the country and its needs.

She returned to Vellore in autumn, to be met at Katpadi station by a haggard but cheerful Paul, who had to leave her immediately for the hospital to operate on a case of ruptured typhoid ulcer. He had no more sleep that night.

"He looks old and tired," Margaret wrote his mother, now usually referred to as "Granny." "He has a pretty non-stop day and often night as well. There is always teaching to be done, and if not teaching, operating, out patients, and ward rounds. But I'm afraid it's no use trying to persuade him to go easy. He and Jack Carman are the heads of their departments, the only two teaching surgeons in the hospital, and either they do the work or it doesn't get done."

They were still living in the house at Katpadi with the Carmans, but a duplex which they would occupy sometime was being built on the college campus. Margaret was now working in the children's section of the hospital. She loved this work and, though the pitiful plight of many of the children shocked and wrenched her, she found the array of unfamiliar ailments —scabies, rickets, eye infections, acute abscesses, the protein deficiency disease *kwashiorkor*—a constant challenge. Had it not been for her own children, Margaret would have found the new life ideal.

But now she was faced head on with that problem confronting so many missionary wives: How to combine responsible motherhood with the professional service she was trained to give? It had been easy back in England with Mother Berry eager to care for the children. But adjustment to this land of servants and ayahs was difficult.

In all these problems of adjustment Naomi Carman was a wise and invaluable counselor. Vivacious but even-tempered, skilled in the ways of India and loving it, patient with all the mistakes the newcomers made, always willing to share her own rich experience but never meddling, Naomi gently and good humoredly initiated Margaret into the art of bringing up a missionary family. One of her most practical contributions was an ayah named Martha whom her children had outgrown.

But Martha's ways of discipline were not always those of the gentle Margaret or the reasonably persuasive Paul. Threatened one day with the "dark closet" as punishment for excessive naughtiness, three-year-old Christopher quietly appropriated one of his mother's ancient pocketbooks, devoid of money, and started for the hospital a couple of miles away. Though he knew which bus to take and kept waving his pocketbook, none would take him. So he started walking, a small but determined drop in the surging stream of buses, lorries, honking cars, bullock carts, droves of animals, bicycles, pedestrians. Trudging with dignity along the middle of the road, the waves of traffic mercifully parting, like the Red Sea, on either side of him, he arrived eventually at the hospital.

A perplexed nurse came to Margaret. "There's a little boy outside. I don't know whether he's your child or not, but he says he wants mummy."

Equally perplexed, Margaret went out, to be greeted by a small bombshell, weeping and flinging dirty arms around her.

"Mummy, don't send me home, please! I—I've got such a lot of work to do here!"

The problem would never quite solve itself, though the badly frightened Martha learned to adjust to more acceptable methods of discipline. But the episode was a big step in Margaret's adjustment also, not only to the demands of India but to the cheerfully permissive philosophy which Paul, like his father before him, was always to practice in the bringing up of his children. The sons and daughters of Paul Brand, she understood sagely, whatever else they might be, would never be cowards. Or goosesteppers. Or carbon copies. And, nerve-wracking though the philosophy would often prove, there would be many times when it paid off, like this. For at least one child had proved that—in the delightfully inclusive British phrase—he could "cope."

10

It was perhaps a year after his first visit to Chingleput when Paul Brand decided that he was ready for the great experiment.

"If you will send me a patient whose hands could not possibly be made worse," he said to Dr. Cochrane, "I'd like to see what can be done with them."

The patient Dr. Cochrane brought fulfilled all the qualifications. "There he is, just what you asked for." He smiled a little grimly. "Whatever you do, you can't make him any worse than he is already."

Studying the patient closely, Paul felt his eagerness chilling to dismay. A stolid-faced young Hindu, Krishnamurthy displayed all the worst hand and foot disabilities of leprosy. There were huge ill-smelling ulcers on the soles of both feet, so deeply infected that the bones lay exposed. The hands were wasted and useless, with the fingers curled into the clawed position, completely unable to grasp any object except by a pathetic attempt to pinch between the thumb and the side of the index knuckle. But it was not because of these outward stigmata that Paul felt dismayed. It was because, looking through the dulled eyes, he could see the man inside.

Man? No. Animal. A creature reduced to the crudest instincts for survival, cringing like a dog constantly kicked and rebuffed, voice tuned to a beggar's whine. If there was pleasure in the opportunity now afforded him, it was because it promised food and bed for some time to come, not hope of usefulness or improvement. Yet the young face was by no means devoid of intelligence. Indeed, as Paul was to discover, Krishnamurthy had come of a good family, had had an unusually good education. He could speak several languages, had held responsible positions. Then the telltale patches had come. His family had turned him away, his job had gone, and nobody would employ him. Slowly his mind had numbed along with his hands and feet. What use a good brain when it couldn't even earn your day's bread, or keeping your wits alive when people turned away from you in disgust and loathing? Better to be a dullard, with your eyes on the ground, to stop thinking, stop remembering, even stop feeling if you could. But just get food, somehow, anyhow, manage to exist.

Paul's dismay was tinged with horror as well as compassion. So this was what leprosy did to a human being, a man made in God's image! No, not leprosy. His fellow human beings. For it was the ignorance and thoughtlessness of people, acting through a herd instinct of self preservation, which had condemned this boy to a living hell. And the bitterest irony was that during most of his exile, like the majority of the most deformed leprosy patients, he had been noninfectious! His family could have welcomed him, embraced him, without the slightest danger.

"Is it worth trying?" Paul asked himself, looking beyond the clawed hands to the dulled mind and deadened spirit. "What use patching up a body that will always be degraded by beggar mentality?"

Will always? He chided himself. What a way for a Christian to talk, as if the spirit of any man were not capable of change, of regeneration!

"Would you be willing," he asked the young Hindu, "to let me do some operations on your hands and feet?"

Krishnamurthy shrugged. Listlessly, almost contemptuously, he extended his claws. "These?" the gesture seemed to imply. "Do what you wish with them. They are no good to me."

So began long weeks and months of testing, of preparation, of experimental surgery, of anxious waiting.

Paul's first interest in Krishnamurthy was his feet. Though the ulcers had healed after long rest in bed and continued dressings, he knew that they would recur as soon as the patient started to walk again. He had noticed that the boy walked with his feet somewhat twisted and, like those of many other leprosy patients, drooping from paralysis. Why not perform a tenodesis on his feet, as was sometimes done in similar cases of poliomyelitis, so that he could walk straight? Normal placement would make his feet less liable to ulceration. Paul tried the experiment, taking a tendon, in this case from a paralyzed muscle, and fixing it at both ends, one end to the side of the foot and the other to the fibula bone of the leg, so that it bridged the gap between the foot and the leg and held up the side of the foot, somewhat like a piece of string.

Mercifully, the operation was a complete success. Krishnamurthy was able in time to walk straight and evenly, his foot landing squarely on the ground, and the ulcers in the old areas never reappeared. It also made a big improvement in his gait. Mercifully, for this particular operation did not later prove successful in many cases. In fact, even in general orthopedic surgery it is rarely used because the tendon ultimately stretches and gives way. But at that time Paul had not done as careful surveys on the muscles of the leg as on those of the hand, and he did not know that there were really good muscles in the leg which could be relied on to correct the deformity. That knowledge, resulting in a more effective operation, would come in due time. It was merciful for another reason that this first attempt at surgery on a leprosy patient was a success, for if it had failed Paul might not have had the courage to proceed.

Now for his hands.

The months of research had seemed to prove the two facts necessary to justify an attempt at surgery: that there were certain good muscles which would never be affected by the disease, and that the tissues of a leprosy patient were not "bad" but subject to the same laws of healing as normal flesh. It was the intrinsic muscles of the hand, controlled by the ulnar nerve, whose paralysis caused the deformity of the claw hand. When the long flexor muscles in the forearm took over in the absence of the intrinsics, they made the ends of the fingers fold in on themselves and curl toward the palm, producing the claw effect.

But there were many good muscles available, as Paul had discovered in that first viselike handclasp! Why not take one of them that could be spared, perhaps the flexor sublimas digitorum which bends the second joint of each finger, and substitute it for the paralyzed intrinsics? This type of surgery was known as Bunnell's operation, though in fact it was first described by Stiles during the First World War, and it was often used to correct similar disabilities from war injuries or polio. In other words, why not apply the same techniques to leprosy as to other paralyzing diseases?

"All right, get set," Paul told his assistant, Dr. Sarveshvara Roy. "And let's be prepared for anything. This may be a bolt of lightning or—just a flash in the pan. Only God knows, and may He help us!"

He looked down at the object on the hand table between them—misshapen, lifeless, a grotesque distortion of one of God's most exquisite and skilled creations. He picked it up and held it for a moment, his sensitive fingers gently probing its contours, like those of a potter gauging the possibilities in a dead lump of clay. Then, reaching for the scalpel, he made a bold swift incision.

He operated on only two of the fingers that first time, carefully following the Bunnell technique of sublimal transfer, making a midlateral incision on each side of each finger, exposing the lumbrical tendon and identifying the canal; freeing the good unparalyzed sublimis tendon from its insertion, splitting it into two parts; withdrawing it into the palm and retunneling it to the fingers, to substitute for the paralyzed intrinsic muscle; testing its tension, testing, again testing (he had no idea how much tension to use, and here the difference could be so slight between success and failure!); suturing; closing the wounds; applying dressings, a light plaster splint. Then there was nothing to do but wait and pray.

In spite of excitement and suspense among members of the research team, the experiment was shrouded in secrecy. Paul had literally to smuggle his first leprosy patients into the hospital, for so great was the popular ignorance and prejudice that knowledge of their presence might easily have emptied adjacent wards and rooms of patients. Moreover, teaching beds as well as funds were still painfully inadequate, and Krishnamurthy, as well as the two other cases on whom Paul first tried experimental surgery, must monopolize for a long period a precious private room. Though Dr. Carman eagerly encouraged the leprosy work and others—notably Ted Gault and Herbert Gass—gave it wholehearted support, some of the physicians deemed it a waste of time, energy, and desperately needed facilities.

By now Paul had a certain number of beds allocated for his firm of surgery, thirty or forty, in A and B Wards, with an allowance of about ten per cent which could be used for wholly non-paying patients, but the demand overwhelmingly exceeded the supply. Leprosy patients, most of them beggars, must be not only non-paying but, for the present, isolated. Though Paul was permitted considerable discretion in allocating his own beds, it required both boldness and a degree of stubbornness to embark on a project of which the hospital authorities understandably disapproved. But Paul had both, together with a concern so consuming that it was rapidly becoming an obsession.

Krishnamurthy's first hand surgery seemed promising, though Paul sternly allowed neither himself nor the team any premature hope of success. The two fingers healed well in their new positions. But it would take more operations, on the other two fingers, then the thumb, followed by a long period of intense physiotherapy, before success or failure could be assured.

But as the weeks and months passed the team could not control its jubilation. News of the achievement leaked out among medical staff members, nurses, students.

"Have you heard? Nothing ever been done like it before!"

"Simple tendon transplant . . . amazing . . ."

"Could be as important a breakthrough for leprosy as the new D.D.S. !"

"No, no, wait!" Paul cautioned his exuberant colleagues. "We've done nothing yet. We know almost nothing. This is only the first step of a baby learning to walk. Next time we may fall flat on our faces."

But it was a step. With profound humility and gratitude as well as professional excitement he watched the miracle of transformation—a claw turning once more into a human hand. Even with the success of surgery assured, the therapy was a slow process entailing the reconditioning of long unused joints, the reeducation of brain impulses to cause muscles formerly bending the fingers now to act on the opposite side of the hand to straighten the fingers, a process infinitely complicated by the hand's lack of sensation. Sometimes progress from day to day, week to week, was barely discernible. Then suddenly the miracle was achieved. The hand was opening and closing with almost normal action, grasping objects of different sizes and shapes to improve its dexterity, blocks of wood, rubber balls, small bottles, pencils, until finally—

"Look!" Krishnamurthy greeted Paul one day triumphantly. Proudly he arched his first three fingers, scooped up a big ball of rice and curry from his dish, held it there with the aid of the opposing thumb, and popped it into his mouth.

The re-creation of the man was even more satisfying than that of his hands, for Krishnamurthy was a new person. His eyes were bright and alert. He could laugh again, enjoy reading books, sharpen his keen wit in sparrings with doctors and internes and nurses. Curious about these unusual people who had shown such concern about him, he listened eagerly to the Christian message and was baptized, choosing to take a new name, John. After remaining in the hospital about a year, he was discharged, equipped for his new life with two useful hands and two healed feet, a good brain, and an abundance of hope and courage.

At this stage Paul was desperately in need of specimens to further his study. The small bits of tissue taken from living patients, while invaluable in establishing the normalcy of flesh in the paralyzed hands, were not enough. He needed to test *nerves*. Of course it was possible to take paralyzed nerves from patients, but they were already destroyed, and using the valuable live nerves even for necessary research was both wasteful and inhuman. He needed autopsies.

He sent out an S.O.S. to every leprosarium and leprosy worker within possible traveling distance, even as far afield as Hyderabad and Bombay.

"Please let me know immediately," he begged, "if a leprosy

patient dies on whom I could perform a post mortem. Telephone or telegraph at any time of the day or night."

Some of the workers involved were cooperative, even those of the government hospital at Vellore, which had a very small leprosy ward. Though the latter did not usually admit likely candidates for autopsies, they promised that if a patient came along who looked as if he were dying, they would make an exception. But leprosy is not a fatal disease, and deaths among patients, almost invariably from other causes, are infrequent. Then, too, even if a patient did die, usually his relatives would not permit a post mortem, which was rare in India. For months, while continuing his experiments, Paul waited.

It was one evening just before dinner when the message came from Harry Paul, superintendent at Chingleput. Without waiting to eat Paul collected two of his team, his Ceylonese assistant, Dr. Gusta Buultgens, and his technician, Jayaraj, gathered a host of instruments and dozens of bottles of formaldehyde, and bundled all into the nearest car available. At about eight they were on their way, driving helter skelter by the straightest route, about seventy-five miles, to Chingleput, over roads which in those days were bad to the point of treachery.

But their conveyance was worse. They had passed through the big temple town of Kancheepuram, its huge carved *gopurams* towering in the moonlight, and were perhaps halfway to their destination when the car caught fire. Apparently leaking petrol from a faulty feed pipe had slowly been drenching the engine until it burst into a violent blaze. Instantly Paul found himself driving behind a raging inferno, flames dancing red around his feet. He pulled up as quickly as possible but could not step on the foot brake without burning his foot. Swerving off the road, he finally got the car stopped, and all rushed about in search of sand and green branches to extinguish the blaze. Paul almost fell into an open well in the process.

By the time the fire was out the time was near midnight and the car, of course, out of commission. Loading themselves down with the bags of instruments and chemicals, the three started walking. It was a wild section of the road. Buses had stopped running. The only life evident was an occasional caravan of bullock carts looming out of the darkness and lumbering past, its lead beasts plodding eerily in a pool of lantern light. Aiming his torch at the rutted and stony ground, Paul felt as hopelessly earth-bound as the plodding beasts, with nothing of their infinite patience.

Suddenly he remembered that in a small town through which they must pass there was a mission school. After a couple of miles of walking they arrived there, located the school, and roused its headmaster. Very kind and helpful, he offered to put them up for the night. No, no, Paul protested. They must get on. Was there a telephone? No. Unfortunately no telephone. But finally the headmaster located an antiquated car whose sleepy owner agreed to drive them the remaining distance.

They arrived in Chingleput at about 2:30 in the morning. With difficulty Paul succeeded in waking the medical officer, who in his turn had to rouse the person who kept the key to the mortuary. By the light of a hurricane lantern the tired little team trailed across the grounds to a tiny outhouse in a far corner of the compound. The work must be done at once because in the morning the corpse would be removed. So there, at three o'clock in the morning, they began an adventure of exploration into the unknown as thrilling to Paul Brand as to some others, a few months later, would be the scaling of Mount Everest.

Paul worked on one arm, Gusta Buultgens on the other, while the technician Jayaraj recorded findings by the light of a little oil lamp. As they removed each nerve, he would label it and put it into a small bottle. Within minutes all weariness was forgotten and they began to be genuinely excited. For as soon as the nerves were exposed end to end from fingertips through wrists and up to the forearms and shoulders, a pattern became immediately apparent.

"Look," Paul pointed out. "Note those nerve swellings, at exactly the same points on both sides, yet at other places perfectly normal? And see the regularity of the pattern? Here where the nerve goes deep to a muscle, it's normal. Only in the superficial parts, close to the skin, do you find the swellings."

Dehio and other experts, he explained as more and more of the details were revealed, had described leprosy as starting in the periphery, or skin, and running up the nerves, affecting them the whole length as the disease progressed, but here it was apparent that although the nerves might be infected all the way up, they were damaged only where they came near the surface. In other words, it wasn't the presence of the bacilli alone which did the damage.

"And that is important?" asked Gusta with her usual meticulous insistence on detail.

"It could be very important," replied Paul. "To begin with it seems to confirm our impression that the pattern of paralysis does not depend on a creeping progress of the disease. It seems to imply that it isn't the leprosy that determines where a patient will be paralyzed. It's something about his own anatomy. And if it has something to do with mechanical factors, who knows, we may be able to change it by some operation."

As the hours passed and the stark little drama moved to its climax, Paul's excitement was filled more and more with awe and reverence. Here was this unknown leprosy patient, with all the marks of human neglect in his ulcerated hands and feet, one of life's rejects, yet now in his death revealing laws of nature that might lead to new life for others!

They found the same precise and perfectly predictable pattern in both arms and both legs. Finishing their examination, they stitched everything up again. As they collected their pile of little bottles, the dawn was breaking. The driver of their disreputable conveyance was asleep at the wheel. Rousing him to some semblance of activity, they crawled back along the road and inspected the wreck of their own car.

"Was it worth it?" asked Jayaraj dubiously.

"Yes," Paul asserted instantly. "Fiery furnace and all, *tremendously* worth it."

After all, he recalled, three other people had once had to pass through a fiery furnace in order to gain the company of a Fourth.

They took the train back to Vellore with all their little bottles of priceless specimens, flooding Dr. Gault and his Pathology Department with work which must be done immediately. Every centimeter of every nerve had to be sectioned and every section put under a microscope. But, though the evidence was interesting, one autopsy did not constitute proof. In subsequent weeks and months other post mortems were made available, until the team had completed seven autopsies. By that time they had good evidence that the pattern was basic and predictable. In more than one instance they even went into the brain tracking the cranial nerves through the skull. In the facial nerve they found a small swelling just where it left the skull and traveled toward the surface, the greatest damage seeming to occur where it crossed the cheekbones on its way to the eyelids—knowledge that was to prove useful in later years in combating blindness resulting from paralysis of the eyelids.

Though it was Paul who played the leading role in this long tense drama, at least three years in duration, it was other members of the team, especially Dr. Gusta Buultgens, who performed the tedious backstage chores. As the leprosy work began to take more and more of his time and interest, Paul felt that he needed someone to keep careful records and asked her to become his full time assistant.

"Let me think about it," she replied with caution.

When she agreed, it was with a wholehearted devotion amounting almost to obsession. Her most remarkable contribution was her meticulous keeping of records: the detailed and tedious marking of the sensory areas and motor defects and the following up of the hundreds of post mortem specimens; the dull repetitive examinations of patients, measuring fingers, testing sensations, recording the infinitesimal and multitudinous variations in hands and feet. Patiently, day after day, week after week, year after year, available at any time of the day or night, asking nothing for herself except to serve, she made her silent and unlauded contribution with never a grumble or complaint.

From herself, that is; often from others. For with her quiet gentleness was mingled a fierce and fiery intolerance toward any weakness either in herself or in others. Few of her colleagues could measure up to her perfectionist standards, and she was by no means hesitant or tactful in pointing out their failures. One of Paul's saddest tasks was intervention in hot quarrels where he was obliged to take a side seemingly against her, often for upholding some principle he himself had voiced. Her loyalty to him and to the work was both selfless and protective. Much of the slow and painful progress during these first years of lonely searching was a consequence of her untiring efforts.

But they were all children, feeling their way, learning by

trial and error. Dr. Gault, expert technician though he was, had had no experience with the pathology of leprosy. Paul himself, in spite of his rigorous apprenticeship in London, had done little reconstructive surgery of the hand. And of course the whole area of surgery in leprosy was an uncharted wilderness.

So Paul was occasionally reminded by the hospital authorities.

"Now look, Paul," they reasoned in fatherly fashion, "we're dealing here with the realities of life, and we've got to run a medical school. And do you really think that with all the problems around us it's worth spending so much time, when you're one of only three surgeons, on something which may be nothing but a wild goose chase?"

However, patience paid off, and finally he was allocated two beds for leprosy patients, with the understanding that the patients would be put in a side ward and should be noninfectious cases.

But there were times during those first years when Paul was sorely tempted to yield to their reasonable arguments. At one point his courage sank almost to the vanishing point. He had performed perhaps a half dozen operations, with moderate success. But reconstructing hands, he discovered, was only the beginning of the problem. It seemed advisable to perform most of their experimentation on the worst beggars, human derelicts whose stock in trade was deformity, not only because they were the easiest ones to get but because the team could operate on them with a clear conscience, knowing their condition could scarcely be worsened. And such patients had no desire to move on. Far easier and more comfortable to remain in the hospital and be fed, bedded, bandaged, and, yes, even washed, than to return, though with a good working pair of hands, to a world which shunned and kicked and buffeted! Instead of cooperating with the regimen of therapy following their operations, they sometimes tried to aggravate their ills. Observing one patient through a window, Paul actually saw him remove his bandages and scratch his sores to make them worse!

His high hopes were dashed. The lackluster faces, the dead hands, the inert bodies preempting precious beds . . . Why rake up such refuse from the dregs of human life when there were hundreds who would respond eagerly to the energies you had to give? It was his young Hindu associate, Dr. Sarveshvara Roy, assistant at the first hand operation and loyal member of the team, who finally put the terrible frustration into words.

"Dr. Brand," he said one day earnestly, "do you really think it is worth it?"

No! The word sprang to Paul's lips. He almost spoke it. But something silenced it. Perhaps it was the memory of reawakening life in the eyes of Krishnamurthy. Or an older memory of three figures turning hopelessly back down a steep mountain path. Or no memory at all, but that strange imperative which compels some men to blaze lonely and unpopular trails which will be the highways of tomorrow.

"Yes," he replied firmly.

11

Paul's third child, Mary, was born in October of 1948. She was to be as adventurous, as fearless, as charged with pioneering energy—yes, and as prone to mishaps and crises—as her unpredictable parents.

The months preceding her birth may have contributed some of the spice and verve which were to make her the family's supreme joy as well as its frequent problem. For the bungalow in Viruthampet overflowed with jostling activity and exuberance. Added to the Carmans and the Brands for a time was the family of Dr. Reeve Betts, American surgeon arrived to open a new department, first in all India, of thoracic surgery. Waiting like Paul and Margaret for the completion of new housing units at the college, Dr. Reeve, his wife Martha, and their three children were welcome but superfluous additions to the already overcrowded household. No wonder the child carried during this happy tumult was so brimming with life and spontaneously friendly—or so full of mischief that she was soon to be dubbed Mary the Menace! Wherever she went things were likely to be smashed—furniture, crockery, probably, at a later stage, hearts. If there was any trouble she would be in the center of it. She might get lost, punished for disobedience, expelled from school, but she would never be friendless or unhappy.

When in September Margaret returned from another summer in Kotagiri, she found Paul already living in one of the new duplex houses on the college campus. Now for the first time in their five years of married life they had a home of their own, seeming unbelievably spacious in spite of its mere three rooms, surrounded by wide grounds bounded on the rear by round upflung rocky hills. The new life, however, was not unmitigated bliss.

It was Margaret's first experience in managing a household alone, and she sorely missed the smoothly efficient cooperation of Naomi Carman. But her medical skills precluded any full-time involvement in domestic affairs. A missionary in Vellore, especially a doctor, was expected to make her professional contribution.

"They would like to know which department you will be prepared to help in," Paul had written during her second summer in Kotagiri.

Assisting once more in the Kotagiri Medical Fellowship and marveling anew at Dr. Pauline Jeffery's accurate diagnoses of obscure eye ailments, her skillful techniques of removing cataracts, Margaret wrote back, "Really, Paul, I don't care which department they put me in, *as long as it isn't in eyes.*"

Two weeks after Mary's birth she received a little note from Dr. Carol Jameson, then acting as principal in the absence of Dr. Hilda Lazarus, who was touring England and America in behalf of the institution.

"I don't want to hurry you," she wrote, "but we are very short of help at Schell, and we would be glad if you would pop in there for a few hours each day and just keep an eye on things."

Schell, Dr. Ida's first small hospital, now the eye department of the great medical center!

Shocked, Margaret explained that she couldn't know less about eyes, but Dr. Jameson was unperturbed. Having come to Vellore herself a quarter century ago, trained in chemistry and surgery, and been sweetly assigned by Dr. Ida to run the clinical laboratory, she had inherited some of the latter's audacious confidence in human potentials. Now she made the same serene reply she had herself received.

"No matter, my dear. You will learn."

And Margaret did. She found the physician in charge, Dr. Rao, a patient and competent teacher, as courteous and gentle with his apprentice as with his patients. Presently she found herself sitting in the out-patient clinic during a rampant conjunctivitis epidemic, with two or three hundred patients to be examined, diagnosed, and treated, and only one other doctor beside herself to do the job. Never, never, she told herself despairingly, would she be able to cope with this kind of situation! But somehow she kept on, and slowly her ability to make diagnoses and prescribe the proper treatments increased. It was a training in personality as well as skill, for the students who came to the department for training often knew more than she did, and many times she found it necessary to swallow her pride and ask their advice.

When Dr. Victor Rambo, the American head of the department who had been on leave, returned to Schell and took her training in hand, Margaret speedily attained knowledge and skill in both diagnosis and surgery. As she became more confident, the work became an increasing joy and satisfaction. With Dr. Rambo she pioneered in his beloved project of eye camps, designed to help reduce the appalling prevalence of eye disease, especially cataracts, in the villages. Every few weeks he would take a team of doctors, nurses, and technicians into a rural center within a radius of perhaps fifty miles, examining any who wished to come from surrounding villages, and performing needed operations, sometimes a hundred in one day. Helping to give sight to hundreds of the estimated half a million blind from cataract in India, including many children, even babies, was a joy she would not have exchanged for any other satisfaction in the world.

Down at the main hospital a mile away from Schell, Paul also was coping with India's vast problems of surgery, often with a minimum of equipment and a maximum of frustration. Before the attempted upgrading of the college and the opening of the hospital to men patients in the mid-forties there had been little general surgery, and the department was still in its infancy. With all the other demands on finances it would be a long time before it caught up on its needs for new equipment.

Much already in use was hopelessly antiquated. For instance, there was the surgical diathermy apparatus. One long out of date had been given the department, a glass-fronted machine with great copper coils inside and impressive looking sparks which showed through the glass and inspired due respect for its efficiency. It was the presence of this machine, simplifying the control of bleeding, which encouraged Paul to attempt an operation for spasmodic torticollis which he should never have undertaken.

The patient was a British engineer working in Madras, a man endowed with all the native dignity of an Englishman plus a love of conviviality, the latter having led to an over-consumption of food and alcohol. Having recently married, he was mortified and distressed to develop this terrible neck spasm which kept jerking his head around his shoulder and completely incapacitated him. The examining psychiatrist had reported that the case was hopeless from the medical point of view. The only possible treatment was an operation, and he begged Paul to perform it.

"No," said Paul. "You should go to England. I have already written Sir Hugh Cairnes, the famous professor of neurosurgery at Oxford, about your case, and I would advise you to go to him."

The engineer flatly refused. He would rather commit suicide, he said, than face his friends in England in such a condition. Unless Paul agreed to help him, this was the end of everything. His wife also begged Paul to perform the operation.

"You are a teaching hospital," reminded the engineer. "I want the operation here."

Paul had had little experience in neurosurgery, but by reading up on the surgical treatment of the ailment he learned that the effective technique was to divide the upper four cervical nerves, motor and sensory, and also to go up through the foramen magnum in the skull and divide one of the cranial nerves. Having done spinal operations many times, he was confident that he could manage this one, given a surgical diathermy to control the bleeding. And, thanks to the donated machine, he had that. He knew that for a surgeon of his inexperience to attempt such delicate surgery was utter audacity, but it was not a time for timidity. A man's well being, possibly his sanity, were at stake. After consultation with other members of the medical staff, who like him had prayed for guidance, he accepted the challenge.

The first problem was lack of a cerebellar headrest, to keep the patient in position, face down, over the end of the table. Paul went to a local blacksmith and had him beat out some iron supports which fitted on the end of the operating table. Lacking a blood bank, he found two blood donors and cross-matched two pints of blood. With Dr. Gwenda Lewis, newly arrived young anaesthetist from Wales, he prepared for the operation. Scrubbed and gowned, he waited impatiently for the signal to begin.

It did not come. A half hour, three quarters, passed. Dr. Gwenda reported that the patient was imbibing plenty of ether, but with no results, an immunity possibly ascribable to the over-imbibing of some other substances. It took an hour and a whole bottle of ether to induce insensibility.

The improvised headrest worked very well except that because the patient was short and stout, the extension over the table brought his center of gravity so far down that as soon as Paul exerted pressure to make the first incision the whole table upended and slid the patient down into Dr. Gwenda's lap.

"An auspicious beginning," murmured Paul with a bit less than his usual equanimity.

Recovering, he found a big stick and propped it under the end of the table, resting it on Gray's "Anatomy" and other fundamentals. But these setbacks were only foretastes. Possibly because the sliding process had dislodged the tube in the trachea, the patient developed respiratory difficulties. He also bled profusely. A transfusion was started, and Paul proceeded. The neck was abnormally thick, and it seemed miles getting down to the vertebrae. After probing deeper and deeper and tying off innumerable blood vessels, Paul called for the diathermy. But when, with the regulator as low as it would go, it was touched to the first bleeding point all the muscles went into spasm, and there was a cloud of smoke.

"Send for the electrician, sister," Paul directed a nurse, his use of the formal term of address the only outward sign of perturbation.

The diathermy was sent out for repairs, and the operation proceeded. He had finally reached the vertebrae when the machine came back. He welcomed it with relief, for by now the wound was full of artery clamps on vessels so deep down they could not be tied off conveniently. But again one touch of the coagulator and the whole neck and part of the body went into spasm, and flashes of fire appeared.

"One, two, three, four, five," Paul intoned, proceeding evenly to "ten," his favorite substitute for profanity. The machine was sent out for further repairs. With the blood nearly used up, the patient's blood pressure falling, his respiration poor, Dr. Gwenda was almost at her wits' end. "Steady! It will soon be over," Paul reassured her, careful to give no indication that he shared her desperation.

He hardly dared open the spinal canal without diathermy, but something had to be done, so he pushed ahead. He nibbled away the bones of the upper cervical spine, then the back of the foramen magnum of the skull, exposing the medulla. By now serious bleeding had developed, and he prayed for the diathermy. It came. Everything, the electrician swore fervently, was in perfect order now. He had tested it on a piece of meat. With a sign of gratitude Paul applied the coagulator to an artery clamp holding a big vein deep in the wound. Again the spasm, only worse this time, and because the current was nearer the spinal cord, the patient seemed almost to rise off the table. There was a blue flash, and every light in the hospital went out.

Paul was left then with a frightened anaesthetist, a blood transfusion used up, a big vein on the back of the spinal column torn and bleeding, a lot of clamps that were difficult to tie off, an unfinished operation, and complete darkness. It was one of the toughest moments of his whole surgical experience. But again there was nothing to do but continue. A flash lamp was brought and held waveringly over the table. He knew he had to finish fast. What to do? Close up the wound without even attempting the job he had started? No. The success of the operation was worth more than life to his patient. He had to carry through.

Mopping out the wound, he swiftly began to divide the spinal nerves. In the thin, wavering light it was very difficult to count which was which. Some were almost out of sight. He could only hope and pray that the right ones were being divided. Then he removed the artery clamps, tying the ones which could be tied, trusting to pressure to block the others. Knowing it was the only way to keep the patient alive, he thrust a gauze pack into the wound after he had closed the dura, leaving the end of it projecting while he sewed up the rest of the incision and relying on the pressure of the pack to stop the bleeding. After being under the knife for five and a half hours, the patient was returned to the ward. The next day the pack was removed, and the wound healed uneventfully.

The operation was a resounding success. The patient never had another spasm, nor was there any excessive weakness of the neck. A year or two later he went back to England, carrying with him a letter from Paul to Sir Hugh Cairnes, asking that he be given a general neurological checkover. The letter which he received in reply from Sir Hugh became one of Paul's most cherished possessions.

"Congratulations on a most remarkable operation," wrote the eminent surgeon. "Do you realize that this operation has been done only a few times in the United Kingdom? I am amazed that in Asia there is a hospital having the equipment necessary for such delicate surgery!"

During these years near the turn of the half century Paul was not the only member of the Brand family given to bold, if not hair-raising, experimentation. Christopher, often nick-named "Chips," was rapidly cultivating an inherited penchant for climbing, heredity no doubt receiving stimulus from the environment of up-jutting rocks, spreading trees, and the example of errant monkeys.

If Margaret had cherished illusions of being a protective mother, she had long since lost them. And fortunately her own upbringing in the compounds of Africa had been sufficiently uninhibited to bring her into somewhat hesitant agreement with Paul's permissive philosophy of child rearing. Christopher's untrammeled way of life would be shared in due time by each of his sisters. There were not many rules, but what few there were they were expected to keep. Paul did not believe in saying, "You must never . . ." If there was an accident, his comment was, "That's good. You'll know better next time."

"I'd rather bring up sixty per cent of our family and have them self-reliant and tough and fearless," he voiced his creed, "than one hundred percent and have them nervous coddled specimens."

But it was a permissiveness rooted in love and concern, not Spartan callousness or indifference. Paul was a wonderful father, and his children adored him. His favorite designations of affection, "Ugly" when they were babies, "Funny Face" as they grew older, were more highly prized than many parents' "honeys" and "darlings." He was never too tired to play with his children. Even on Sunday mornings, the only day in the week when he could have slept, he would get up, collect as many of them as could walk or be carried, and a bunch of bananas, and go up to explore the caves on College Hill.

But the youngest generation of Brands, try as they would, failed to outdo the oldest in daring and adventure. After returning to India in January, 1947, just one month after Paul, Evelyn Brand had worked for a full year in Sendamangalam; then at the next conference of her church, having reached the age of compulsory retirement, she had ended her active relationship with the mission. But—retired? Hardly. She welcomed it as a beginning, not ending, of her missionary career. Now, at sixty-eight, she was free to pursue the life time purpose interrupted by Jesse's death. For a dozen of the nearly twenty intervening years she had been marking time on the dead level of the plains, lifting impatient and longing eyes to the mountains. Not that she had neglected them entirely! Taking with her the tiny mosquito-netting cage built in sections on the roof of the Madras mission bungalow, she had for years spent all her vacations on the Kolaryans, second of the five ranges which she and Jesse had dreamed of winning for Christ. She would go by train to Atur, where some of the girls she had brought up in the Kollis would meet her, travel by bullock cart to the foot of the mountains, then ride up in a *dholi*. Here, during the brief weeks of her vacation, she would travel from one settlement to another in this area completely untouched by the civilization of the plains, making friends with the people, applying her simple remedies, fervently and unceasingly preaching the gospel of Christ and his love. But this had been a mere holiday pastime. Now she could really resume her life's work in earnest.

The little house which was to be her headquarters was already partially built. Differing little from the huts of the native tribes in nearby villages, it was made of woven bamboo strips overlaid with clay and whitewashed, surmounted by a high, thickly thatched, peaked roof. Later, when two retired Indian mission workers came to live with her, she added an extra room. But first she had with her only Elizabeth, a Bible woman who had worked with her at Sendamangalam, and, for a little time at the beginning, Ruth, her adopted Indian daughter, now married to a Christian teacher named John.

During the next fifteen years "Granny" Brand was to travel hundreds of miles on horseback along steep rocky mountain paths; camp night after night in her little frame mosquito-net hut where, drenched but undaunted by the monsoons, she would often pull on a mackintosh, raise an umbrella over her head, and go contentedly to sleep; break her hip, her arm, take severe tumbles over her pony's head, be thrown on her back into the bushes, but return always after the briefest of intervals to the life of rugged trekking. By the light of hurricane lanterns she would teach village children to read and write and pray. She would establish schools, one of them a boarding institution, and an agricultural settlement, clearing jungle land to make way for fruit trees and vegetable gardens. She would dig wells, abolish guinea worm from the surrounding villages, wage unceasing warfare on "poochies," typhoid, malaria, tuberculosis, malnutrition, and, in time, leprosy; save the lives of unwanted babies, conduct educational programs, run work camps. Slowly, one by one, she would glean a few converts to the way of love she lived and taught. And then, at nearly eighty-five, leaving behind her a small core of Christian workers to continue the community she had started, she would go down from the Kolaryans and climb another range of mountains, to start the whole process all over again.

No wonder her son and daughter-in-law and grandson were not afraid of attempting the untried!

12

It was perhaps two months after John, formerly Krishnamurthy, had been discharged from the hospital, hopeful and confident with his new hands, that he returned. He looked woefully thin. He tried to smile, but there was no laughter in his sad, hungry eyes. He held out his good new hands.

"These are not good hands you have given me, Sahib doctor," he said mournfully. "They are bad hands."

"Bad!" Paul stared at him in amazement. "They look good to me. What do you mean?"

"Bad *begging* hands," explained the young man sadly. Because he still bore the marks of leprosy, nobody would employ him or even give him a place to live. Before, seeing his useless hands, people had taken pity and thrown him coins. But now that his hands were whole, they had no pity.

Paul was aghast and speechless. What was he doing? Repairing men's bodies only to make their spirits more disabled than before? It was possible to solve John's problem. Taken back into the hospital, he was soon restored to health. Before contracting leprosy he had learned to type, and Paul felt it would be a challenge to his new hands to try developing the skill again. Soon he was beginning to earn money by doing typing jobs for patients who could afford his services.

But this did not solve the larger problem. Presently another patient, returning for his checkup, made the same startling indictment.

"Sahib doctor, do you know how much you have harmed me?"

"Harmed you!"

"*Ammam*, yes. Before my operation I used to beg for a living. I sat under a banyan tree at Ambur, on my own special stone, and held out my poor useless hands, and sometimes people would give me as much as two rupees in a day. Then you gave me these good hands, and I was so happy because now I need no longer beg. I went to look for work like other men, but the shopkeepers and tradesmen all saw the signs on me, the marks on my face, no eyebrows, and they drove me away with curses. I went back to my banyan tree and sat on my old stone and held out my hands, but they threw me only a few coins, not enough to buy decent food. What shall I do, Sahib doctor?"

What, indeed? The question struck at the very heart of Paul's purpose. Was he merely creating beggars with less ability for begging? The hospital certainly could not fill up its precious surgical beds with them after they were healed. Anyway, it wasn't beds these men wanted. It was the chance to work and live.

The answer was obvious. They should be taught new means of livelihood, trades which they could pursue without depending on employment. But how? There must be a place for them to live while learning the trade, skilled instructors to teach them, and, even more important, physiotherapists who would watch the movements of the repaired hands at work and decide what trades were suitable for them; then finally, the means to set up each man in his own village with his own cottage industry.

All this would take money, and there was no money. True, Pastor Warwick, his old building employer in England, hearing of the new work, entirely unasked had canvassed his friends for contributions and sent donations which had fully financed John-Krishnamurthy's treatment and the early expenses of the research team. But these funds did not begin to cover the increasing demands of research and surgery. One morning he discussed the problem with a sympathetic patient, Mother Eaton.

"Mother" Eaton was an American missionary, eighty-four, from Pasadena, California. She had come to Vellore seeking help for a severe and incurable rheumatoid arthritis. Unfortunately little could be done for her except for the slight relief afforded by a few pills and injections. But she was not one to be hardened or embittered by pain. The next morning she called Paul to her bedside.

"I couldn't sleep last night," she told him, "because of the pain, and as I lay awake I kept thinking about your leprosy patients. I have a little money in the bank, about five hundred pounds. I haven't much longer to live, and I kept wondering what my Lord would say if I came to him with that money still lying idle."

"Yes?" Paul responded gently.

"I want you to take it and use it. Put up some huts village style, the way you were talking about, and let your cured patients live there as a little community centered around a training shed where they will learn to become self-supporting. After a few months they can go home and make room for some more."

So it was that *Nava Jeeva Nilayam*, the New Life Center, came into being.

Paul had some difficulty getting approval for the project. Even Dr. Cochrane was not in favor of immediate action.

"Karigiri is being built just for this purpose by the Mission to Lepers and the American Leprosy Missions," he reminded. "Why not wait for that?"

Paul did not want to wait. Two years had passed since plans for the new Schieffelin Leprosy Research Sanatorium had been drawn up and its site chosen. The barren stretch of ground eight miles from the hospital, the only procurable land in a thickly populated area where the word "leper" was anathema to cautious landowners, was still as empty of human life and activity as for the last hundred years. Ground for the new buildings had not even been broken. Besides, what he wanted and needed for this purpose was not a streamlined institution but a small village, simple and intimate, like those most of his patients had come from and would go home to, and he knew just where he wanted to build it, a spot in a remote corner of the two hundred acre plot of land which Dr. Ida had chosen long ago, in the face of much opposition, for her medical college.

There was opposition now. Some of the senior physicians disapproved of having leprosy patients on the campus with medical students. When permission was granted, it was with the provision that a barbed wire fence should enclose the new settlement, that none of the occupants should cross the fence and enter the campus, and that all the patients should be non-infective. Significantly, in the years that followed it would be the students, losing prejudice and gaining knowledge, who would break down these barriers, first crossing the fence to visit and help the boys and to share with them entertainments and religious services, finally eliminating the fence entirely.

Thanks to Mother Eaton the project took shape, a small cluster of neat mud-walled buildings, washed white and topped with grass-thatched roofs. And thanks to Dr. Ida's insistent example that utility should always be coupled with beauty, plus the interest and energy of the college principal Dr. Lazarus, the paths were soon bordered with flaming poinsettias, and Dr. Ida's favorite blue morning glories were clambering up the walls and over the thatch. Paul derived keen pleasure from drawing the simple plans and supervising, often participating in, the building operation. A far cry from a steel-girt building in Piccadilly to a mud and thatch hut in a corner of India, yet one seemed to fulfill itself in the other. He had come to think of the building episode as almost a waste of five good productive years, strands of his life pattern long clipped and useless. Strange now to discover them ready and waiting, invaluable to the weaving of its new design! No, not strange; humbling and awesome.

That year of 1950 saw other developments in India important to his work in leprosy. In Madras Dr. T. N. Jagadisan, organizer of the first All-India Leprosy Workers' Conference in 1947 and long a colleague of Dr. Cochrane in the British Empire Leprosy Association, Madras Provincial Branch, was instrumental in reorganizing the latter into the *Hind Kusht Nivaran Sangh,* which undertook research, treatment, training, and education, and would serve as an invaluable coordinator of such voluntary agencies as the Gandhi Memorial Leprosy Foundation. Dr. Jagadisan, brilliant scholar, English professor, lecturer, author, and Indian patriot, had himself been afflicted with leprosy of the tuberculoid type, noninfective but neurally disabling. His success on Dr. Cochrane's advice in retarding the growing stiffness of his fingers by constant massaging and exercise was of intense interest to Paul in his own studies of physiotherapy.

Paul was now faced with a crisis in his surgery department. The two beds were woefully inadequate both for research and for the increasing demands of leprosy patients. Fortunately he now had expert surgical assistance. Dr. Howard Somervell, noted surgeon who had first come to India to climb Mt. Everest with the Mallory expedition, then spent twenty-five years as a missionary doctor in Travancore, had visited Vellore, seen its needs, and offered his services for a year. His presence lent color as well as prestige to the department. Artist as well as doctor, he would illustrate his operating notes with pictures. Between operations he could often be found drinking coffee from a K-basin. On Saturday at noon he would leave Vellore to go mountain climbing. Unlike most westerners, he often wore Indian clothes when off duty. The patients, especially the children, loved him and called him *"Ta Ta,"* "grandfather."

"When they begin to call you *Ta Ta,*" he remarked ruefully, "it's time you retired."

But fortunately for Paul and Vellore, he did not. He even returned later for another five years of missionary service.

His presence encouraged Paul to expand his leprosy work. Unable to return to England to secure financial help, he stumped India, appealing both to individuals and to charity organizations. In Bombay he showed the photographs of his first hand operations to Professor Choksi, a Parsi who was chairman of the Tata charities, a foundation established by the great India industrialists of the Tata family. Together with the Wadia charities, they contributed enough money to build a seventeen-bed ward unit for leprosy, construction of which was begun in the following year, 1951.

The mid-century year was one of progress in both hospital and college. In January, a few days before India became a republic, all Vellore celebrated Dr. Ida's jubilee, marking fifty years since her arrival as a doctor in India. Madras University crowned the event by granting the college full affiliation, the goal of a decade's untiring labor. When a *lakh* of *rupees* ($20,000) came to her in gifts from all over the world, she decided, at Dr. Lazarus' suggestion, to put it toward a much needed new hostel for the men students and, belonging to the same breed of impatient activists as Paul, she made the decision one morning and was out breaking ground for the building that afternoon. Under the direction of Ted Gault, warden of the hostel, the campaign to finance the new building was successfully concluded.

Dr. Ida was fascinated with the new hand surgery. It being her habit to visit the hospital each day she was in Vellore, disturbed patients were always requesting that she sit beside them and hold their hands during operations. The leprosy patients were no exception.

"Do you mind?" she would ask Paul anxiously. "You're sure I won't bother?"

At his reassurance she would sit beside the patient's head, take the free hand in hers, and, if the patient was under local anaesthesia or perhaps none at all, whisper an occasional encouragement. Holding their hands, she would tell them what marvelous miracles were being performed these days, what a wonderful doctor was operating on them and how the power of God was working in him. It mattered not a whit that the hand she held had no feeling. Dr. Ida's *darshan*, blessing, was of a spiritual essence which knew no boundaries of the senses.

The year 1950 was productive also in the Brand family. The new arrival was a third girl named Estelle, a sleepy gentle little soul as different from her next older sister as violet from crimson. Perhaps because of the proximity of the ebullient Mary, she would be the sweet, quiet, studious one, exceedingly dear to her father.

Time for extracurricular pursuits during these early years of Paul's leprosy work was almost nonexistent. Once the New Life Center was sufficiently finished to house the first small group of boys, he poured into it every extra moment and ounce of energy. But with his days full at the hospital, his weekends devoted largely to the trips to Chingleput, his work at the Center must be crowded somehow into the brief hours between teatime and dark.

One of the purposes of the Center was to teach the patients with reconstructed hands a trade which would make them self-sufficient. Because of the prejudice against leprosy they must be taught crafts which each patient could pursue alone in his own village. At first Paul did most of the teaching himself, introducing skills connected with his own carpenter's training. He instructed them in the use of tools, then taught them to make toy animals, trains, cars, jigsaw puzzles. Under his careful supervision the toys were well made, beautifully finished, and they found a market. At first they were all sterilized and so advertised, even though this was an unnecessary precaution, since leprosy could be spread only by personal contact. But as time went on and people became more willing to buy, the very act of purchasing the products helped to break down prejudice.

The boys also learned farming skills as vegetable gardens and fruit trees were planted to help supply food to the colony. It was an adventure in cooperative living as well as training. Leprosy being no respecter of persons, high caste and low, wealthy and poor, college men and illiterates, all learned to live harmoniously together. The first groups included an engineer, a chartered accountant, a B.Sc. student, and a former Brahmin turned Christian, as well as uneducated villagers. All took turns doing the menial tasks of cleaning the compound, drawing water, sanitation duty, growing part of their own food.

But a second main purpose of the Center was research. Paul needed to study these reconstructed hands in order to evaluate his surgical techniques. What difference had the operations made? Did the techniques need to be changed to suit the peculiar disabilities of the leprosy patient? And still at the forefront of his quest was the question: Why did the fingers and toes of leprosy patients waste away?

Many cases of shortening, of course, were obviously results of infections and accidents. Early in his study Paul had asked Dr. Cochrane and other experts, "How could I tell the difference between a finger which has been destroyed by accident or infection and one in which leprosy has caused absorption?" Well, if he saw a hand in which all the fingers were equally absorbed, Cochrane had pointed out, he could assume that it was due directly to leprosy. On the other hand, if he saw a good hand with some normal fingers and some much shortened, it could be assumed that the shortening had resulted from some accident or sepsis.

Paul was not wholly satisfied with these assumptions of the specialists, which ascribed most instances of shortening to the direct action of the disease. An incident which had happened in his early years at Chingleput had strengthened these doubts. One day he was looking at the records of a patient, indicating that for years the man had been negative. In fact, he had never been highly positive. Yet he firmly assured Paul that his fingers had shrunk half their length in the past two or three years.

"Can you remember anything which has happened to them?" asked Paul.

Oh, yes, the patient could. Several accidents had happened. There had been little burns and things, nothing very important.

"How long were your fingers when you became negative?" Paul prodded.

The patient reflected. He was an intelligent man and his memory was good. "I had lost about a half inch of this one and three quarters of that one," he reckoned. Now his fingers were each of them about an inch long.

Intensely interested, Paul had gone to the superintendent, Harry Paul. "Now look, are you *sure* this man is negative?"

"Yes, of course. He has had repeated tests."

Paul's eyes narrowed. "His fingers have been shortening for the last five years, but he has been negative for seven. How can that be leprosy?"

The leprologist had had no answer. Neither had Paul. But whatever the truth might be, he intended to find it.

Now one day in the New Life Center he made a startling

observation. He was trying to open the door of the little store room, but the padlock was rusty, and the key would not turn. One of the patients, a cute little chap, undersized, malnourished, about ten years of age, came along smiling and reached for the key.

"Let me try, Sahib doctor," he offered. "Bet you I can do it."

He closed his thumb and forefinger about the tiny handle of the key and with just one quick movement of his hand he turned it in the lock.

"There you are!" He looked up with an impish grin as if to add, "What are you anyway? A weakling?"

Paul's eyes sharpened with sudden interest. Was that a drop of blood he had seen fall to the floor? "Here, let me see your hand," he demanded.

Examining the boy's fingers, he found that the turning of the key had torn a flap of skin and fat and joint capsule so deeply that at the bottom of the wound the bone was showing! Yet the boy was completely unaware of it. Why? How? Answer to the first, of course, was obvious. He had no feeling in his hand. If he put it in his pocket, he wouldn't know whether he was touching a key or a coin or a handkerchief. If he laid it on a hot pot on the stove or on the stove itself, he wouldn't know his hand was being burned unless he smelled the scorching flesh. There had been no pain to warn him before damage was done. But that did not answer the second question. How had a ten year old boy been able to exert enough pressure not only to turn the key but to cut his finger to the bone?

Though he had neither the knowledge nor the equipment for measuring actual pressures, Paul and his team proceeded to do some careful figuring. Measuring the amount of total force available to twist various handles, they found that such force might vary from fifty to two hundred pounds. Given a big handle, the normal hand can exert its whole force easily, but given a small handle with a cutting edge like a key, the strength applied is greatly reduced because the pressure begins to hurt. Using simple arithmetic and dividing these figures by the area of the hand exerting the force, they discovered that with a big handle, where perhaps eight square inches of skin might be involved, a hand might exert about twenty pounds of pressure per square inch. But with this tiny key, a half inch in diameter at the handle, with metal an eighth of an inch wide, the area of steel available to be pressed was a total of about a sixteenth of a square inch. The boy might actually have been applying up to a thousand pounds of force per square inch! No wonder he had torn his finger to the bone!

The incident marked the beginning of a new phase in Paul's thinking. Here was this boy, doing something which ordinary people are constantly doing without harm, yet damaging himself seriously because the insensitivity of his fingers made him unaware of the pressure they were exerting. And if he, why not others? Might not the fingers of leprosy patients be constantly receiving excessive force from apparently trivial daily tasks, incurring damage which would often stop short of actual wounds but which would slowly accumulate scar tissue under the skin, replacing the fat and blood vessels of the fingers and, little by little, resulting in a sort of shrinking process which would in time shorten the fingers? And if so, might it not be possible to check the process by making sure that the forces exerted by the patient's fingers remained in the same range of power as those experienced by normal hands? The pursuit of this line of reasoning held thrilling possibilities.

Every evening Paul would leave the hospital, go to the New Life Center, and sit in the workshop. At first there were six boys in the colony, then ten, then twelve. For him it was the most exciting, most satisfying part of the whole day.

"Go ahead with your work," he would tell them. "Just forget I'm here."

For an hour or two he would sit watching them, not their work, not their tools, only their hands. Then at the end of every day he would ask them to put their hands up in a row, and he would inspect every finger. So well did he get to know them that every little scar was familiar, every tiny twist, every limitation in movement. With the team helping, fingers were photographed; laid flat on a piece of paper they were outlined, dated, and placed on file, so that if ever one lost even an eighth of an inch of length it could be spotted on the outline. If ever a finger dropped off Paul was determined he would see it and, if possible, know the reason why. Week after week, month after month this continued, with Dr. Gusta Buultgens keeping her meticulous records. And, to Paul's excited satisfaction, scarcely a change took place in a finger which could not be traced to some cause unrelated to the disease: an abrasive tool, an over exertion of pressure, splinters, tacks, broken handles.

As he watched them work, Paul, once again the carpenter,

figured out ways to improve both efficiency and safety. Timing them, he would note how many nails they could drive in, say, five minutes time. Most of their clumsiness—and they were terribly clumsy—came from their inability to feel. Picking up a nail or a screw they could never be sure without looking whether it was headed the right or wrong way, and it took longer to pick it up than to drive it in. Suddenly Paul got an idea.

"Try holding the nails in pliers," he suggested.

It worked amazingly. He found that in almost every case if they could get their fingers away from their work and put them around a tool, it speeded them. With pliers they were soon as fast as normal workers. Also it kept them from pounding their fingers unwittingly. After this he made a little box with sloping sides and a slit along the bottom and suspended it above the bench. Nails thrown into this box hung down through the slit automatically the right way up for grasping with the pliers. All the tools were fitted to large round smooth handles. Files were set in blocks to protect hands from pressure. When it was discovered how dangerous it was for the hands to be near any moving part of metal, such as planes, the latter were all fitted with big handles and second auxiliary knobs.

During this period of watching, testing, experimenting, which lasted upward of two years, Paul's training in building assumed tremendous importance. He could tell the patients about holding tools, changing leverages, adjusting to different ratios. And his observations taught him the necessity of connecting surgery of the hand with the work they were going to do. For patients who would do carpentering he presently discarded the standard operation he had been performing because it was causing uneven pressure on the fingertips. The new technique, instead of concentrating force on the end joint, tended to close the fingers evenly at all joints.

His staff was a rare fellowship of dedicated persons. In 1951 when her Swiss husband Dr. Ernest Fritschi came as house surgeon to the hospital, Mano Fritschi became the first director of the New Life Center. Daughter of an Indian canon of the Church of England and a trained social worker, she brought to her work skill, warm friendliness, and deep devotion. When she was obliged to leave, Chandra Manuel, a biology graduate with work in anatomy, who had a deep interest

Jesse and Evelyn Brand with Connie and Paul

Paul's childhood home in the Kolli Hills

Evelyn Brand with the Ko
Hill women

Paul and Margaret's wedding, Emmanuel Church, Middlesex, England, May 1943

Paul and Margaret with Mary, Jean, Estelle and Christopher, early 1950s

(back, l to r) Margaret,
Granny, Paul,
Christopher, Jean,
Mary, (front) Patricia,
Estelle holding Pauline

Paul with his
mother during a
visit in the early
1970s

Paul and Margaret with Pauline at her 1980 graduation from Wheaton College

Dr. Brand escorts Indira Gandhi at the Christian Medical College, Vellore

Dr. Brand with Dr. Mary Verghese and other Vellore staff members

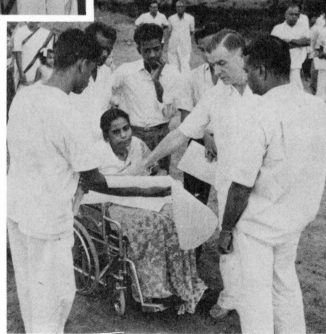

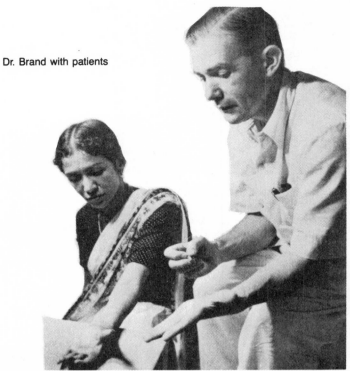

Dr. Brand with patients

American Leprosy Missions

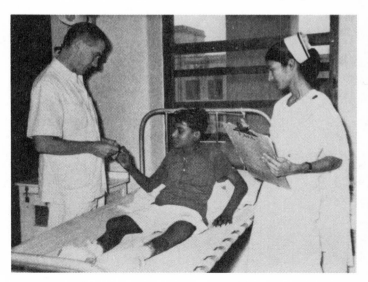

Sadagopan

Dr. Brand and two young patients
at the New Life Center

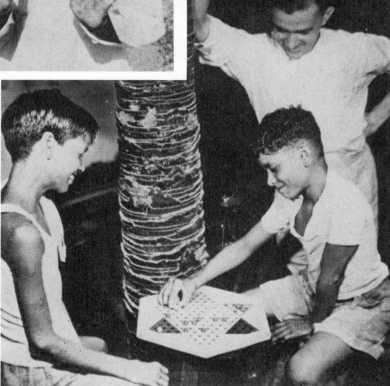

American Leprosy Missions

Dr. Paul W. Brand

in people and a sincere dedication, took her place, to remain as an efficient worker in the center for the next nine years. The year 1951 also saw the arrival of Ruth Thomas.

Long before this the team had realized the need of a skilled physiotherapist. Letters had been sent out to many missionary societies telling of this need. Obliged to leave her work in China because of the communist regime, Ruth Thomas, a Welsh physiotherapist, was in Hongkong about to take passage home when she heard a rumor of this message. Changing her route, she disembarked at Colombo, crossed to Madras, and came to Vellore. Throwing herself heart and soul into leprosy study, she worked out courses of exercises and pursued research projects on the best way to deal with stiff fingers. Faithful, quiet, so shy she would turn scarlet if pushed into a position of prominence, she made an inestimable contribution to leprosy rehabilitation. Gathering around her a little group of patients, she gave them a good formal two year course in physiotherapy. Though most of these young trainees had no college education, they were remarkably keen, and some of them came to know hand structure, muscles, and nerves better than most surgeons.

The tracing down of injuries incurred from the day's work at the New Life Center became a sort of detective game. Most of the patients were cooperative, but occasionally one would feel a bit ashamed of his wound and would try to hide it. For instance, there was the boy in an early group who appeared at evening inspection with a severe laceration on the front of one finger. Obviously it had been bleeding during the day.

"What have you been doing?" Paul asked him, much concerned.

"Just digging," he evaded.

"May I see your spade?"

The boy produced a spade with a reasonably smooth handle and obstinately maintained that he had been digging with it all day. But when Paul went into the tool shop he found there a spade with a cracked handle bound together with a piece of bailing wire. The twisted end of the wire, though tucked back neatly, was covered with blood. Obviously the boy had been digging with that twisted wire sticking into his index finger. He had known that he shouldn't be digging with it, but hadn't thought the box of tools would be inspected. But this was a rare case. Once the boys realized the importance of keeping their hands free from injuries they became the most ardent of sleuths.

Once they realized the importance! Some of the patients, lads in their early teens, would be mischievous and full of fun when they came and completely without regard for their hands and feet. These, referred to by the team as the "naughty boys," were often the most interesting and challenging. Many of them were sheer show-offs, deriving impish enjoyment from shocking others with their ability to bear pain. There were boys who could stick a thorn through a finger or palm and pull it out the other side, pick up a hot coal or thrust a foot into the fire, daring others to do the same. When asked how they had acquired a wound on hands or feet, they would shrug and reply with evasiveness or bravado, "Oh—I guess it came by itself."

These boys were the delight and despair of Paul and his team. Often they were the brightest mentally of all the patients. As the weeks passed and it seemed they would never learn, slowly a change would occur. They would begin to smile spontaneously and enjoy the fellowship of the place; then, perhaps suddenly, they would develop a new kind of alertness, take pride in their hands, and be ashamed when they hurt them.

One of these boys was Venkatasen, who came to the Center with commencing absorption of fingers, clawed hands, and bad thumbs; left it to become one of the most skilled and valued workers in the splint shop, working with intense heat in the baking of plastics. Yet never would he be found with a single wound or blister on his hands, and his fingers would remain exactly as when he left the Center, the same degree of shortening of one finger and a little bulbous end on another.

Only occasionally did a patient come who failed to adjust to the spirit of the Center. One of these was Nannu. Though it was always the team's principle to *live* their religious conviction rather than *preach* it, Nannu claimed that Mano Fritschi tried to force him to become a Christian. He maintained also that he was deprived of proper food and that Paul had threatened to shoot him. He even sent an appeal to the court for redress of damages, of course with no result. The team were relieved when he left the New Life Center, chagrined when he returned a short time later with an ulcer.

"I'll have nothing to do with him," flared Dr. Gusta Buult-gens when he arrived in the hospital clinic. "And neither will the rest of the team if I have my way."

She did not have her way. Hearing that Nannu was in the clinic, Paul quietly had him brought up to B ward, where he remained for two months. Dr. Buultgens obstinately refused to go there to treat him. After making her rounds in F ward with Paul, she would take the house surgeon and the physiotherapy boys away with her, marching off with lips compressed and head held high. Paul, left alone, would then make his way to B ward, where day after day he would treat the sullen and still hostile Nannu, changing the dressings with his own hands.

"A very special patient he must be," some one was heard to remark, "for the sahib doctor to give him such gentle care and attention!"

13

Though his first furlough was due in 1951, Paul felt he could not possibly leave India yet. The New Life Center was just getting well started, and research was becoming increasingly exciting as evidence mounted that it was not the leprosy itself which destroyed fingers but injuries done to them because of their insensitivity.

Acting on this as yet unproven theory, Paul and his fellow-detectives painstakingly tracked down each burn, scratch, callus, blister, trying to account for it by some other cause than leprosy. Once they thought they were really stumped. Although they were able to trace all the wounds occurring in the front of the hand, some of the boys kept turning up with blisters on the first three knuckles. Even though they inspected the hands each day and took the boys back to their working benches asking, "How could this happen?", no cause was apparent.

"Perhaps we should inspect our hands oftener," one of the

boys suggested. Whereupon they discovered that the blisters were present at a morning inspection though not the evening previous. Therefore they must have occurred during the night. How? By now the patients were more excited than the doctors and physiotherapists working on the team, for they knew this was their one chance of abolishing the great bugbear of their lives, the fear of losing all their fingers. And it was one of the patients who tracked down the criminal. At that time there was no electricity in the Center, and the boys used hurricane lanterns with glass globes. Always taught to guard against heat and fire, they would light the lamps carefully, put the globe down, and do their evening's work. When they went to bed they would place the lamps beside their mats, lie down, reach out, and turn them out. In turning the little wick handles tucked away beneath the glass globe there was a tendency for three knuckles, or even four, to rub in succession against the hot glass. Since it was dark, no one noticed the blisters. Easy enough to find a remedy once the cause was discovered! They merely took some wooden blocks and fastened them to the little knobs which turned down the wick. No more blisters!

There were times, however, when Paul really feared his theory was in jeopardy. Occasionally parts of fingers did seem to be disappearing with no logical explanation, usually during the night. One morning a boy came to him with nearly a third of his index finger missing. Paul looked from the raw stump to the young patient's tearful eyes.

"What happened, son?"

"Doctor Sahib, I don't know. It was there yesterday. You know it was. You measured it last night."

"Where is the piece that's missing?" persisted Paul.

"I don't know," mourned the patient.

They went into the room where the boy had slept and searched the floor around his mat. There were a few tiny spots of blood, but not even a scrap of flesh! Paul could sense the feeling of fatalism closing around him. It would only need the apparent disappearance of one or two fingers in the night to reawaken in these boys all the old superstitions about leprosy. They searched again, more carefully, and this time not far from the mat and leading away from the blood spots, they noticed in the dust of the earth floor a few little footmarks. Rats! How horribly simple! Not feeling any pain, the boy had slept on completely unaware that a rodent was enjoying a good meal on his finger. And how often this must happen in village homes where rats could gain access as easily as human beings! This danger also was easily corrected. Thereafter cats were introduced into the compound, and every patient who left the colony took a kitten as part of his necessary equipment.

Sometimes proof of the theory came through a patient's unhappy choice of occupation, as with Thangavelu. He came to the center with commencing absorption on all his fingers. The team tested them, made maps, tracings, photos. He was put on controlled employment in the carpenter shop, and for about two years he did not lose the smallest fraction of an inch from his fingers. Their mobility was greatly improved by successive operations. But Thangavelu came from a farming family, and he complained that carpentry was of little use to him.

"Very well," agreed Paul. "We will try to teach you better methods of agriculture. But—I'm warning you, it's a risk."

"I'm willing to take the risk," the young man replied.

Paul was able to secure for him a pair of bullocks and a plow. For about three months he plowed the land at the Center and hired himself out to the local farmers, yet even though he had learned a fair amount of hand care, his fingertips began once more to harden. Then his family was willing to take him back, and he returned home, hiring himself and his bulls to a building firm, driving them round and round a lime mill and using them to draw water. When he came back some months later for reassessment, every one of his fingers was from a quarter to a third of an inch shorter than it had been.

So the evidence accumulated, by no means through Paul's efforts alone. It was the team working together which accomplished the results. And the astonishing thing about it was that the most valuable members of the team were not doctors, social workers, physiotherapists. They were patients. In a sense each one of them became doctor, social worker, physiotherapist. And all were amateur detectives, tracing down the villain of their own worst fears.

"I have a clue!" one of them would proffer at the day's meeting, when there was equal give and take between staff and patients. Then the idea would be tossed around, accepted in whole or in part, or perhaps discarded. These little group meetings, or seminars, became some of the most treasured experiences of Paul's life.

One of the most valued members of the team, who became an apt pupil of Ruth Thomas in physiotherapy and Paul's able assistant at the center, was Namasivayan.

Namo, as he was usually called, was intelligent and well educated. He had passed his intermediate exams with distinction in 1946 when he discovered a small lesion on his hip. A physician diagnosed it as leprosy. The word aroused in him unspeakable horror. It conjured up images of all the leprosy victims he had ever seen, no fingers, stumps of feet, begging. All his dream castles of becoming an electrical engineer collapsed. His mother persuaded him to go to an untrained native physician whose medicine caused a flare-up of big raised lesions on his face. Shut up in his room for five months, hands paralyzed so he could not even write, he nearly went mad with fear and despair. One day when his mother brought him a glass of milk, he put in it five grams of arsenic which he had once bought for chemistry class, and lifted it to his lips. As he was about to drain it he seemed to hear the voice of his college principal in Bangalore, who had once said in a lecture, "Committing suicide is cowardice." After that he became imbued with one purpose: to make himself useful somehow to others who had been cursed like himself. After many bitter experiences of being shunned and rejected, he heard of Dr. Brand and came to him. There was a flaring patch on his face, and his clawed hands, as he held them out, were trembling.

"I—I've come to serve," he stuttered.

He became one of the first members of the New Life Center. Psychologically disturbed and very bitter against people because of their heartless attitude toward leprosy, he was moody and withdrawn. One night months after his arrival Paul was using a tape recorder at the center to entertain the patients. The mood was one of gaiety and lightheartedness, each patient taking his turn talking into the recorder and hearing his voice played back. Suddenly Namo broke into the light chatter. "I want to say something."

Cupping the mike in his clawed hands, he began talking in a tight, strained voice. Instantly the mood of gaiety was dissolved. "I came into the world without asking to be born," he said with painful slowness. "I am—moved and—tossed about by forces outside my control." His voice became a cry of despair. "I—I don't know where I'm going."

But as more months passed Namo changed. He began to see that love, not hate, was the motivation of all who labored in the New Life Center, that they were really concerned about him. Though no pressure was ever exerted in the center to change a patient's religion, many, seeing Christianity in action, did become Christians. Namo was one of these, taking the name of Paul when he was baptized into the Church of South India. Where his crusade for helping fellow patients had been a bitter, vindictive fight against society, it became in time a loving service, a dedication. His patience sometimes exceeded even Paul's, as with the case of Balasundram.

Bala was nine or ten when he came to the hospital clinic. His hands were already clawed, one finger had been lost through a burn, and the others were all a bit shortened. Though one hand was somewhat mobile, the other was absolutely stiff.

"This hand is no good," Paul told Namo. "We had better fix those joints in some position that will be useful to him, since we shall never be able to move it."

"Sir," said Namo, "not yet please. Give me three months."

So Bala was admitted to the New Life Center. Every day Namo worked on the right hand, massaging, rubbing in oil, giving it wax baths, exercising it. After three months Paul examined the patient again. To his surprise he found just a bit of movement in the fingers.

"Can I have three more months?" Namo begged.

"As long as you like," said Paul, "provided he keeps improving."

Bala stayed at the center a year and a half. Then Namo brought him again to Paul. The fingers could now be opened completely, with a full range of passive movement. Paul was able to operate on the boy's hands to restore his grasp. But it was Namo who had worked the miracle. Paul's job had taken a couple of hours, Namo's hour after hour, day after day, for a year and a half.

Trained by Ruth Thomas, Namo was to become increasingly skilled and devoted until some years later, after a half dozen operations on his own hands, he was given a good position as physiotherapist at the sanatorium in Chingleput. As elder brother in his family he assumed the educational support of a distant relative, an accomplished and attractive girl who, after graduating from the School of Nursing at Vellore, became his devoted wife. So this bitter young introvert who once thought his world had ended found increasing fulfillment not only in service but in rich personal satisfaction.

Another early patient who made a big contribution was Sadagopan.

It was in February 1951 that Margaret was approached by a young man as she left the college offices to walk the short distance to the bungalow. Though he was a fine looking youth with an intelligent face and handsome features, the ravages of leprosy were obvious. His hands were reduced to stumps, with most of the fingers of one hand missing from the middle joint. His eyes were filmed and reddened, doubtless nearly blind. A pair of old misshapen sneakers encased feet shaking from strain and fatigue, only partially concealing their deformity and infection.

"I am looking for Dr. Brand," he said in a politely cultured voice. "I have come with a letter to him from Dr. Jagadisan."

"Oh, I'm sorry." Margaret tried not to show her overwhelming pity. "Dr. Brand isn't in Vellore right now. He's away on a trip."

The youthful figure sagged, and the fine features seemed to crumple. "Not here?" the visitor repeated.

"He should be back in a day or two. If you would care to find some place to stay in Vellore and return tomorrow—"

"Yes. Thank you." He turned away, his shaking feet carrying him unsteadily along the path, leaving a wet mark with every step.

"Wait!" Something about the sagging shoulders touched Margaret to inquire with concern, "You—you can find a place to stay, can't you?"

He turned. No, he told her with a matter of fact honesty, there would be no place for him in Vellore. He had tried the hospital, and they had refused him. When he had attempted to come here to the campus by bus, the driver had stopped the bus and put him off. But, thank you, he would manage somehow.

Margaret's ears echoed with a confusion of sounds, the disconsolate voice of the stranger, Paul's frequent warnings that the children should never come in contact with his patients, and, loudest and most insistent, some words she had been reading only that morning. It was these last which finally, almost against her will, brought her to a decision.

"You may come home with me," she said, "and stay until my husband comes."

The youth's eyes lighted, first with incredulity, then with gratitude. They walked along the path to the bungalow, and she noted with relief that there were no children playing on it. She could hear their running feet and gay laughter inside. "I'm afraid," she said frankly, "that I shall have to ask you to remain here on the verandah. You understand, I hope, that I can't ask you into the house because of the children?"

His gratitude was like that of a dog experiencing kindness for the first time. "Oh—yes! All I could ask or want is a place on the verandah."

Sadagopan stayed there for three days. Margaret brought him a mat and a pillow and took food to him herself each meal. She took time often to go out and visit with him. It was late at night when Paul returned. Margaret took him upstairs and explained the situation.

"But, darling," he protested, "you know children are more liable to infection than adults. Why did you do it?"

"Paul," she replied, her eyes very clear and bright, "The Bible says, 'I was a stranger, and you took me in.' I had been reading that very passage the morning of the day this man came. It seemed to speak so clearly."

Paul was tired, and he had been sick. But he did not wait until morning. He went down at once to the verandah, greeted Sadagopan kindly, and examined his feet and hands.

This matter of the contagion of leprosy was a concern to all the team, especially in these early years. It was Dr. Cochrane's theory that a person was either immune to the disease or not—usually the former—and, though he assured his colleagues that with proper precautions they were in almost no danger, the possibility was at least in their subconscious minds and not far beneath the surface.

If Paul ever pricked himself with an instrument in operating, Gusta Buultgens was after him immediately to apply some kind of medication.

"A good thing for our research," he told her calmly, "finding out where I get my first patch of leprosy."

So he made a map of both hands, and whenever he was

pricked he would mark the spot on the diagram, noting the date, the patient's name, whether he was positive or negative, and his type of leprosy. He kept this map until he had so many pricks on his left index finger alone that if he had acquired a patch it would have been difficult to know which prick had caused it.

He was concerned, however, when his workers failed to take due precautions. Ruth Thomas was the worst offender. As the work grew she spent much time in the hospital treating leprosy patients. One patient, a lepromatous case, was extremely positive and so tender that he could not bear the usual splints and bandages. Every day Ruth would go and sit beside him, gently massaging his hands, In spite of Paul's remonstrances, she would never listen. And, though a candidate for permanently rigid fingers, the patient came out of this period of reaction with fingers as soft and supple as those of a normal hand.

As time progressed and the team acquired more knowledge and experience, together with more proof of the low susceptibility of adults to the disease, the danger of contagion seldom entered their minds.

And there was indication also that prejudice was breaking down, especially among the students. Not long after the New Life Center had been established a group in the Student Christian Movement decided to build the patients a chapel. The work was done entirely by students who volunteered to spend their two week vacation on the project. It was an adventure of social pioneering in more ways than one. Dr. Lazarus, the principal, joined in the labor, her lithe diminutive figure clad in sturdy slacks, an unheard-of innovation for a woman of India. And it was no small triumph for young intellectuals, even Christians, reared in a society where menial labor had for centuries been allocated to certain castes, to soil their hands and shoulder picks and shovels.

The final breaking down of prejudice would come a little later when the Student Christian Movement, which had usually gone to Katpadi for their annual retreats, chose one year to hold it in the New Life Center, using the chapel which they themselves had built. Prejudice among the students, that is. It would be many years before fears and superstitions would be tempered in the town.

These early years were a constant struggle against frustration and prejudice. One of Paul's hardest tasks was to refuse surgery to the crowds of people who soon began coming. With only a few beds he was obliged to select those for whom he thought he could do the most good. This meant rejecting others, like John Partharsathy.

John, who had been one of the free patients at Chingleput, was middle-aged and almost blind. When he came begging to have his claw hands opened, Paul had to say, "John, I'd love to be able to help you, but we just can't. We have so many able-bodied young men coming for surgery! Your hands would take a lot of time, because they're very stiff. And suppose we did open them out, how could you use them? If you can't see or feel—"

"But, doctor," the old man persisted gently, "I have a great desire to bring some happiness in return for all that's been done for me. I—" he hesitated, then continued modestly, "I believe I could bring music to people."

"What kind of music, John?"

"Well, I used to be able to play the organ, and I'm sure that if you could open my fingers, I could play again."

"Without being able to feel or see?" Paul had to be brutally honest. "I'm sorry, John, but how could you possibly play?"

The clawed hands crooked in a beseeching gesture. "I know how you feel, doctor, but—please just give me a chance."

Unable to resist the plea, Paul relented. With great misgivings he operated on John's hands. The surgery and therapy were moderately successful.

"Now—let me go to an organ," John pleaded.

An old pedal-operated harmonium was located, and John was led to it. Putting out his hand, he could not even feel the instrument, but Paul backed him to a stool and helped him sit down. His nerveless hands caressed the keys. A few squeaky little sounds emerged.

"It's like a broken dream," thought Paul, glad the sightless eyes could not see his instinctive pity. Again the fumbling hands moved—and discord filled the silence.

Then suddenly the organ swelled, not merely into melody but into the full harmony of the glorious hymn, "Jesus shall reign where'er the sun." And as the music came flooding out of the crude little box there spread over the uplifted face an ineffable smile of peace and satisfaction. Paul almost wept.

John's dream was to be richly fulfilled. As organist at a mission leprosy sanatorium in Dichpalli, he was to create harmony not only at Sunday services but during the weekdays, bringing cheer to any patient who might care to listen. But dozens with equally potent dreams had to be turned away.

Paul's growing conviction, supported by his mounting mass of evidence, that injuries, not leprosy, destroyed hands met with as frustrating opposition from leprologists as did his attempt to introduce more surgical patients from the hospital authorities. Even the open-minded and cooperative Bob Cochrane was somewhat suspicious of the new ideas.

"But look, Bob," Paul would reason, "you agree that a lot of the fingers lost by leprosy patients are lost because of accidents and sepsis and injury in fingers that cannot feel?"

"Yes, that's true enough," Cochrane said.

"And you agree, don't you, that it's a rather unique thing that people should lose their fingers at all? Aren't there mighty few diseases in the world where fingers are lost?"

"Yes, that's also true."

"Then why," Paul argued, "should we assume that fingers in leprosy are lost from two completely separate and apparently unrelated causes? Surely this is too much of a coincidence."

Dr. Cochrane only frowned and pursed his lips.

But as time went on and the team's proofs were more and more conclusive, the experts became less dogmatic. When Paul was able to show from further study that negative patients actually lost fingers faster than positive ones, they grudgingly admitted there might be something in his theory.

"All right. Granted they can lose fingers after they are negative," became their argument. "Even though it may not be leprosy which causes it, at least it's inevitable due to trophic changes."

Paul was reasonably sure it was not inevitable, for at the Center they were constantly proving it. Perhaps at this time he was too dogmatic in his claims that leprosy did not destroy hands and that loss of fingers was preventable. His critics accused him of saying things which simply were not true. Time was to prove them both right. For leprosy does damage hands, but only in about one per cent of cases and in a different way from what was then commonly thought. At a very short highly positive stage of certain cases the bones may be softened so that with accompanying lack of sensitivity the slightest act, even tying a bundle, may damage and even break a finger. But therapists can prevent even this damage by applying simple splints during this short period.

If Paul was too dogmatic, it was for the sake of the patients. You could not say to them, "It isn't always leprosy which destroys hands. You may be able to help save them." They would shrug and say, "*Pavum*, it is fate. What can I do?" No, you had to say, "Look, brother, you *need* not lose your fingers. If you do, it's your own fault."

So while working at their benches the team were cold statisticians, slow, cautious, scientific, unwilling to publish anything as fact until it had been proved, reproved, and proved again, out in the field they were dogmatic passionate advocates of a new way of life, promising hope for people who had thought life hopeless.

Facts! How Paul needed them, facts about hands, feet, nerve injuries, paralysis, plastic surgery! And then unexpectedly in 1952 a big break came. The Rockefeller Foundation heard about his work. This huge organization, centered in New York but with offices all around the world constantly on the watch for progressive movements which deserved promotion, approached him with the offer of a grant.

"You must go to different parts of the world and get help," their representative Dick Anderson told him. "See anybody you want to, surgeons, pathologists, leprologists, and take what time you need. We'll foot the bills."

This vote of confidence from such a great organization, coming at a period when many of his colleagues believed he was just wasting his time, was for Paul a shot in the arm. And, since he was due for a furlough, he jubilantly began making plans at once. England first, of course, then America, then on perhaps to other countries. With the advice of pathologists, neuropathologists, surgeons, leprologists, he made a list of all the people in the world who might be of assistance. It was with a zest for more knowledge rather than for rest or holiday that he looked forward to this belated furlough in 1952.

Margaret, however, prepared for the trip with mixed emotions. The prospect of transferring four uninhibited children, aged two to eight, into an ayah-less world of plush carpets, bric-a-brac, maiden aunts, and British manners was appalling. The children also had doubts as well as anticipations.

"Will there be trees to climb?" asked Jean with foreboding.

"At least there'll be walls," Christopher assured her.

Margaret remembered suddenly that to return to England she must have birth certificates for Mary and Estelle and hastily began unwinding the red tape necessary to secure legal documents. When finally she received copies of the registrations, she found to her dismay that they contained no names. Returning to headquarters, she complained to the officer.

"How old were these children when registered?" he inquired.

"Ten days," she replied.

"Oh, that explains it! They naturally wouldn't have taken any notice of those names, knowing that you would probably change your minds."

Margaret carefully explained how the English system differed from the Indian. Again she received the document, to discover with further dismay that the mother's name was listed as Margaret Elizabeth Berry. Again she went to headquarters, explaining that it should be made clear that this was not her married name.

"Oh, yes, I shall fix that easily," the officer promised.

When the document was returned to her, she found it had been corrected to read: "Mother, Margaret Elizabeth Berry, Spinster."

In good-humored despair she started all over again.

They were off at last, by train to Bombay, by ship to England. True to form, Mary got lost in Aden. It was only a half hour to sailing. They searched for her frantically all over the boat, combed the docks, broadcast a description of her over the ship's loud speaker. Margaret was beside herself.

"She's been kidnapped!" she insisted. "I'm sure of it. Some of those Arabs hanging around the wharf must have come aboard and taken her!"

Knowing this to be extremely unlikely, Paul faced the crisis with his usual equanimity. "We've done all we can," he told her calmly. "Come along and eat your lunch in peace."

They were pulling up the ship's anchor when a woman came along leading a sleepy-eyed Mary by the hand. The child had apparently wandered into her cabin, crawled into the bunk, and taken a nap.

But for the most part the voyage was without incident.

Going through customs in England, however, there was a moment of tragicomedy.

"And what's in this package?" inquired a testy official, his hands obviously prepared to open it.

"Oh," Margaret replied wearily, for there were still mountains of baggage to be inspected. "That's just toys, toys made by leprosy patients in India."

The official dropped it like a hot cake. "All right," he said hastily. "That will be all for you." And he rushed them through customs without further examination.

The East, it seemed, had no monopoly on ignorance and prejudice and superstition.

14

History was repeating itself. One morning in Carlton Hill, London, the milkman came running up to the door of a house called Nethania.

"Miss Harris, Miss Harris, come and look! Does this maybe belong to you?"

Aunt Hope rushed out. She should have been prepared, but thirty years can efface many memories. Her mouth fell open at sight of Jean hanging upside down ten feet in the air, swinging by her knees from the crosspiece of a lamppost, engrossed in a distorted vision of shocked passersby.

It was even worse than Margaret had anticipated. With no trees to climb, no wide spaces to run except the street, no pets, the children were desolate. The restrictions of a beautiful home with soft rugs, delicate pottery, polished cabinets filled with no-touch curios, were almost unbearable. The aunts, who remembered Paul and Connie only as little angels, were shocked but sweetly cooperative. They put aside one of the biggest rooms in the house for the children, knowing it would be wrecked. But it was impossible to contain them in any room.

Paul plunged immediately into his problems of research. One of his chief goals in England was to find surgeons who could advise him on better techniques of surgery to relieve stiffness in leprous fingers. Hoping to learn new techniques for skin-grafting the fingers of patients, he asked the help of Sir Archibald McIndoe, the famous plastic surgeon who had performed amazing operations on burned airmen, and invited himself down to East Grinstead to visit his unit. Eagerly he showed the great man photos of leprosy cases and asked his advice, but the results were disappointing.

"You seem to be doing about everything possible," McIndoe said. Then he invited Paul to give a lecture on his work to the plastic surgeons of his unit.

The result was breathtaking. Sir Archibald was utterly entranced.

"Here you come to East Grinstead to learn something," he exclaimed, "and you end up by teaching us! I say, this lecture is something every English surgeon should hear. Would you give me permission to put it up as a possible Hunterian lecture?"

Paul gasped. The Hunterian Professorship, given each year by the Royal College of Surgeons in memory of John Hunter, father of British surgery, was one of the greatest honors in surgery. And the honor would be the smallest part of it. What a chance to bring the whole challenge of leprosy rehabilitation to the attention of the surgical world! He dashed back to London, rewrote the lecture with some embellishments, and submitted it. To his amazement it was accepted.

The honor was conferred on October 24, 1952 in London in an ancient and colorful ceremony. Paul went first to the Royal College to meet the president, Sir James Paterson Ross. After having tea with him from the fabulous silver service of the Royal College, he was led to the robing room and attired, like all the council members, in the traditional scarlet gown. To his delight, some of his old University College teachers, including the beloved Professor Pilcher, were in the group. The procedure which followed was dictated by ancient and solemn tradition. Not a word was spoken during the whole ceremony except those of the lecturer. The lecturer was not introduced, nor was he thanked. Nor did he say anything in the way of gratitude or comment, nothing but the actual words of his academic lecture.

Preceded by a beadle carrying the gold mace on a cushion, the president and council members trooped into the hall and filed into the front seats. Paul brought up the rear. When he arrived at the front, he approached the president, who silently bowed in his direction. Silently Paul bowed back, then immediately plunged into his lecture, a highly technical paper on "The Reconstruction of the Hand in Leprosy." When he had finished, he indicated the fact by bowing again toward the president, who rose and bowed toward him. The beadle then stood and bore the mace on its cushion down the aisle, and the procession reformed, only now it was Paul who led the way with the president, the Council following. After a brief celebration in the hall of the Royal College it was over and Paul left, now dignified by the title of Hunterian Professor of 1952. A dozen years later he was to be accorded the exceptional honor of receiving the citation a second time, his presentation then to be entitled: "The Reconstruction of the Feet."

Gratifying, and very useful for publicizing the problem of leprosy, but he had come chiefly to seek knowledge, not to give it. He continued his search in England, with increasingly disappointing results. Taking with him his big box of slides from all his post mortems, he visited pathologists and neuropathologists, many of the famous authorities in the field, calling their attention to the nerve swellings, asking what they meant. They made polite noises, said yes it was strange, yes it was most interesting and doubtless important, but none could make any real contribution concerning the nature of the swellings or their cause. When Paul told them of the team's tentative conclusions, they would nod and agree, yes-yes-yes, that was probably so.

He consulted Pulvertaft and Seddon and other eminent hand surgeons in England, thoroughly enjoying their stimulating company and learning a great deal, if not specifically about problems of leprosy, at least about hand surgery, an area in which he still considered himself a beginner. Even more important than the learning of specific facts was the opportunity to observe masters of the art at work, the way they handled their instruments, the meticulous attention to detail of experts like Pulvertaft, the beautiful techniques of nerve surgery of artists like Seddon. But he had hoped among other things to learn how to mobilize stiff fingers. Not only could no one give him an answer to this problem, but he found few who had had as much experience as he on paralysis of the hand's intrinsic muscles.

After some months in England the family separated, Paul leaving for the United States to spend four months in further travel and research under his grant from the Rockefeller Foundation, Margaret to depart somewhat later for South Africa, where her parents had returned for their retirement.

Paul spent a month in Boston studying with such specialists as Flynn, Marvel, Barr, and Denny-Browne; a month in Chicago at the famous Pasavant Hand Hospital, where he studied under Koch and Mason. Then he went on to San Francisco for two weeks with Bunnell, probably the leading hand authority in the world, and other experts such as Howard. Further travels took him to Boyes in Los Angeles and to Riordan in New Orleans. The latter was the one man he found on his trip who was actually working on the reconstruction of hands in leprosy. A fine hand surgeon who had trained under Bunnell, he was going out one day a week to the only leprosarium in America, at Carville, Louisiana. As a result of Paul's visit and demonstrations of his techniques at Carville, Riordan adopted some of the Vellore methods, and Paul adopted some of Riordan's. It was a profitable sharing experience for both of them. But though he gained much knowledge and was able to share some of his techniques, from only one person in America did he receive a glimmer of light on his basic problems.

"Now look," he said to Dr. Derek Denny-Browne, the eminent Harvard professor of neurology, "here are some slides taken from autopsies of leprosy patients all over India. I want to know what's happening to these nerves, why they are swelled like this, and I can't find anybody who can give me an answer." He listed some of the authorities he had consulted.

The professor smiled ruefully. "Well, if those boys can't help you, there's not much chance I can. But let me have a look, anyway."

Obviously a man who loved pathology, he spent a long time poring over the slides. "You know," he said finally, "these slides look just like my cats."

Then he began telling of work he had done years before on the nerves of cats and rabbits, applying pressure to them to check the blood supply, then later examining them under the microscope. Getting out some of his old slides and comparing them with Paul's, he said, "There you are. Just like your swellings. There has been an inflammation inside the sheath, and that causes a pressure on the nerve, diminution of blood."

This was the first real breakthrough Paul found as to the cause of paralysis. Though in the end it would not prove as simple as it seemed at the time, they were to find that the chief cause of paralysis was ischemia, temporary lack of blood supply in the tissue.

While the new information he gained was limited, the trip was abundantly worthwhile in knowledge and experience both learned and shared. Besides the demonstrations of surgery and rehabilitation he gave in Carville, in New York he participated in a television program on which he showed pictures of his rehabilitation work and some of the toys made at the New Life Center.

He finished his tour in New York with a speaking engagement arranged by the American Leprosy Missions. During the meeting he began to feel ill, and as he left he knew he was coming down with flu. Though the Rockefeller Foundation was paying him an adequate per diem allowance, he was trying to save much of it and had registered at a little inexpensive hotel. Returning to it on the subway, he became so dizzy that he swayed and fell over, lying on the floor of the car, yet not a single person moved to help him. No doubt they thought he was drunk. It was too cheap a hotel for the room to boast a telephone. He had had no experience in seeking medical assistance in America and assumed, mistakenly, that the surgeons on whom he was scheduled to call were all too specialized to be bothered with a case of influenza. Besides, he was too ill to care if he had a doctor. The next day he rang for the bell boy and asked him to bring orange juice and milk and aspirin. For six days he lay burning with fever, feeling more and more wretched and depressed, seeing no one but the bell boy, who was dispatched each day for the three commodities. Then suddenly he looked up to see Dr. Eugene Kellersberger of the American Leprosy Missions, standing in the door, a broad smile on his face, arms filled with paper bags full of groceries.

"How—how did you find me?" Paul asked. Never had a human face looked so angelic.

After Paul's meeting with the Missions Dr. Kellersberger had said to a colleague, "That man looked ill. Where is he staying?" The colleague didn't know, so he made inquiries of the Rockefeller Foundation and found that Paul was supposed to be visiting a certain surgeon, Dr. Littler. Interrogated, Dr. Littler said, "Yes, I'm expecting him, but he hasn't turned up yet." Dr. Kellersberger had continued his search, becoming more and more worried. Finally he had combed the New York hotels. And here he was. By now Paul was sufficiently recovered to appreciate the delicacies in the bags, but he was far more grateful for the concern and friendliness of this world famous leprosy specialist.

He managed to sail as planned on the *Ile de France*, leaving New York for Plymouth on April 2nd, but he was by no means fully recovered when he reached England. Margaret was visiting her parents who now lived in Capetown, South Africa, and he planned to join her by plane after a few days with the aunts. The train trip to London seemed interminable. When he arrived in his room in Nethania, he sank gratefully into a chair and pulled off his shoes. Then suddenly it came, without warning, perhaps the blackest moment of his whole life. For as he leaned over and pulled off his sock, he made a discovery. *There was no feeling in his heel.*

He rose mechanically, found a pin, sat down again, and pricked the small area below his ankle. He felt no pain. He thrust the pin deeper, until a speck of blood showed. Still he felt nothing. For a few moments, which seemed an eternity, he remained seated, dabbing at the prick with a handkerchief, over and over, the only activity in a world which seemed suddenly devoid of all life and motion. Then he got up and flung himself on the bed.

So—it had come. He supposed, like other workers with leprosy, he had always half expected it. As Bob Cochrane often said, you either were or were not immune. And he, Paul Brand, obviously was one of those few adults who were not. Unconsciously, he realized now, the expectation of this moment must always have been close to the surface of his mind. In the beginning probably not a day had gone by without the automatic searching of his body for the telltale patch, the numbed area of skin. Hands, face, back, arms—even now he gave them an occasional once-over, without realizing it. But—to find one's heel the vulnerable spot, like Achilles! He laughed aloud, hoarsely.

"Paul?" It was Aunt Hope's gentle voice at the door. "Are

you all right? Can I get you something, dear? Some hot tea?"

"No, auntie, thank you." He made his voice sound cheerful. "Just a night's sleep is all I need. It was such a long tiring trip."

"Of course, dear. Sleep well. You'll feel like yourself in the morning."

She tiptoed away, and he lay there in the dark, yielding fully to the blackness of despair. The small tidy world of Nethania, the exciting outer world of trams and lorries and undergrounds and clicking heels and laughing children, were as remote as planets in outer space. He would never be a part of them again. Ostracized, taboo, "outside the pale," *leper!* How glibly he and others had dismissed these worn phrases as unrealistic and outmoded! Had they really thought that by changing the name of the thing they could destroy its agelong curse? Alone? No. He realized presently that he was not alone. He had joined a bitter fellowship of at least ten million others who had tasted just such a moment. This was the way Namasivayan had felt when he had found the lesion on his hip. And Sadagopan with the patch on his back . . . and Dr. Jagadisan . . .

But this was not a time for self pity. The hours were passing. Before morning came and he had to face another day, he must plan. What should he do now with his life? One thing was certain. He must not live intimately with his family again. Should he go back to India, continue, himself as a patient, to work with other—*lepers*? Or was it better to remain here in England where the disease would not be recognized by the public? He could picture the furor when the news got out, especially in England! And what a blow to leprosy work! Here he had been telling his team it wasn't contagious! Few of them would ever dare engage in such work again.

He clenched and unclenched his hands, savoring the pain of the nails digging into his palms. Would the time come when he could dig to the limit of his strength and feel no pain? At least he had enough knowledge so he could prevent deformity!

It would be easier just to disappear. He had actually begun to consider plans for doing it when cold reason shocked him into sanity. "Coward!" he gritted the word through his teeth. "And you're the one who has been telling everybody that leprosy is curable!"

Sweating, breathing hard like a runner, he kept the tread-mill of agony in motion, a round of self pity, reason, planning, which went on and on with no beginning and no ending. He was still lying there half sleeping, half waking, and fully dressed except for shoes and socks, when the windows with their undrawn shades turned gray. It seemed like a lifetime rather than a single night. Dragging himself to his feet and looking in the mirror, he was surprised to find that his features looked fairly normal, his brown thatch of hair untouched by gray.

"All right," he told himself grimly. "Let's get on with the business."

With clinical objectivity he found another pin. Then with steady fingers he bared the skin below his ankle, jabbed in the point—and yelled.

The relief of the blessed pain was staggering. His first reaction was to fall on his knees and thank God. The next was to fling open a window and breathe deeply of the warm April air, as if he could not get his lungs full enough. The third was to berate himself for being a stupid fool. The explanation of his mistake was simple enough. Sitting in the train all the way from the coast, still too weak from the flu for normal restless motion, he had numbed a nerve. Depression had dulled his wits, stimulated his fears. And of course such an area of insensitivity *was* a common symptom of leprosy.

And, as he was to discover, most leprosy workers could report a similar episode at some time in their careers. They might put an arm on the back of a chair and have it go numb, discover a small innocent patch on the skin, and leap to conclusions. Yet after two decades of experience he was never to know of a contemporary leprosy worker who had contracted the disease from his patients.

For years he told no one, not even Margaret, of that night of horror. He was too ashamed of it. He wanted to forget it. But fortunately he could not. For hereafter his sympathy for his patients would become empathy. He would know exactly how they felt at that first most shattering stage of their sickness. And as time passed the episode was to spark an awareness which became the basis of profound religious experience. What an absolutely glorious sensation it had been to feel that sharp painful thrust of the pin! Again and again, cutting a finger, turning an ankle, sticking a foot into too hot water, even suffering from agonizing nausea as his body reacted in violent self-protection from mushroom poisoning, he was to respond in fervent gratitude, "Thank God for pain!"

Paul's keen interest in pain had been first roused by his teacher, Sir Thomas Lewis. Experience with leprosy patients, resulting in the discovery that most of their disabilities were due to unconscious self-destruction because of the absence of pain, so intensified this interest that his thinking on the subject became basic to his philosophy. Some of this thinking was expressed later in a lecture at a meeting sponsored by the Christian Medical Fellowship during a conference of the British Medical Association in Oxford, England, where he quoted the observation that animals who have lost their sensation of pain in their limbs have actually been seen to eat their own insensitive parts as if they no longer realized that these were part of themselves.

"It is clear," he continued, "how important pain must be in the whole pattern of the survival of living organisms composed of many cells. As soon as pain is lost there seems to be a loss also of that body consciousness which makes every part share the success or failure of the whole. It is clear that once pain is lost, different parts of the body may revert to competition with each other. Thus, our very survival depends upon pain."

While the body of the lecture involved a technical discussion of cells, neurones, chromosomes, the transmission and translation of nerve impulses, it became in its conclusion a remarkable testament of personal faith and life philosophy.

Paul said in part, "Just as the pattern of the atom and the molecule with whirling electrons is repeated in the vastness of the universe, so as we ascend the scale of life we see the same laws of biology repeated with differing degrees of significance at every level. The law of pain is no exception. Individual cells had to give up their autonomy and learn to suffer with one another before effective multicelled organisms could be produced and survive. The same Designer went on to create the human race with a new and higher purpose in mind. Not only would the cells within an individual cooperate with one another, but the individuals within the race would now move on to a new level of community responsibility, to a new kind of relationship with one another and with God.

"As in the body, so in this new kind of relationship the key to success lies in the sensation of pain. We all of us rejoice at the harmonious working of the human body. Yet we can but sorrow at the relationships between men. In human society we are suffering because we do not suffer enough.

"So much of the sorrow in the world is due to the selfishness of one living organism that simply doesn't care when the next one suffers. In the body if one cell or group of cells grows and flourishes at the expense of the rest we call it cancer and know that if it is allowed to spread the body is doomed. And yet the only alternative to this cancer is absolute loyalty of every cell to the Body, the Head. God is calling us today to learn from his lower creation and move on to a higher level of existence and to participate in this community which he is preparing for the salvation of the world.

"With the acceptance of the discipline of pain, suffering for one another, will come also the ecstasy of shared happiness and of new understanding as we glimpse the vision of God for his world."

It was during this furlough of 1952 that Paul and Margaret became officially associated with the Mission to Lepers. Dr. Lazarus, the director-principal of Vellore, had advised them to find some mission group to act as their sponsors. In fact she had made tentative approach to the Methodist Board of Missions in the United States, who had expressed their willingness to interview Paul and probably assume the family's support, but in the meantime Donald Miller, Secretary of the British Mission to Lepers, had suggested that, since so much of Paul's work was now in leprosy, the mission would be glad to sponsor him, agreeing to assume his support not only in leprosy work but as professor of orthopedic surgery to the Vellore Medical College.

This was the beginning of an increasingly happy fellowship, marking also a new and constructive phase of the organization's own development. Founded in the 1870s to provide asylum and spiritual help for hopeless outcasts, the mission had slowly moved from mere institutional care of leprosy to its medical treatment. Now it was to become increasingly involved in research and new techniques of control, prevention, and rehabilitation.

On the way to South Africa to join Margaret and the children, Paul stopped to continue his research. In Johannesburg Dr. Jack Penn, a highly successful plastic surgeon who had studied with Bunnell, had performed some interesting operations on the collapsed noses of leprosy patients. Paul's own experiments with inserting a bone graft from the leg to support the ridge of the nose had been only moderately successful. Dr. Penn's method was to cut the whole nose off, then use a big flap of skin turned down from the forehead to construct a new nose, and finally to cover the defect in the forehead with a split skin graft from the thigh. Paul was impressed and he decided to try this technique as soon as he returned to Vellore.

He spent four days with Margaret's parents in Capetown. Then he and his family took the two-night trip to Durban, boarded the steamship *Karanga* for the last lap of the journey, and arrived in Vellore in May, 1953. After traveling over more than half the world, he had come to one conclusion: he and his team were on their own. There was plenty to learn from people who were doing good hand surgery and rehabilitation, but so far as applying these things to leprosy patients, there was nobody who could help them very much. He returned to his work disappointed, but with greater skill and knowledge and added confidence.

15

The five years of the Brand family's second term in India were a period of painful but visible progress. For Paul it was a time of steady building, a trial-and-error structuring of new techniques; for Margaret one of professional pioneering; for the children one of lusty growth; and for the whole family an increase of twenty-five percent. It was astonishing that there was no decrease from fatalities, for the children's propensity for hazardous sports also mounted with the years.

"They must have a whole army of guardian angels," Margaret declared with fervent gratitude, "on duty day and night."

Their new house, the upstairs flat of a small bungalow, offered enticing possibilities. There were innumerable parapets to stand on, a sleeping porch at the top, to the roof of which one could climb by taking a long jump and then managing to balance oneself, a huge tamarind tree near the back door whose top branches were not too far from a chimney jutting from one of the parapets. Chips soon learned to jump from the top of the chimney into one of the branches, copying the technique of the occasional monkeys.

Estelle was not so agile. One day Margaret approached the house to see her perched on the chimney two stories up, poised between there and a tamarind fruit hanging to the tree. If the fruit came away, there was nothing to hold her. Horrified, but in a calm voice, Margaret issued directions to the other children. "Mary, get Estelle around the middle . . . Now pull her back . . ." Only when the child was safely returned to the ground could she give vent to her emotions. "Estelle Brand, don't you ever dare do that again!"

The house soon became the rendezvous of all the campus children, and it was a wonder that Dr. David, the college principal, and his wife, who occupied the first floor flat, survived. Ingenious games were devised. When it rained the children would block up the terraces on the roof, stuffing rags, jackets, pants, anything they could find, in the outlet holes. Then they would swim in the pools thus formed. One favorite game was to slosh water over the porches and down the stairs, then slide down them with a whoosh. Margaret endured tortures seeing other children balancing on the parapets, knowing they were less sure footed than her own.

Chips' climbing skill increased with the years. One of his favorite sports was climbing the pipes of the new men's hostel, entering the students' rooms and leaving unmistakable marks of his presence, a recreation Jean soon learned to share. For a long time he pursued this pastime, escaping detection. Finally the students caught him, carried him down three flights of stairs by the seat of his pants, and ducked him in the lily pool.

"Now go home and tell your father," they adjured him with relish.

But he was a favorite with them nonetheless. They took him fishing, boating, picnicking, and he was disconsolate when, about the age of nine, he had to leave his mother's tutelage to attend Breeks' School, the British boarding school at Ootacamund.

Paul, joining the children's fun whenever he could find time, helped them build a tree house in the spreading branches of the tamarind. It was a beautiful house, nine or ten feet in the air, roomy and sturdy. When the day came for the housewarming party, it easily accommodated ten people. A bucket served as food lift. It was walled with mosquito nets for sleeping, but when the children retired there the first night they found more mosquitoes inside than out, so sleeping was temporarily abandoned.

The children did not pursue these fascinating sports without casualties. Paul, ill in the house with fever, was once summoned outside by a scream. Jean, climbing in the tamarind tree, had been discomposed by the attack of some huge black ants. She had fallen and broken both bones of her forearm across the middle. Paul rushed out with a roll of plaster and water. As she lay on the ground he took the roll of plaster, wet it, and laid it quickly over the arm, keeping it motionless. Lifting her into the old Vanguard, he drove her to the hospital, obtained a good X ray, and set the arm. The results were perfect.

On another occasion Chips almost put his eyes out with a firecracker. Though he had been told not to set it off, obedience was not one of his virtues. When it delayed action, he went and blew on it. Fortunately he had the presence of mind to shield his face with his hands, but his hands were badly scorched.

"Could I have a piece of ice?" he asked Margaret meekly, reluctant to confess his disobedience.

The parents' permissiveness did not include moral laxity. Paul especially was a stickler for the truth wherever it mattered. Once when Jean, about six, had falsified some incident, he spent a whole afternoon sitting with her sifting all the evidence. Finally, when it was apparent that she had not told the truth, he said, "You must go away by yourself until you can come and tell me exactly what happened." Stubbornly insisting that she was right, she flounced away. After about fifteen minutes, however, Margaret saw them sitting side by side in the bottom of the clothes press, quietly talking.

Paul practiced the same permissive philosophy toward his team of workers, easy-going, fraternal, tolerant, unless some issue he really considered important was at stake. Melville Furness, his associate for many years, remembered only one harsh word he had ever spoken. Furness had recorded incorrectly that a man's left hand had been operated on instead of his right.

"You've got this hand wrong," Paul said sharply. "Brother, don't let this happen again."

Furness came to Vellore in 1953 from Chingleput, where he had been a patient of Dr. Cochrane. At sixteen he had discovered that he had leprosy. Nonetheless, he had been able to attend college. When the disease had become worse, he had gone finally to Chingleput. There, treated with the new sulfone drugs, he had become negative, had married a talented girl named Lucy, and had worked for five years in Dr. Cochrane's clinic at Saidepet. He came to Paul's department to keep records after Gusta Buultgens left to care for her ailing father, and proved as meticulous as she had been. Trained in physiotherapy by Ruth Thomas, he became so skilled in hand diagnosis that frequently Paul would ask his advice in deciding what techniques of surgery and rehabilitation to use. His wife Lucy was for years Paul's efficient secretary.

Chandra Manuel continued on the team as social worker in charge of the New Life Center. She had had a difficult time in Paul's absence. The patients were uncooperative, resenting the fact that a woman was in charge. "Dr. Brand said so and so," or "Chief does it this way," they would grumble. Frustrated, she wrote her complaints to Paul. He neither criticized nor reproached, merely asked her to keep on and do her best. Inspired by his confidence, she learned more about leprosy, visited the sanatoria, began asking herself, "Why do the patients act like this?"

After that Chandra learned to identify herself with the patients. She ate with them, took them on picnics, worked with them, loved them. And she had much less trouble.

But it was only with Paul's return that the center was restored to full harmony. Though he could give it only one day a week, with what time he could spare in the evenings, there was immediately a different spirit in the place. The quality of the toys improved. Accidents to fingers and feet lessened. There was more eager participation in the evening seminars. "He'll see everything," the boys told each other with less of warning than of anticipation.

Paul reveled in the renewed fellowship. He would go to the

Center in shorts and colored shirt, join in work at the carpenter's bench, joke with the patients, make them feel wanted and accepted. The hunt for the destructive villains became again his obsession.

"Go with that boy to his village," he might tell Chandra, "and find out what happened to his fingers. Sit with his people, talk with them, watch them working. Find out if he's been pulling on hard ropes." Or Paul would experiment on his own hands, perhaps dipping bits of bread into hot coffee to find out if this habit might be causing blisters.

But in his leprosy work at the hospital Paul still encountered both frustration and opposition. True, he had a loyal team of workers. There was Dr. Herbert Gass, specialist in dermatology, who had done research on bones and leprosy as a young man and had always been a faithful supporter of Paul's work. There were Ruth Thomas the physiotherapist, and her trainees, Palani, Namasivayan, and Furness. And in 1953 Dr. Ernest Fritschi returned to Vellore as recipient of a grant given to Paul's work by the Indian Council of Medical Research, to become one of the most valued members of the team.

"Amazing what wonderful people are attracted to leprosy!" Paul often marveled. Certainly not the kind who desired money or fame!

But the clinic was a small building in an obscure corner of the hospital compound, the patients' waiting room the meager shade of a wall or a tree. The Tata ward was not yet finished. Only a small number of beds was available for leprosy patients, and these must be isolated.

"We must make an operating theater in the New Life Center," Paul told Ernest Fritschi, only partially because of the limited space at the hospital. He was anxious to experiment with simple techniques which could be used under crude village conditions.

Startled, Ernest contemplated the white-tiled operating room with its gleaming array of instruments, compared it with the bare interior of the small building near the New Life Center which Paul proposed using, a whitewashed hut of brick and tile which the students had formerly used for social work and clinics.

"Yes, sir," he agreed. "But—*how?*"

"You'll see," said Paul.

He secured a shadowless lamp devised by an ingenious missionary doctor in North India, made by beating a big sheet of aluminum into a concave shape, polishing it, installing a 200-watt bulb, and suspending it by a series of simple pulleys to the ceiling. It cost about thirty rupees, just one-hundredth of the usual price for shadowless lamps, and was efficient but a little hot. A one bin sterilizer was provided. A wooden operating table made at the New Life Center was fitted with an adjustable head piece and a special hand table support. The only alteration made in the eight-foot-square room of the little hut was the addition of mosquito netting to the windows to keep out the flies.

"Now go to it," Paul told Ernest. "It's yours."

Ernest was equal to the challenge. He operated, Paul assisted. The patient walked into the room. Chandra, who had never assisted at surgery before, scrubbed. She and Mano Fritschi did the sterilizing. There was no anaesthetic, only a hypodermic syringe. After the operation, which proceeded without incident, the patient walked into the "Lazarus Ward" close by, a small hut built by Dr. Hilda Lazarus as a rural maternity center and donated by her for use by the leprosy patients. It was the first of many such simple operations. Ten years later the lamp of beaten aluminum would still be in use in the new Rural Hospital a few rods from the center.

On the day that his first operation was performed in the New Life Center, January 30, 1954, another event occurred which was to prove of vital importance to the team and its work. It was the anniversary of the assassination of Mahatma Gandhi, a day of mourning yet for the medical students a sort of holiday, without classes. Dr. Carol Jameson, head of gynecology, had planned a picnic for the residents of her department in connection with the rotation of the doctors working in a branch hospital in Gudiyattam, about twenty-five miles away. Less than halfway there the station wagon in which they were riding left the road, overturned, and was demolished. The twelve young staff members with Dr. Jameson were brought back to a hospital stricken with grief almost as poignant as had seized the nation on that day of tragedy six years before. Paul rushed down from the center to join the other doctors in their agonizing task of salvage and repair. It was like the old war years in London, only worse, for most of these young victims had been his early students.

Only one, Dr. Mary Verghese, a beautiful girl from the Syrian Christian community in Kerala, failed to return to near normalcy. At first they did not discover the full extent of her injury. Her face was badly gashed, her cheekbone shattered, her clavicle broken. But only after she had lain unconscious for many days, almost motionless for many more, was it learned that she was paralyzed from the waist down. Later Paul performed two fusion operations on her spine which, together with a cordectomy to relieve her severe pain and spasm, kept her helpless in a hospital bed for many agonizing months.

Never had Paul been so conscious of his inadequacy. With all his knowledge and skill there was so little he could do! He could fuse her spine into a rigid column so she could sit up without the support of a solid perspex jacket, perhaps even lean forward and backward. He could send a physiotherapist to move the paralyzed limbs through a daily range of motion to prevent deformities and pressure sores, to strengthen her arms for the tremendous extra load they must carry. He could sit by her side or, when her revolving bed was turned so she lay face downward, crouch *sadhu*-like on his haunches and bring her news of advances in their work and help her to think constructively about the future.

Yes, and like her other friends he could derive spiritual uplift from her incredible faith and courage, for never in all those months did any of them hear her utter a word of complaint. But what could he or they do to fill her greatest need, to make her feel again a useful and valued member of society?

"You should begin to plan your future professional career," he said to her one day some months after the accident.

She stared at him incredulously. Then a wild hope flared in her eyes. "You mean—it might still be possible—"

"Of course." Paul discussed with her the possibilities. Her specialty of gynecology was out, but there were bacteriology, pathology.

"I suppose I can't do any clinical work," said Mary wistfully.

"Why not?" Paul's eyes lighted with understanding. "I know how you feel. I'm glad you like to work with people."

They had other conversations. After she was able to sit in a wheel chair Mary could look out her window and see the leprosy clinic where Dr. Gass, the dermatologist, and his assistants treated patients three days a week. One day Ruth Thomas wheeled her over to the clinic, and Mary offered her services. Sitting in her wheelchair she helped examine patients, wrote chits for medicine, issued directions for nurses. The patients welcomed her, finding in her weakness, so much greater even than theirs, a rebuke of their self pity, a renewal of hope.

After she had worked here for about a month Paul suggested that she try his department of surgery, in which she had shown promise as a student.

"Surgery!" she exclaimed. "Have you forgotten? I'm a *paraplegic!*"

"What of it?" he answered. "You don't operate with your feet. And this operation on the hands is one of the few that has to be done sitting down."

First she assisted Ernest Fritschi with tendon transplants, then she learned to perform the operation herself, becoming probably the only paraplegic in the world who performed major surgery. A keen student, she soon became one of the most capable and valued members of Paul's team. And when Ernest left his post to assume direction of the new Leprosy Research Sanatorium in Karigiri, she applied for his position in leprosy research under the Indian Council of Medical Research, and was appointed.

Perhaps more than any other member of the team Dr. Mary was able to understand Paul Brand's philosophy as it concerned leprosy patients, she who knew so well the blessing of pain through its absence, who had so nearly lost her sense of personal worth and identity.

"I feel," Paul expressed it himself, "that the most precious possession any human being has is his spirit, his will to live, his sense of dignity, his personality. Once that has been lost the opportunity for rehabilitation is lost. Though our profession may be a technical one, concerned with tendons, bones, and nerve endings, we must realize that it is the person behind it that is so important. Of course we need technicians: surgeons, physiotherapists, nurses, occupational therapists, vocational guidance specialists. But above all we need men and women who are concerned with people and who accept the challenge of the whole person, his life, his faith, and his hope."

The completion of the Tata Memorial Ward with its 17 beds was a landmark of progress, marking Vellore as one of the first medical college hospitals in the world to admit leprosy patients openly to its wards. And, contrary to the fears of some authorities, the other patients did not run away. They soon realized that the doctors and nurses and technicians concerned with the leprosy patients were not afraid of contracting the disease, so why should they be? Friendly and reasonable explanations helped keep them calm.

But, though the enlarged space increased the opportunities for surgery, it also increased problems. Once the news spread that there were surgeons who could perform miracles on the dread claw hand, leprosy patients began swarming from all over South India. Many were beggars. Most were poor and desperate. There was no room for them. Penniless, friendless, they squatted about the compound, slept under the trees, crouched with their begging bowls on the pavement outside the walls. Paul and his team were becoming extremely unpopular for having them around. It was Sri Jagadisan, always the pioneer, who finally helped solve this problem.

"Perhaps the *Hind Kusht Nivaran Sangh* can do something," he proposed.

The local branch of this all-India organization, of which Rajkumari Amrit Kaur, minister of health for India, was chairman, purchased a house on one of the side streets opposite the hospital and rented it to Paul and his team for a rupee a year. Given over to leprosy patients, it was a tremendous asset. A patient was put in charge of it, and a small rent was charged the occupants. In time little occupations were provided, such as the making of plaster bandages for their own use. Known as "Number 10," for years to come it was to provide living quarters for twenty or thirty patients during pre- and postoperative treatment.

But the reaction of the neighborhood was violent. A house in the middle of the bazaar section occupied by *lepers*! Even the municipal councilors came under pressure to forbid the team's using it for patients. The local shopkeepers and residents tried every expedient for obstructing the project. Little did they realize that a few years later when public meetings would be held at Number 10 the whole neighborhood would be pushing and crowding to get in!

Paul had little time to devote to the project. Its success was due to other members of his team, to Ruth Thomas and her ex-patient physiotherapy trainees; to Dr. Selvapandian, Paul's able assistant who was to become head of the Department of Orthopedics. The latter took on Number 10 as his special interest, raising money to buy the occupants a radio, books, bookshelves, and giving it many hours of personal service.

Paul often visited the place. It was one way of practicing his philosophy of recognizing the human dignity of every patient. But he did not go out of a sense of duty. He enjoyed every minute of his visits. The occupants were often a pathetic lot with many of the combined liabilities of leprosy and beggary —ragged clothes, stumps of hands and feet, blind eyes, hairless brows—but their faces shone with hope and at least temporary well being. "Have a cup of coffee?" they would inquire eagerly. "*Daya vu say thu*, please," he would reply heartily, knowing that they were watching his every word and motion for the slightest sign of hesitation. Often he arranged little parties for them.

It was here at Number 10 at a Christmas party that he first outlined one of his best known and best loved sermons. He had gone straight from the office after a hard day's work and was very tired. Slipping in late and hoping he would not be noticed, he took his seat on a mat on the edge of the crowd gathered in the big central courtyard open to the sky. After the rush and tension of the day he would have liked to just sit for a while, absorbing the strength and uplift he always found in this place, derived from its atmosphere of human courage and mutual helpfulness in time of need. But they would not let him. The air about him, a bit heavy with the combined odors of crowding bodies, poverty, stale spices, aseptic bandages, became suddenly charged with sweetness as a huge garland was slipped over his head. Some of the patients had pitched in their beggars' *pice* and bought him one of the fat gaudy chains of roses and jasmine and silver tinsel sold in the flower bazaar.

"For your Christ *mela*," one of the Hindu patients told him eagerly.

"Won't you please say something?" another begged him. "Just a few words?"

Paul felt empty of ideas. But he knew he must think of something. As he rose to his feet he became suddenly conscious of hands, dozens of them, many raised palm to palm in the familiar gesture of *namaste*, some arched in the shape of claws, some with all five fingers, some with no fingers, some with a few stumps, some half hidden to cover their disfigurement. *Hands*.

"I am a hand surgeon," he began. While Palani repeated each sentence in Tamil and somebody else translated it into Hindi for the benefit of the patients who might have come from North India, Paul had time to assemble his thoughts. "So when I meet people I can't help looking at their hands. The palmist claims he can tell your future by looking at your hands. I can tell your past. For instance, I can tell what your trade has been by the position of the callouses and the condition of the nails. I can tell a lot about your character. I love hands."

He paused, looking down at the eager upturned faces, wondering what Another would have said to them, one who had often stood in just such an open courtyard under an open sky, surrounded by just such a group as this and wanting to give them of himself, stretching out his *hands* . . .

"How I would love to have had the chance to meet Christ and study his hands! But knowing what he was like, I can almost picture them, feel them, see the changes that took place in them. Suppose—suppose we follow him through his life and look at his hands together."

First, Paul continued very simply, for most of his listeners were simple men and non-Christians, there was the phase of babyhood, when his hands were small, helpless, futilely grasping at the light, no separate movement even of the fingers. Many of them knew what it was like to have skillful hands and lose them. Could they imagine the goodness of a God who was the creator of all things, yet was willing for the sake of human beings to give up his infinite skill, to make himself completely helpless?

Then there were the hands of the boy Jesus, clumsily holding a brush or a stylus, trying to form the letters of the Hebrew alphabet; human hands, which had had to learn things the hard way, like those of other people. For Christ had had to grow in knowledge and wisdom like any boy, learning some things imperfectly, no doubt, because he could learn only what he was taught.

But the hands of Christ the carpenter, how well Paul understood how they had looked, having himself been a builder and stone mason! Rough, tough, gnarled, with broken fingernails, bruises. You couldn't learn to be a good carpenter without hitting your thumb sometimes, and you were bound to let the saw slip and cut your hand. Learning was made up of making mistakes. It was wrong to think of Christ as physically perfect. His perfection was that of the spirit, of the absence of sin and the discipline of the will, and that didn't mean he never made physical mistakes. He must have pounded his fingers time and again, cut them, made them bleed.

And then there were the hands of Christ the physician, the healer, the preacher. How much compassion, sensitivity, there must have been in them, so much that when he touched them people could feel something of the divine spirit coming through! Just as the doctor could tell when he touched an abdomen or a chest what was going on underneath, because he was trained to sense the vibrations of the heart or the motion of the bowels, so Christ by touching a human being was able not only to sense the sin or guilt or anger inside but to transmit some of his own faith and courage and love.

Paul gestured as he spoke. He always did when he became intensely moved. And many of the turbaned heads jerked sideward in that affirmative motion which is so characteristically Indian. For his listeners knew exactly what he meant. They had seen and felt such hands. In fact, they were looking at them now.

"Then," continued Paul, "there were his crucified hands. It hurts me to think of a nail being driven through the center of any hand, because I know what goes on there, the tremendous complex of tendons and nerves and blood vessels and muscles. It's impossible to drive a spike through its center without crippling it. The thought of those healing hands being crippled reminds me of what Christ was prepared to endure. In that act he identified himself with all the deformed and crippled human beings in the world. Not only was he able to endure poverty with the poor, weariness with the tired, but—*clawed hands with those crippled*."

A long sigh drifted through the courtyard. It seemed to blow the air newly clean, like a breath of sudden freshness.

"And then there were his resurrected hands," Paul concluded. "One of the things I find most astounding is that, though we think of the future life as something perfected, when Christ appeared to his disciples he said, 'Come look at my hands,' and he invited Thomas to put his finger into the print of the nails. Why did he want to keep the wounds of his humanity? Wasn't it because he wanted to carry back with him an eternal reminder of the sufferings of those on earth? He carried the marks of suffering so he could continue to understand the needs of those suffering. He wanted to be forever one with us."

As he finished Paul was again conscious of hands as all over the courtyard they were lifted, palm to palm, with the same stumps or lack of fingers, the same scars, the same crooked arches. Yet not the same. No one tried to hide them. They were held higher, close to the face, almost with pride. Even the stumps seemed to have acquired a certain dignity.

16

Adikesavelu was a technical school graduate and an expert in Hindi and Tamil as well as his native Telegu. He came to Vellore with a letter from Dr. Jagadisan, his hands so badly crippled that he could no longer type or even hold a cup of coffee. He was without a job, without money, without hope. Here Dr. Gass started him on the new diamino-sulfone drugs. Dr. Brand's team measured the angles of his hands, gave them paraffin baths to remove the stiffness. Ruth Thomas and her physiotherapist aides worked on them for months. Sensing his financial worries, she asked him to give her Tamil lessons. When Paul returned from furlough, he operated on Adi's hands, one at a time, doing his best to help him type again. Then Ruth told Paul that Adi was selling his wife's ornaments to pay his living expenses.

"Would you teach me Tamil?" Paul asked him.

"Of course," replied Adi. "I shall be glad to do it free."

"No, no," insisted Paul. "You have to live."

Adi started teaching Paul Tamil by his bedside. After his

discharge Paul gave him a job teaching language in the hospital. For over twelve years now he has been teaching Hindi, Tamil, Sanskrit, and Telegu to staff and patients. He has written, typed, and cut stencils for a book called "Common Spoken Tamil Made Easy," the sale of which has netted him a modest sum. He has been able to support his wife Vanaja (Lotus) and his two children with self respect and dignity.

But not all of Paul's patients were so fortunate. There was Lakshmanan. He also was an educated man, though reduced by leprosy to beggary. He came to Vellore with hands that were terribly clawed. Paul operated on one hand, then later on the thumb and two fingers of the other hand.

"Your hands are good now for any ordinary work," Paul told him.

Lakshmanan's reply was illuminating. "I daren't go back to my family or to my old friends if I still have the marks of leprosy. You—you don't know what it's like to be in a cage," he continued, trying to make himself understood, "in a prison of loneliness. You have now removed some of the bars of my prison, but I can't get out and be really free unless I look normal. Please—you must correct these last two fingers."

Paul hesitated. The fingers were bent so closely on themselves that he was afraid he could not straighten them without stretching the blood vessels to such extent that the fingers would be endangered. They would need an extensive skin graft. But the young man still pleaded. Paul performed the operation, but the stretching, plus the extensive skin grafting, caused gangrene to develop, necessitating amputation. Lakshmanan accepted the situation with apparent stoicism.

"It's my *karma*, my fate," he said calmly. "I asked you to do it. It's not your fault. Take them off."

No one suspected how deep were his emotions until, a week after his discharge, he committed suicide by throwing himself into a well.

This passionate desire of leprosy patients for normal appearance incited Paul to further experimentation with face surgery. Worst of all the grim stigmata was the collapsed nose. What caused it? Not injuries surely, as he believed was the case with fingers. Fortunately one need not know the full cause before seeking a remedy.

Soon after his return from furlough he tried the technique

he had observed in Johannesburg. Choosing some of the worst cases of collapsed noses, he cut them off and fashioned new ones, using a flap of skin turned down from the forehead. These were only moderately successful, the chief difficulty being that with the dark skin of Indian patients a split skin graft on the forehead was likely to darken more than the skin around it. The operation using a flap of skin from the forehead was by no means a new one in India. Called the Hindu rhinoplasty, it was first performed thousands of years ago in North India by a famous Indian surgeon, Susrutha, being one of the first recorded operations in all history. The technique had changed little after all these centuries.

Sometime later Dr. William White, plastic surgeon from Pittsburgh, visited Vellore, and he was able to shed real light on the problem. It was not Dr. White's first visit to Vellore. In 1951, on his way to visit a friend in North India, he had stopped over in Vellore for a few days. Tremendously energetic and interested in Paul's work, he had spent all of the days and most of the nights seeing cases, discussing problems, planning operations. Now on this second visit he told the team of a nose operation originally used by Sir Harold Gillies, often considered the father of plastic surgery. In working on syphilitic noses Gillies had discovered that the real defect was not the loss of cartilage or support for the nose but the loss of the lining. White believed that the same premise could be assumed for leprosy.

Paul was jubilant, for this seemed to support the team's increasing certainty that the susceptibility of different parts of the body to the leprosy bacilli had much to do with temperature. It was the sections nearest the surface, the coldest areas, which suffered the worst damage. And not only was the inside of the nose one of the coldest parts of the body because of the evaporation of moisture as the air passed through, but the lining membrane was intimately adherent to the cartilage and supporting structure of the nose. When these membranes became infected through ulcerations of the lining, the connecting cartilage would be destroyed and the whole nose drawn inward.

Dr. White was able to demonstrate the new operation to the team. Immediately Paul applied the technique to leprosy. Going up into the nose through the mouth between the front teeth and the upper lip, he lifted the nose right off the face and divided every bit of its lining. Then to his amazement he found that the whole nose could be lifted forward and stretched out to unbelievable proportions.

"Look!" he exclaimed with glee. "Big as an elephant's trunk!"

When he stuffed it with gauze he could make a nose twice as big as the man had had before. It was easy enough to restore the collapsed nose to normal size. Then by making a model of a nose, covering it with split skin graft from the thigh, putting it inside the nose to constitute a new lining, and later inserting a bone graft, he had a patient as free from nose disfigurement as if he had never contracted leprosy.

Still later Sir Harold Gillies, then an old man, having heard of Paul's work, came to Vellore and worked for awhile with the team. His interest and enthusiasm were unbounded. Many years ago, he admitted, he had operated on a leprous nose in South America. Paul was delighted to accord this eminent colleague the honor of having performed the first nose reconstruction in leprosy.

Almost as hated a stigma as the depressed nose was the lack of eyebrows which persisted even after the disease had burned itself out. Without them patients were fearful, probably with reason, that they could not convince their families and friends that they were cured.

"*Ayyo!* Leprosy!" people would exclaim at sight of the naked brows.

Sometime after their first work on noses Paul ran across an article written by an American naval surgeon who had made eyebrows for a Korean war victim of burns by transplanting a piece of scalp just on the end of its artery and vein. This "island flap" operation, he discovered later, was a familiar technique, possibly originating in Holland, but it was the first time he had heard of it. He decided to apply it to leprosy.

The experiment was a triumphant success! The first patient started growing eyebrows at a tremendous pace and was enormously excited. The demand was soon far exceeding the supply. Many of the patients with new eyebrows would refuse to clip them. They would enter a room, proud as could be, shoulders back, head up, eyebrows coming first and the patient following after.

"Look at me!" their whole mien proclaimed. "I used to be a 'leper' and had eyebrow baldness, but look at me now!"

Eyebrows and noses, Paul decided, were as important as well functioning hands and feet; perhaps more important, for they were often the outward and visible signs of inward health. Rehabilitation was as much a spiritual as a physical process.

In all this facial reconstruction the team was in debt to Antia, a Bombay surgeon, who had been a pupil of Sir Harold Gillies. Besides performing more facial operations on. leprosy than any other surgeon in the world, Antia pioneered in developing the post-nasal inlay operation of Gillies, as well as exploring the possibilities of face-lifting and other plastic operations on leprosy patients.

Through the years the technique of all the team's surgery kept improving. The original tendon transplantation completely changed to follow a new procedure known as the "Brand operation." It involved freeing a good muscle from the patient's forearm, making a curved incision over the back of the hand above the thumb and extending up the forearm, laying back the skin flap, and detaching the tendon of one of the muscles used for upward motion of the wrist; then, grafting to this the free tendon from the forearm and splitting the graft into four slips, passing the slips through the proper tunnels in the hand and suturing them to the tendons on the backs of the fingers.

"Good!" exclaimed Sri Jagadisan, exulting in the normal supple grip of his fingers after Paul had operated on his hands which had been clawed and paralyzed, one for ten, the other for twenty years. "So—I have a pair of *Brand* new hands!"

Paul was always ready to discard any method for a better one, and the team was constantly making improvements in the techniques. When Mary Verghese discovered that the scar on the hand could be made smaller by suturing the tendon outside the hand, then tunneling it under the skin without making the long flap incision, he welcomed it as a major development. Ernest Fritschi, born improvisor and keen thinker, was always suggesting improvements. And Paul went out of his way to give publicity to all of his assistants' changes.

"You do this operation," he said once to Ernest when a difficult case appeared. "You've had more experience." This from the chief, marveled Ernest, speaking to the man he had trained!

Paul's informal manner in the operating room was conducive to a sense of security and confidence. He was always relaxed, apparently unhurried. But there was never a wasted moment. Assisting doctors and nurses found it almost as difficult to keep pace with him as had their predecessors with the incredibly swift Dr. Ida.

Young Alice Jane David found it so when one day in 1953 she was asked to relieve the nurse assigned to assist him. Having admired Paul as a teacher, she anticipated the prospect. But though the operation, an extensive skin graft, was interesting, it was also demanding, involving hundreds of interrupted sutures. Never had she known a surgeon's hands to move so fast, or his orders to require such swiftness and attention.

"He's testing me," she thought, and she prayed, "Oh, God, help me to keep up with him."

After the operation Paul spoke to the supervising nurse, Miss Hutchison. "Hutch, who was that little lassie who helped me today?"

"Alice Jane David, Doctor."

"So? Well, she's the first one I've found who could thread needles as fast as we can put in the stitches. Why don't you put her with me from now on?"

She worked with Paul in all his operations for the next three years, until she went to Australia to take a special course. Never in that time did she see him become angry. Many a time when she did not have the required tool on her table and would improvise something else, he would quietly take it as if it were the one he had requested. He always called her "Alice," except when he was under tension, when he called her "Sister." Then she knew she must really be on her toes.

A full decade after she became his nurse she was to receive her finest tribute for those years, when one day in a Montreal Children's Hospital she was assisting a plastic surgeon to reconstruct a badly injured hand.

"We are indeed honored," he told her, "to have Paul Brand's scrub nurse here. She knows the trade."

The team's leprosy work during those formative years of the fifties was inseparably linked with the development of the Schieffelin Leprosy Research Sanatorium at Karigiri, a joint project of the Mission to Lepers, the American Leprosy Missions, and the Vellore Christian Medical College. Sod for the new institution was turned by Dr. Ida in Paul's absence in September, 1952, and in July 1953 Dr. Herbert Gass and his wife took up residence in the medical superintendent's house. In December the still uncompleted gray stone buildings were dedicated by Donald Miller, general secretary of the Mission to Lepers. The bare remote wilderness had sprung like Ezekiel's dead bones into life.

The Karigiri units consisted of a hospital, a research laboratory, staff houses, and cottages for patients. Later it was to include workshops for the making of shoes, artificial limbs, table mats, baskets, and other crafts; a department of physiotherapy; a thatch-roofed earth-floored community center used for recreation, school, and worship; much later a beautiful stone-pillared House of Prayer. The function of the institution was to observe, study, and investigate various types of leprosy, to treat medical and surgical complications, and to train workers for full-time leprosy work. Though its in-patient capacity was only one hundred, applications for admission were so many that the number soared as high as a hundred and eighty, and had to be stabilized finally at about a hundred and fifty. The out-patient clinics were wildly popular, until after four years the number of patients receiving regular treatment was over four thousand. Ernest Fritschi became the hospital's first resident surgeon.

Of course Karigiri increased opportunities for Paul and his team immeasurably. Paul himself, a staff member by virtue of his service with the Mission to Lepers, attended clinics there every Monday afternoon and remained to operate on Tuesday mornings.

Though his second term in India was a period of steady but unspectacular growth in surgical and rehabilitation techniques, largely in the area around Vellore, his work in leprosy was becoming known outside the bounds of South India. In October of 1954 he visited the Mission to Lepers' home and hospital in Purulia, North India, where he had been asked to introduce a program of hand surgery. Some of the workers from Purulia had already been to Vellore as trainees. This further training session was followed by lectures at the School of Tropical Medicine in Calcutta.

To Paul's surprise he was invited by the government of Nigeria to go to Africa for two series of lectures and demonstrations. He took flight with excitement but with some misgivings, knowing that he was going among some of the world's leprosy experts and wondering how his revolutionary concepts would be received. His first stop was Kano, a bare, dry, dusty place near the border of the Sahara Desert, where there was a large mission leprosy hospital under the direction of Dr. John Dreisbach. All the government and mission doctors who were doing any leprosy work in northern Nigeria were invited to attend the lectures, and at the first one the little lecture room was packed. The audience listened with rapt attention, and at the close Paul was rather pleased with himself. He felt he had gotten off to a good start.

The next lecture was the following morning. To his chagrin the audience consisted of two wan missionary females. What a flop his first attempt must have been! He soon discovered, however, that the cause of absenteeism was not dissatisfaction but an improperly baked meringue pie made with duck eggs, served at a dinner the night before. The staphlococcal intestinal infection was so serious that several members were laid up for the duration of the course, though the majority were back by the end of the first week.

Paul thoroughly enjoyed his month in Kano. He visited the village huts erected by the patients themselves out of plaited cornstalks and mud, and marveled at the excellent service given by the hospital with very little money and almost no Nigerian doctors and nurses. And he found Dr. Dreisbach a stimulating co-worker. One of Africa's foremost leprosy specialists, he had already made progress in designing orthopedic shoes, and their mutual interest in the problem acted as a sort of catalyst on each other's creative faculties. Free from administrative responsibility, Paul took keen enjoyment in experimenting in the sanatorium workshop with tools and woods and plastics, and he and Dr. Dreisbach together designed a new kind of orthopedic shoe and worked out procedures for making it.

One of the greatest delights of the Nigerian trip was a visit to Connie and David Wilmshurst in Gindiri, where they were working in a big training center of the Sudan United Mission. David, who was warden of the institute, had a heavy responsibility looking after all the trainees and young teachers, and Connie was teaching, writing, and illustrating attractive children's booklets, as well as caring for their own four children, the two oldest of whom were soon to be placed in boarding school in England. Connie was still blonde, serene, and beautiful, but she was much too thin. Paul enjoyed a picnic with them on the river, where they caught up on each other's news and discovered a new bond of fellowship in the worldwide mission they were now engaged in together. Connie and David were also in an area of high incidence in leprosy, and one of their doctors had been in Paul's training course.

His journey home took him through the Belgian Congo, South Africa, and Kenya, leaving him with an impression of tremendous surge and activity, of countries rising from the most primitive background, where no form of wheeled transport had been heard of until the arrival of the trucks and cars of the modern industrial era. He found Africa a striking contrast to India, with no counterpart of the latter's ancient bullock cart or centuries-old richness of learning and culture.

Though most of his lectures were well received, he encountered some of the usual opposition to his theories. In a big leprosarium in South Africa he saw patients with great blisters on their hands.

"Surely these come from burns and are preventable," he suggested to the leprologist in charge, telling of his own experience in the New Life Center.

The expert coolly appraised him. "And how long did you say you've been working in leprosy?"

"About eight years," Paul replied.

"And with only eight years of experience you're telling me that all my years of knowledge are ridiculous?" snapped the doctor. "I've been doing leprosy work all my life, and I *know* leprosy produces blisters regularly in the palm of the hand."

"Look, sir, would you accept one suggestion?" Paul pressed the point gently but stubbornly. "Could we take some of the fluid from this blister and also a biopsy, a specimen from the tissues of the palm, and examine them under a microscope for signs of leprosy inflammation?"

The leprologist snorted. "What good would that do? Ridiculous!"

Paul was amazed at the man's logic. Here was a reputable

doctor, a scientist, who seemed to be saying, "Some leprosy patients get blisters, therefore blisters are caused by leprosy." An improper syllogism if there ever was one!

It was good to climb aboard the last of the sixteen airplanes which had borne him around the tour and finally to land in Madras, with joyous friends and colleagues and family waiting to meet him. Never again would he feel frustrated by the lack of equipment, deficient staff, and other difficulties confronting him at Vellore. He had seen too many places with worse problems.

17

Hopefully Paul removed the new shoe, stooped over and examined the sole of Sadagopan's foot. He shook his head and smiled wryly. The ulcer was back again.

"*Pavum*, a pity. I thought sure this would be it. But—better luck next time."

Sadagopan smiled back in his sweet gentle way. "Don't worry, Doctor," he said almost apologetically, as if it were somehow his fault that the experiment had not succeeded. "Some day we will win."

It was perhaps the thirtieth time that the ulcers on his feet had been carefully healed and a new device enthusiastically produced, with Paul's assurance, "This time we're *really* going to prevent it!" Whereupon Sadagopan, always the guinea pig, would confidently try out the new type of dressing, solution, cast, or shoe, wear it for hours or days or weeks or even months, and then there he would be back again with a recurrence of the same old ulcers.

Feet! Paul's struggle to prevent injuries and deformities in patients' insensitive feet was far longer and more frustrating than the ones dealing with hands, noses, eyebrows. In the early days at Chingleput he did not realize the enormity of the problem. Assuming that the foot ulcerations were like the trophic ulcers resulting from other anaesthetic conditions like paraplegia, where people by simply resting on an anaesthetic part ulcerate it by loss of blood supply, he ordered chairs to be installed in all the buildings and benches put along the paths, so the patients would not stand or squat, resting their weight too long on the same part of the foot. If he saw a patient squatting, he would push him over into a sitting position.

"Ulcers can't happen when you're walking," he told them, "because at every step you lift your foot off the ground, and it gets momentary blood supply."

How wrong he was! To get an ulcer from standing still, a patient would have to stand at least five hours without moving a muscle. Only a fraction of ulcers in leprosy, he discovered later, are caused by ischemia.

Next he concluded that dressings were important. Coming straight from the aseptic hospitals of England, he was horrified by the ulcer shed at Chingleput, with its assembly-line techniques and lack of sanitation. Shocked and revolted, he tried to institute aseptic reforms: masks, sterile swabs, boiled instruments. But while this was all to the good, the effort was really wasted, for mechanical forces, not infection, proved to be the prime cause of ulcers.

Then he began to notice the piles and piles of shoes left each morning outside the ulcer shed, shoes that no sensitive feet could possibly tolerate. Finding one with nails sticking up, he took it into the shed, located the owner, matched it to the foot, and discovered that the nails fitted the ulcers. Then he issued a rule that shoes were not to be left outside but put beside the patient at the time of dressings. The results were astonishing. In many cases it was proved that the shoe had either caused the ulcer or occasioned its persistence. Nails were the worst offenders. A half inch of nail might stick up into a foot. Then the orderlies would put on the dressings, the patient would go out with his bandaged foot, and put it straight into a shoe in which the nail would penetrate the dressings. This had been going on day after day, week after week, without anybody connecting the shoe with the man!

But it was in the New Life Center that Paul and his team were able to conduct real research on feet, following up each case, like Sadagopan. All sorts of experiments were tried. For a time the ulcer ward waxed purple with gentian violet dressings. Penicillin cream gave way to Dakin's solution and that to magnesium sulphate. Every new house surgeon on duty was certain his own treatment was the answer.

But the biggest improvements came when they stopped doing regular dressings and merely encased the foot in elastoplast, leaving it on for several weeks. Then—"Why don't we try plaster of paris casts?" suggested Ernest Fritschi.

Paul agreed. Why not? Dr. Milroy Paul had reported using this treatment in Ceylon. To their surprise they found that the patient's ulcers healed just as well when he walked around in a plaster cast as when he was lying in bed. No injection, no dressings were needed, just the prevention of localized pressure.

It was a logical progression to the next step: If an ulcer could heal in plaster of paris, why not prevent its occurrence by producing a shoe like a plaster of paris cast?

So began the long long quest in which the patient and hopeful Sadagopan was the guinea pig. After many trials they found that he did better with a shoe of accurate molding, so they concentrated on these. They tried leather, building up the shoe under the hollows and scooping it out under the pressure points. They tried wood. Paul made these clogs himself, scooping them out with gouges and chisels to fit the various feet, sandpapering and fitting them with his own hands. Sadagopan went for a long time with these without a recurrence of his ulcers. But Paul could not make them all, and few other carpenters or cobblers could be found who would take so much trouble. A shoe with splinters or an irregularity in the wood was worse than no shoe at all. Then they tried standing the patients in wax and making plastic shoes from the positive cast of the footprint, an idea Paul had gotten from Dr. Dreisbach in Nigeria. Oh, for a plastic that would fit the foot like putty and set in that position! Paul set out to find one.

After reading all the books he could find and consulting with the Imperial Chemical Industries Laboratories in Calcutta, Paul found that a mixture of PVC (polyvinyl chloride) with an inert filler might serve the purpose. It could be formed around the foot, then heated in an oven, where it would set into a heavy rubberlike substance. Obtaining a formula, the team made shoes there at Vellore and used them for a long period. They were fairly good, but heavy. Paul was not satisfied. If there were only some substance that could be sprayed on the foot!

While he was in England on furlough he consulted many research laboratories and was recommended to a plastic production plant called "Brand and Company." A good omen, he thought. They manufactured a plastic similar to that used for putting the American fleet in "moth balls," a spray preservative for ships and guns and tanks. With their cooperation Paul put on a pair of long socks and let them spray his feet again and again. The result resembled a pair of Wellington boots, a perfect fit, and they would have been durable if he had put a piece of vulcanized rubber in the sole. They were not strong enough to walk on without some extra support. But their greatest liability was expense. He must find something much cheaper for India.

The next experiment he called the Kano shoe, for he designed it while in Nigeria working with John Dreisbach, who had spent years studying feet. It consisted of a tennis shoe made by a Lebanese manufacturer near Kano, with a polyethylene inner sole which could be molded exactly to the patient's foot, lined with something soft, and slipped inside the canvas. It was normal looking, cheap, and combined two of the three principles which they now believed essential: spreading the pressure by molding the shoe to the foot, and preventing the foot from bending while it moved. But the Kano shoe lacked the third essential feature, softness. The polyethylene did not have the yielding faculty of leather, and its edge made blisters. Both Paul and Dreisbach finally abandoned the idea.

Then Mary Verghese came into the story. She was opposed to molding.

"It's all right," she maintained, "as long as the mold stays in place. But let the straps get loose or the patient move his foot, and the very things which make it good become bad. I believe softness is the important thing."

So they began to experiment with all kinds of soft materials, starting with sponge rubber. And *san thosham*, happiness! Sadagopan was completely free of ulcers. "Now we've really found it!" Paul congratulated him when a whole month had passed. But another month, and the ulcer was back again. His foot had worn right through the rubber. Send a patient away in that kind of shoe, and he would soon be walking on the ground!

They first tried microcellular rubber by buying one of the Hawaiian sandals called "thongs" and using them as insoles.

"We can make this in India," Paul decided. He went to Calcutta to consult Bata's, the big shoe manufacturers. The manager agreed to donate a quantity of rubber, also to arrange for special mixes in any degree of softness. Batches of different "degrees shore" were sent to Vellore to be tried out. The members of the research team could be spotted in any crowd by their peculiarly shaped shoes, as all tested the different kinds of thickness. After about a year's experimenting they settled on fifteen degrees shore, a decision which was never changed.

Fortunately Vellore had friends in the Madras Rubber Company. The managing director, Mr. Eapen, was a member of the Vellore Council. The company agreed to mix the rubber if the team could secure a machine for stamping it out and heating it. This was done. In time a rubber mill was purchased so the whole process could be completed at Karigiri, where it became one of the rehabilitation industries. This solution of the problem of the inner sole was one of the team's most important milestones of progress.

But there was still the problem of the right kind of shoe, and through the years many people contributed help in its solution. For instance, there was Dr. Robertson, "Uncle Robbie," who had been chief orthopedic surgeon in charge of all splint and prosthetic workshops under the government of New Zealand. He came to Vellore in his retirement, hands unsteady, voice shaky, but with a residue of energy which he longed to put to service.

"Anything you tell me, I'll do," he said to Paul. "And you needn't pay me. I just want to spend the rest of my life helping people."

Paul put him to work on the foot problem, and this eminent specialist, used to the ultramodern in hospital and laboratory equipment, shut himself away in a mean little shed at Karigiri and studied the trophic ulcer problem. He wandered around among leather merchants and found the kind of leather he wanted, then started making shoes. Molding was important, he believed, but not with plastics. Leather was kind to the foot and adjusted itself to its contours. He produced what was called the "Uncle Robbie" shoe. He would take a piece of semi-tanned leather, bark tanned, soak it in water, bandage it on the patient's foot, and let it dry slightly. Then he would take it off and dry it in the sun exactly to the mold of the foot. Finally he would build up under its hollows with more leather, finishing with a leather sole underneath.

It was a good shoe and the final answer for many patients, like Dr. Jagadisan, who before wearing it had never been free from ulcers. But it was not durable enough for rough use. Worn into the muddy paddy fields of South India, it would soon fall apart.

Then there was John Girling.

"Daddy, daddy," Mary cried, rushing up to Paul one day, "Robinson Crusoe has come!"

Paul found a man with a huge beard, clothed in leather shorts and a rumpled shirt, sitting under a tree, a pack by his side. "And who are you, my friend?"

"Well—" began the stranger. John Girling had been educated at Gordonstoun, the famous Scottish school where Prince Charles was to study, designed to develop character as well as intellect. Dissatisfied with the prospect of entering business, John had packed up his belongings with his father's blessing and had started around the world to find something satisfying. He had worked his way across Europe, Turkey, Iran, Pakistan, to India, and finally arrived in Nagpur, where for the first time he had seen victims of leprosy. Shocked, he had hunted up a leprosy hospital and offered his services, performing such menial tasks as sweeping and cleaning the latrines.

"This won't do," he decided. "I must find something which will restore these people to worthwhile living."

"The person who could tell you about that," he was told, "is at a place called Vellore. His name is Brand."

So here he was on Paul's doorstep, a shaggy youth of about twenty, with no money, one pair of leather shorts, a change of shirts, and his pack. "I don't need money," he told Paul. "I just want to help leprosy patients."

"What training do you have?" inquired Paul, rating him as a crank.

"None. I never passed my school finals. But I have a good pair of hands, and I think I'm rather ingenious."

"Sorry," said Paul, trying to put him off, "but in India we can pay only coolie wages to people without training. I couldn't pay you more than a hundred rupees a month for manual work."

"Fine," replied the youth.

Paul raised his eyebrows. "Well—suppose we put you in the shoe shop."

In Karigiri John sat down crosslegged in the shoe shop and started making shoes. Paul forgot about him. When he went back one day, he found some high quality shoes on display. John had made them. He came around asking Paul intelligent questions. Before long John Girling was in charge of the shop.

The rubber mill was turning out an inferior product, full of holes. "Mind if I try to improve this rubber?" John asked.

"Fine. Go ahead."

In a couple of weeks the mill was turning out good rubber. "We must pay you more money now," Paul told him, but the youth replied cheerfully, "I don't think I could spend more than a hundred rupees a month." He ate Indian food, lived in servants' quarters, wore a *dhoti,* and was completely happy. He helped with research work and was the backbone of the new pressure disk studies. When an article on the studies was published in the "Journal of Bone and Joint Surgery," John was the co-author. Later when a Danish expert was sent by the United Nations to study the splint workshop, he told Paul, "If you really want the splint workshop to be a success, there's only one man who can run it. Girling."

John went to Denmark to learn better methods of making shoes, later to London for training in making artificial limbs. Married to a Danish girl, he returned to Vellore for further service in 1964. His contribution to leprosy rehabilitation was equaled only by his joy in having found self-fulfillment.

It was John who helped Paul develop his "rocker" shoes and boots.

The best way to prevent high pressures under feet, Paul concluded, was to make the foot rock like a seesaw on a central pivot instead of bending. He obtained this result by placing two small parallel bars under the sole of the shoe, which could be of either wood or very heavy leather but must be rigid. And now, finally, Sadagopan's long patience was rewarded. Wearing a "rocker" shoe when walking, he remained for days, weeks, months, years, without a sign of trophic ulcer.

But this also was not the perfect solution, for with some patients the "rocker" shoe tended to twist the foot. If a person with normal sensation steps on a loose stone and starts to turn his ankle, the pain causes him to remove his weight from it and fall down, perhaps spraining his ankle but avoiding a fracture. But the leprosy patient does not fall. He goes on walking, putting his whole weight on the twisting foot, perhaps tearing a ligament or even fracturing a bone. The "rocker" shoe increased this danger of twisting. A high boot supporting the ankle could mitigate this danger, as it did with Sadagopan, but in most cases it was prohibitively expensive. So, as so often happened in the team's long crusade, the solution of one problem merely led to another.

The first tenet of Paul's foot philosophy came to be his "doctrine of the first ulcer," a term ridiculed by the team but expressive. Their main energies should be concentrated on the man with his first ulcer. The man with a badly destroyed foot may be too late to save. The man who has never had an ulcer may not really believe he is going to have one, but the man who has had one ulcer is ready for education. He would need no expensive shoe, only a simple sandal to keep his foot from thorns and nails, a *chappal*. Many patients were in this category. With the campaign barely begun, the team was soon able to reduce the total incidence of ulcers in village areas around Vellore by fifty per cent. And shoes for leprosy patients, Paul was convinced, were infinitely more important for the feet than surgery. For it would take years to train surgeons in the new techniques, and they would always be few in number. But by giving a few months' training to a host of willing and able volunteers, like John Girling, shoes could be introduced *now* all over the world.

Provided patients could be persuaded to wear them! That, Paul discovered, was one of the worst problems. For instance, there was Karuninasan.

He was not the first leprosy patient Paul's mother had brought to Vellore. At least two or three times a year she would turn up at the hospital with one or more derelicts gleaned from her mountain dispensary or her horseback travels over the Kolaryans, sometimes with a long string of them. Beds or no beds, she would somehow maneuver them into the hospital. If Paul was not there, she would employ a highhanded technique, drawing herself up to her full five feet slightly plus and, in spite of her shapeless bag of a dress and short stringy white hair, managing to look like a duchess.

"No room? I guess you don't know who I am. Dr. Paul Brand is my son, understand? And these are his very special patients."

Or if Paul was there she might become sweetly, deliberately wheedling. "Look, dear boy, I have quite a lot with me this time."

"But, mother, there are no beds!"

"Oh, you'll find beds," she would toss back airily. "Just say it's for your old mother."

Nor were her persuasive tactics confined to doctors, nurses, and orderlies. On one occasion when she had smuggled a man with badly deformed hands into a crowded, third-class compartment, a train guard endeavored to evict the undesirable passenger, in no uncertain language.

"Get out of here, son of a pig! Out, you filthy—"

He stopped short, suddenly confronted with an avenging fury rearing up from the floor where she had been lying. "Don't you dare touch my patient! I'm taking him to my son Dr. Brand in Vellore, Dr. *Paul* Brand, do you hear?" Meekly the guard backed from the compartment.

Paul's mother had found Karuninasan on one of her mountain camping trips. Turned out of his village because of his leprosy, he had been reduced to beggary. When Evelyn Brand spied him huddled in a wreck of a shed, she immediately concerned herself with his plight and insisted on bringing him the several hundred miles to Paul in Vellore.

"See, Paul, this poor boy! He's begging because he can't do anything else. Paralysis of both feet and hands, and ulcers on both feet."

Paul examined them, the hands that would not open, the feet that were being slowly destroyed by huge open sores. They took him into the ward and started to treat him. It took months to heal the sores, and then one by one he had operations which restored first one hand, then the other, then one foot, then the other. He was in the hospital for more than a year. One of the earlier patients taught him to read, and when he learned the story of Jesus, he came to have a new hope and faith. He wanted to go back home and use his new hands and feet, his new knowledge.

Paul said to him, "Now look, you have to take care of your hands and feet. You must meet Dr. Robertson."

Uncle Robbie fitted Karuninasan to some molded shoes, beautifully and lovingly finished with his own hands. "You must wear these," he explained to him carefully, "to spread the strain of weight-bearing evenly over the whole of your feet. If you walk barefoot or in a flat shoe, the same old ulcers will come back again."

Karuninasan was proud and pleased. Happily he returned to Granny Brand in the mountains. She sent him back to his village with new clothes to start his new life. Finding himself the only man in the village who could read, he started a little night school, working in the fields during the day. Every Sunday he rode on a little pony to Granny's village to worship at her tiny church.

One day when Paul was visiting his mother in the Kolaryans, he climbed over the rocky paths to Karuninasan's village. The youth met him joyfully, showed him his hands, his school, his books. Then Paul looked at his feet.

"Why are you wearing those bandages?" he asked.

He removed the bandages, and found the ugly sores returned, the bones exposed.

"Karuninasan! Where are your shoes?"

"Oh, I have them!" He took Paul into the house and pointed to a little shelf. There was the beautiful pair of shoes wrapped in brown paper. Proudly he undid them. "See? I have kept them so carefully. I wear them on Sundays when I go to church."

18

The Brands and the Webbs spent their first holiday together in 1954, an arrangement so happy it set a pattern for almost a decade.

Paul had met Dr. John Webb on furlough when asked by the Church Missionary Society to speak to a group of potential candidates. John, an Oxford graduate and specialist in pediatrics, claimed afterward it was partly Paul's enthusiasm that brought him to Vellore as head of the department of pediatrics. When he and his wife Alison, also a pediatrician, with their two boys Mike and Andrew, arrived in June, 1953, Paul and Margaret immediately found them kindred spirits.

"Why not go with us to Kotagiri?" Paul suggested the following spring when the Webbs were casting about for a suitable vacation spot.

Together they booked a house called Westcliff in the mountain resort. It was a comfortable house as hill houses go, but, as Paul commented, "They don't go very well." Even the refurbishing done by the owners, a tar and paint job on the lower floor, was more liability than asset. The Webbs had a big black dog named Max, who rushed about transferring much of the wet tar to much of the fresh paint, which did not improve the decor. It was discovered also, too late, that the lavatory seats, the usual wooden commodes, had been given a fresh coat of paint.

One day Alison, fresh from England and a life of hygienic cleanliness, made the mistake of following the sweeper woman to the terminal of waste disposal and, discovering the open, seething pit which was obviously the origin of the superabundant flies, was almost ready to leave the place. But aside from these drawbacks it was a pleasant and productive vacation.

Productive especially from the Brands' standpoint because it marked the advent of Patricia, a fourth sister for the lone Christopher. Margaret interrupted her holiday service at the Kotagiri Medical Fellowship long enough to enter the maternity department as a patient—barely long enough. On the third day after Patricia's birth Dr. Lydia Herlufson, who had delivered her, came down with a severe attack of malaria. Dr. Pauline Jeffery, the eye specialist, was afflicted with a bad case of jaundice. A patient arrived at the hospital with severe panophthalmitis, total infection of the eyeball, and in excruciating pain.

"What shall I do?" one of the nurses asked Margaret in desperation. "I can't send him away like that, but both of our doctors are seriously ill. Could you suggest something?"

Margaret got up from her bed and went to the dispensary, where she examined the patient. Finding that he needed immediate surgery, she proceeded to operate. Meanwhile her attendant nurse came to the confinement room to minister to the needs of her bed patient. She looked around the room in bewilderment. No Margaret. She looked in the adjoining bathing cubicle. Empty. The baby was in its basket peacefully sleeping, but the mother was missing. She went around the hospital inquiring. Presently another nurse emerged from the operating room.

"Oh, yes," she replied in answer to her colleague's question. "She's just finishing an operation. Do you want her?"

It was that same year, 1954, that Margaret began to study the problems of eyes in leprosy. Ernest Fritschi, now acting superintendent at Karigiri, asked her to come out and take care of some cases at the Research Sanatorium. Nothing was being done for eye complications in leprosy patients. In fact, Fritschi and his team did not even know what eye complications there were.

"But Karigiri is the place where we should be finding out," he insisted.

A dark room was improvised by installing heavy curtains and painting all the walls of one room black. There was one Snellen Testing Chart. During her years at Schell Margaret had acquired much general knowledge and experience in treating eyes. In eye camps she had performed hundreds of cataract operations, some of them on leprosy patients. But this was scant equipment for the pioneer task she faced had she not brought to it also a passion of concern which transcended all difficulties. Of the two million leprosy patients in India forty per cent were lepromatous (that is, severe cases where the bacilli multiply in the skin and gain an ascendancy over the tissues of the body), and of these ninety per cent would show some ocular involvement sooner or later, some of which would undoubtedly lead to total blindness. The very thought of a person without the sense of touch losing his sense of sight also was appalling. He would have no contact whatever with the outside world except through his ears. And this happened not only to the elderly, who had enjoyed years of eyesight. It was just as often the fate of young people in their teens or twenties. It must mean a living death.

Plunging into research on the problem, Margaret found that there are several ways in which eyes are affected by leprosy. One is by lid paralysis, when the nerves supplying the opening and closing muscle of the eyelids become ineffective. The lids at the beginning can close but cannot maintain the closure. Later on they may close just enough to cover the cornea, finally not even that. The results are obvious. The eye gets dry, because the lids are important in brushing tears across it. If the duct doesn't operate properly, the tears merely run down over the eye and collect in the lower lid, then run down over the face. But the cornea, which must be kept moist to remain healthy, becomes dry and much more liable to damage. Even a simple act like rubbing a sleeve across an eye may damage a dry cornea, resulting in scratches, scarring, unnatural blood vessels, all conducive to serious infection which may develop into corneal ulceration. When not treated properly these ulcers may go deeper and deeper until the whole eye is lost.

It was possible, Margaret found, for patients in the early stages of lid paralysis to regain a certain control of the lid by active and repeated exercise. Oil used at night might also help, and tinted goggles might prevent damage from glare or foreign bodies. But these measures were likely to be ineffective or temporary. Surgery then was necessary.

The simplest operation, Margaret discovered, consisted of closing the eyelids, merely stitching the lids together so that any remaining action could complete the closure to a safe degree. The lids were closed at both ends, leaving only a small opening in the middle for the patient to see through. This might work well for a time, but the scar tissue between the lids was inclined to stretch, resulting again in unsightly, staring eyes. The patients did not like this operation. They were desperately anxious to look natural.

As time progressed she found that the operation they preferred was a temporal transplant. Though this was usually performed by the plastic surgeons, she and the other eye specialists made use of it also. For many years now it has been performed frequently at Karigiri. A part of the temporalis muscle (the one which controls chewing and clenching of the teeth) is detached from its origin, together with the fascia, swung around, and attached to a piece of fascia running through the eyelids. From now on the patient's lid-closing muscle is the same one as his chewing muscle. This means that sometimes when he is having a meal and is chewing at something rather hard, his eyes will keep blinking. But that is a small handicap. Not only are his eyes now protected from damage, but they look and act like other people's. Provided he remembers to chew often enough! For the act of blinking is now voluntary, not automatic.

It was also possible for leprosy itself to invade the eye, usually attacking the front third of the eyeball, since it is a surface disease. Confirming in her own experience the findings of many leprosy experts, Margaret learned to tell the signs: a cloudy inflammation of the cornea, and, when the lid was lifted, a crescent-shaped white patch at the cornea's top threaded by minute blood vessels. Leprotic nodules, like tiny volcanoes, appeared in the iris, and later in the center of them a shining white bead, like a minute golf ball teed up on the iris. All were grave signs of danger and, though the process of disintegration might take years, it was likely to be hurried up by acute episodes of the disease when the eye, fighting a renewed attack by the bacilli, often damaged itself more than did the leprosy. To combat this danger Margaret and her team soon began giving the usual treatment of cortico-steroids, trying to make the eye stop fighting and accept quietly the invasion of the bacteria, and hoping that the bacteria would themselves be dealt with gradually by the general treatment of the disease.

Cataracts also were a frequent by-product of leprosy, occurring not only in older patients but in those of the twenties or teens. In her first work at Karigiri Margaret performed many cataract operations on leprosy patients, only to find that the results of such surgery could sometimes be disastrous. There is a form of cataract which follows on repeated attacks of iritis, usually in patients with the lepromatous type of leprosy. Operate on one of these, she discovered, and in three months iritis might again develop. Then the eye might be doomed. How many cataract operations had she performed in eye camps, she wondered in dismay, for patients who had seemed to recover normally but perhaps in a year had been plunged into total blindness! As time passed, she became more and more cautious about performing cataract operations on a patient of the lepromatous type unless she was certain that he had not had any kind of iritis for over a year, and then only with the most skilled and careful control during the operative period and for many months afterward.

She was talking once with a doctor from Malaya who had sincerely tried to help leprosy patients. "I have operated on at least two thousand of them for cataracts," he observed with some pride.

"And what sort of follow-up results have you had?" inquired Margaret.

"Well," he confessed, "as a matter of fact, I never saw the patients again."

The necessity of this follow-up program became more and more evident to Margaret as the years passed, but it was a long time before she came to realize the tremendous need of examining every patient's eyes whether he reported any trouble or not. It was Murugan who brought this realization to sudden focus.

Preparing to participate in a big World Health Organization meeting on leprosy to be held at Vellore, she was collecting cases for exhibit. Since few eye symptoms had been reported, she decided to tour the cottages at Karigiri to see if there were any old cases who had not been coming for treatment.

"I wish you'd look at this man's eye," an orderly in one cottage said. "It's been a bit red for a few days."

Margaret approached the patient, a boy about eighteen named Murugan. "Are your eyes sore?" she inquired.

"Oh—a little bit. Not much."

For all his admitted symptoms she might easily have passed him by, but, rolling back the lid of his left eye, she found to her consternation a serious condition in the upper part of the cornea which might develop rapidly and lead to blindness. Rushing him to Schell, where there was a corneal microscope, she diagnosed his trouble and started him on the necessary treatment of atropine drops and hydrocortisone by subconjunctival injection, the latter a new drug which was proving an invaluable ally in the fight against blindness. Murugan's condition improved rapidly.

"You can't rely on patients to come and report their troubles," she told the conference, exhibiting him as a case in point. "You must go to them."

After that Margaret realized that the eyes of every single patient must be examined, checked, rechecked, ad infinitum. It was a staggering, long-time project, its development covering much of her third missionary term, well into the 1960's.

Equipment was scant at Karigiri, and transport to Schell constituted a major problem. But finally a proper corneal microscope was provided for Karigiri by the Mission to Lepers, and the Indian Council of Medical Research granted the salary for a full-time ophthalmic assistant for research work. Three very fine Vellore graduates were appointed in turn to this post, Dr. Pamela Sinclair, Dr. Vimala Chowler, and Dr. Annie Verghese, a gold medalist with a very promising future.

Now progress could really be made with giant steps. Making a careful survey of five hundred cases, they discovered that eighty-one per cent of the patients coming to Karigiri had some eye involvement. Some, like Murugan, were saved from early blindness because of this routine examination. Paramedical workers going into the villages around Karigiri were alerted to report any danger signs in patients and trained to recognize early eye involvement, no matter how trivial. And, equally important, patients discharged after apparently successful treatment were impressed with the importance of returning for frequent checkups.

The research and experience necessary to understand all the different symptoms, to know when to perform surgery, to maintain the delicate balance between treatments and eye reactions, to establish a system of routine examinations, were a slow and painful process covering nearly a decade of Margaret's professional career. Though not so sensational as some of Paul's revolutionary surgery, because prevention is seldom as dramatic as cure, it was a pioneering venture of the utmost significance to thousands of leprosy patients the world around who, because of the tireless devotion of Dr. Margaret and her colleagues, are now able to say, "Whereas I might have been blind, now I can see!"

That summer of 1954 when Margaret rose from childbed to perform an operation was the last one the Brands spent at Kotagiri. After the episode of the seething pit their appetite for the place was somewhat jaded. Besides, they wanted to go to Ootacamund the following year, where Christopher would be in school. But the Ooty houses were equally discouraging.

"We've about decided to go camping next summer," Paul remarked to Eric Stanes, chief of a big tea estate for whom he had performed a medical service. "We're fed up with all this business of holiday houses." He grinned. "Yes, and with missionaries too. We'd like to get away into the wild open air."

Mr. Stanes looked sympathetic. If they wanted to camp, he suggested, why not use a big empty bungalow abandoned by the estate because its elevation had proved so high that the tea was getting frostbitten? They were welcome to use it without cost, and if they wanted something wild, this was it.

Before the next holiday Paul went up to see the place and returned, his description bubbling with superlatives. Though it was named Korakunda, the planters had renamed it Heaven, and no wonder, because it had everything one could possibly possess on earth! It was utterly magnificent. All the streams in the estate had been dammed up, to form great lakes, in the hope that they might equalize the temperature and prevent frosts, and there were great open downland areas green with thick grass, and *sholas*, jungles, known to be the haunts of tigers and panthers. In fact, one of the house's previous occupants had been sitting on a window seat with his dog beside him when a panther began pulling the dog out the window. He had just saved it by hitting the beast over the head with a magazine. A day or two later the same or another panther had picked the dog up again outside the kitchen, and the cook had saved it this time by hitting the wall with a frying pan, the noise so frightening the beast that he dropped the dog.

These episodes served only to whet the family's appetite, Margaret's possibly excepted, but no decision was actually made until one morning at breakfast a telegram arrived stating that a house was available in Ooty at a place called Missionary Hill. However, the telegram contained an error. It read: "House available lower Missionary Hell."

"Well," said Paul, "that certainly presents an alternative. Heaven—or 'lower missionary hell.' Which shall it be?"

Hell was bad enough, they all decided, but a "missionary hell" would be even worse. The Webbs agreed, and "Heaven" became the two families' summer paradise.

The first year they used it, 1955, they sent ahead all the luggage, including bedding, stowed parents, children, and pets in the sturdy old Vanguard, and drove the two hundred and eighty miles to Ootacamund in the Nilgiris. After this the advantages of the new site became even more apparent, for

Korakunda was thirty-two miles from Ooty over the most detestable of mountain roads, rough, rocky, abounding in hairpin turns, skirting hair-raising precipices.

"Visitors will either have to like us very much or need us very much," Paul commented cheerfully. "In either case we'll be happy to have them."

Christopher was to meet them at Korakunda, coming up from his school in Ooty on the one bus a day. He, like the luggage, was expected to precede them. Arriving at the house, they found no luggage, no Christopher. Seven thousand feet up in the mountains, the place was cold. Furniture was at a minimum, though there was one bed with a mattress. They built a fire, deposited all the children in the bed, and put the carpet over them. Then Paul and Margaret huddled by the fire and wondered. Presently rain began to pour. About nine that night a lorry appeared, and out came the luggage and Christopher. Having missed the bus, he had set out at age eleven all by himself, taken another bus to the point nearest the house, about fifteen miles away, and set off walking through the tiger jungle. Fortunately this lorry had overtaken him, and he had thumbed a lift. It had turned out to be the tea lorry, carrying the family baggage.

A slightly inauspicious beginning to years of magnificent holidays! But both families reveled in the wildness, the freedom, the privacy, the congenial companionship, the diversity of sports. There were swimming in ice-cold but clear sweet water, fishing in the lakes and mountain streams, expeditions into the jungle for tender bamboo shoots, wild strawberries, and hill guavas, innumerable picnics. The old Vanguard was the standby for all their expeditions, and both families would pile into it, six inside, four or more on the roof rack, and often a couple in the luggage trunk. They would go as far as the car could travel, then take picnic equipment and sometimes a tent, and go on trekking, finding a place to camp beside the river. Then John and Paul and the boys would go fishing. Usually by lunch time there was a string of fresh trout to grill.

From their first meeting Paul had found John Webb a kindred spirit, one of the few people to whom he could really unbare his soul. They would roam for miles sparring good-naturedly, airing their pet philosophies, probing each other's inmost thoughts. And they had common hobbies. Both liked to dabble in paints, John in water colors, Paul in oils. Usually they would try to paint the same scene, with varying but indifferent results, about which Granny, who gave them lessons on several of her visits, made many insulting remarks.

Korakunda was a paradise for pets as well as people. Usually a small zoo accompanied the families on their holidays. Once they drove the two hundred and eighty miles with a dog, a cat, and two parrots in the car. The cat was a Siamese, acquired because Paul had heard that Siamese cats were the best ratters and he hoped to breed a large number of kittens for his leprosy patients. They named him Seesaw, the nearest equivalent to the Siamese word for "cat" as reported by a Vellore student from Siam. He proved to be a magnificent ratter, and undoubtedly sired a far larger progeny than was ever utilized for the benefit of patients.

One of Paul's most popular roles on holidays was that of story teller. Each year he would compose a serial narrative about a semi-fictitious group called the Wends, who bore astonishingly familiar names but became involved in highly exaggerated exploits. The characters included all the members of the Brand and Webb families, but there the similarity ended, since each was usually ascribed traits in marked contrast to his role in real life. John, for instance, who had played cricket for Oxford and soccer and fives, was depicted as weak and cowardly and somewhat of a simpleton, with Paul always outrunning and outwitting him.

"Must be some suppressed desire or frustration," teased John. "That's your way of getting it out of your system."

As soon as they arrived at Korakunda the children would begin to prod: "Daddy—Uncle Paul—will you start the story tonight?"

Once he tried facetiously to stall them. "All right. Well, Mary was running along through the forest, and she could hear two great big tigers close behind her, and she suddenly came out of the forest, and there was a two thousand foot precipice in front of her. And she didn't know what to do. That's all for now. Good night."

But they would not be stalled. "Now, Daddy, you can't just start there and end there. You've got to make a proper start and end the story properly."

So from having blurted out the words on the spur of the

moment Paul had to weave a story about them. It was one of the most fascinating and exciting of the series and lasted the full month's holiday. At supper time he would lapse into silence, and they knew it was no use talking to him. He was busy working out the next chapter of the story. Sometimes he would say as the hair-raising narrative progressed, "Well, I certainly didn't know *that* was going to happen!" Visitors to Korakunda were involved in the story, then disposed of when they left. When Ruth Harris came up, however, from her mission station on the plains, she became intensely interested in her role, and they kept her in the story, keeping her informed as to what was happening to her namesake.

The character delineations were often clever little projects in psychology. He would choose one of the children who was least forward in family affairs to become the hero or heroine. One year Estelle, the shy, quiet little Brand, always sure she was going to do something wrong and hence burdened with an inferiority complex, was heroine of a series which required her to make a long journey alone and to form all sorts of decisions which she might well be capable of in real life but lacked the self-confidence to make. When the story was concluded there was a flush of pleasure on her sober little face. If her father had that much confidence in her, the sparkle in her eyes implied, she might really accomplish something big and important one day.

19

In a little basement shop in Howland Street, Paul found the object of his search. The proprietor, a potter named Kenneth Clark, was glad to grant his request. For several hours Paul watched the clever fingers, the spinning wheel, the rapt face of the craftsman. He asked questions. He examined bowls, vases, jars of faultless pattern; he inspected others discarded for their imperfections. And then for a little while he himself became a potter, not a good one, but finally with the aid of the master he produced a passable bowl of which he was inordinately proud. After its firing he called for it and took it to the autumn reunion of the Mission to Lepers, where he was to deliver an address. The subject had been previously assigned: "The vessel marred in the hands of the potter."

Paul exhibited his bowl and told of his experience. "There were four things that I noticed in the potter's shop. The first was the preparation of the clay. The second was the molding. The third was the firing. The fourth was the care and use of the finished pot."

Then he compared these four with the work of his team in leprosy: the preparation by the social workers and physiotherapists; the molding of hands, noses, feet, eyebrows by the surgeons; the firing, the agonizing, shattering trials which must be endured by outcasts of society; the carefulness with which the finished product must be used and the tragedy when the restored feet or hands are again destroyed.

Here Paul raised the bowl in his hands, brought it down hard on the table, and smashed it. The act was as shocking to his own emotions as to those of his audience. So actual was his distress at this mutilation of something he had so lovingly created that for a moment he was unable to speak. Even when words came he could not trust his voice.

"Why did this bowl break? Because I was handling it as if it were metal instead of fragile pottery. It could have lasted all my life. It was a beautiful bowl, and I was fond of it. Can you share my sorrow over its breaking? Then I ask you to share my sorrow when I see a beautiful hand or a strong pair of feet that could serve a man through the whole of his life, being needlessly broken."

That they did share it was evident in the almost inaudible murmur which broke the hush, in the deeply involved awareness which Paul sensed in the uplifted faces.

Certainly his greatest satisfaction during these years of intensive experimentation came not so much from the new knowledge gained and the techniques slowly being developed as from the marred human lives which the team was able to restore to usefulness. For example, there was Robert James, who wanted desperately to play the violin again. Paul opened his badly clawed fingers so that he could hold the bow and reach all the strings. Robert joined the Vellore staff, and for many years he went out on Roadside twice each week and gave inspiration with his music.

There was Sadagopan, who wanted to find some way to make himself useful in the hospital. "I—I believe I could type," he said hopefully.

Paul looked at Sadan's hands. They were no longer clawed, but many of the fingers were mere stumps. He thought: "If this man can learn to type, anything is possible in rehabilitation." He found him an old typewriter. Sadan practiced constantly. At first he picked and fumbled; then slowly he became swifter and more accurate. He learned shorthand. The new skills opened the way to a responsible job as typist and record keeper in a sanatorium of South India, a wife and healthy child whom he was able to support, a satisfying life.

And there was the Calcutta lawyer.

Unlike many of the poorer and less cultured leprosy patients, this man was able to find medical treatment for his disease, for in any large city there were leprosy practitioners ready and willing to treat paying patients. During the period of acute infection he had ceased his law practice; then when the leprosy was arrested, he had returned to it.

But the crippling effects of the disease remained, becoming more and more obvious. His fellow lawyers began to whisper, then to mutter, finally to voice their objections openly. It was a disgrace to the profession for a man to plead a case with clawed hands! Complaints were filed against him, and his case was soon to come up for a hearing. In desperation the lawyer wrote to Paul.

"Come immediately," Paul wired back.

He made an exception and operated on both of the man's hands in the same day. The results were gratifying. The patient dashed back to Calcutta in time for the hearing. The charges were stated. He should not be allowed to plead cases, the accusation ran, because of his deformities.

The lawyer rose to make his defense. He lifted his hands, shapely, supple, the fingers bending and straightening in free, normal motion.

"What deformities?" he demanded.

The charges were dropped, and he continued his successful practice.

But, satisfying though such achievements were, they were not enough. There were at least ten million leprosy patients in the world, many of them crippled. Paul had scarcely scratched the surface of the problem. Some remarkable advances in Vellore and Karigiri, yes, and some pilot projects in other parts of India. A few isolated leprosaria in Africa experimenting with the new methods of surgery and rehabilitation. A little group in England gallantly educating and raising funds. But few leprosy experts had even heard of, much less accepted, his ideas, and rehabilitation was not even included in the agenda of the leprosy world conferences.

Paul decided to show, not tell, a wider audience about the team's achievements. With the help of the Marconis, a motion picture producer and his wife in Bombay, he proceeded to make a short film of the team's work in leprosy. The story had been growing in his mind for a long time. It would start with close-ups of hands, beautiful unblemished hands, moving with inimitable grace in the *mudras* of the Indian dancer; fade into the distorted claw hands of a boy, who would be brought to the New Life Center, become the friend there of another boy, a patient about to return to his own village with new hands, new skills, new hope. Seeing the changes being wrought there in the lives of others like himself, spiritual as well as physical, the boy would decide to stay, looking forward to a future as full of possibilities for himself as for his departing friend. Though the main idea was Paul's, Paxey, Carlo Marconi's wife, helped write the script.

Another colorful member of the Marconi team was Gigi, a leopard cub. Though the Indians were terrified of the animal, not so the Brand children, who were always receptive to unusual pets. Gigi was especially partial to 'Tricia, now a little three-year-old, and the two became fast friends. However, the animal was growing to an unwieldy size by the end of the six weeks, and Paul and Margaret did not regret its departure.

A student in the medical college was the beautiful and talented dancer in the motion picture. A boy named Raymond, his name changed to the more Indian Raman, played the principal character. His friend was Sunderi, who played himself, one of the boys in the New Life Center. All the actors were amateurs, students for the crowd scenes, villagers from the surrounding areas.

The film was shot all in daylight in a season of intolerable heat. Even the indoor scenes were played on little stages built outdoors to take advantage of the sunlight. Hour after hour, day after day, week after week Paul and the Marconis and the cast baked and sweated. To add to the frustration it was monsoon weather when, even if it didn't rain, there were constantly shifting clouds, and Carlo Marconi was a purist who insisted on exactly the right quality of light. Some scenes were shot innumerable times. If a cloud didn't cross the sky at a critical moment, an actor would make a wrong motion. But the film was finished at last, becoming one of the truly satisfying achievements of those often frustrating years. They called it "Lifted Hands."

"How about shooting an operation?" Paul suggested on an impulse to Carlo. Since he was to go on furlough soon, it occurred to him that it might be valuable to show an actual operation to surgeons back in England.

Carlo considered. "Well, I've never shot an operation, and as I'm not an expert I won't charge you for it. But give me the raw film, and I'll shoot it."

So in this impromptu fashion Paul performed a tendon free graft, and Carlo shot it. Paul was able to take it with him to England when he went on furlough at the end of 1957.

Besides a new baby, Pauline, they took along another new product: marmalade. During their furlough in 1952 the dearth of this precious commodity, due to the relics of wartime rationing, had been a source of great pain to Paul. "We should take home a whole trunkful of it," he said to Margaret.

"A trunkful."

"Well, you know," he gestured vaguely, "just pack a layer of clothes and a layer of marmalade, and a layer of clothes and a layer of marmalade."

Margaret went ahead and planned a great marmalade making day. With the help of Aruldoss their cook she produced about thirty pounds and stored it in three of the large tins used for plaster bandages. She hammered down the lids.

Halfway through the journey she went to the ship's baggage room to get something out of one of the trunks. Paul's advice was followed to the letter: a layer of clothes and a layer of marmalade, a layer of clothes . . . She spent the rest of the journey washing and ironing. Anxiously she watched the tin in their cabin trunk, relieved when it showed no signs of blowing its lid. The last morning she packed into it all the clothes that would be needed on arrival.

"Now I'm really being a good manager," she congratulated herself.

They were spending the furlough in a big house in Kew belonging to the Mission to Lepers. The children soon discovered the garden and ornamental pool with a bird bath in its center. The birdbath looked steady enough, but when Christopher attempted to cross the pool by leaping to it, it collapsed and plunged him into dirty, freezing water. Dripping mud, he came running in to demand clean clothes. Feeling very virtuous, Margaret told him exactly where to find them. But when he opened the trunk, there was a layer of clothes, and a layer of marmalade, a layer of clothes . . . Happy beginning for a furlough, a new house in a new country, a new baby squalling, a wet foggy February day, and not a stitch of clean clothing! Moreover, to her chagrin, the first sight that met Margaret's eyes when she went to a store was rows upon rows of golden marmalade.

Most of this furlough was a succession of speaking engagements, which Paul welcomed with the zeal of an evangelist given opportunity to preach a saving gospel. For he knew that there would never be new life for the victims of leprosy around the world until the public was educated to a sane and intelligent attitude toward the disease.

He showed his film called "Tendon Free Grafting" at the annual meeting of the British Orthopedic Association and was amazed by the tremendous ovation it received. After the meeting a representative of CIBA approached Paul and asked if he might submit a copy to his organization with the option of purchase.

"But—it's only a thing we shot for private showing," Paul disclaimed. "In fact, this is the original."

However, the representative persisted. CIBA bought the film, edited it, put a sound track on it with diagrams, and ran off fifty-seven copies in four languages. That year it was entered in various competitions around the world. It won second prize in the British Medical Association contest, first in the German film festival competition. It took the million-lira prize for technical films in the Milan Film Festival of Italy. In fact, it proved to be one of the most successful films CIBA ever sponsored. For Carlo Marconi it was a photographic triumph, and for Paul a first major step toward his ultimate goal. Linking together hand surgery and leprosy at a time when leprosy was just coming into perspective as both a medical and a social problem, it marked an important milestone in the educational task which from now on was to be his greatest concern.

Paul made the appeal for Vellore that year at the sixth benefit concert in Royal Albert Hall, for which the world-famous pianist Eileen Joyce generously appeared with the London Philharmonic Orchestra. She was later to tour India on behalf of Vellore and to play at the College, for Ida Scudder and the staff. Paul had had many eloquent predecessors in presenting this appeal, including the Countess Mountbatten. The organizers, however, endured some anxious moments because the appeal must never last more than six minutes, and Paul abandoned his script after the first two. But he ended on the dot. One of the chief promoters of these annual concerts, as well as a tireless worker for Vellore, was A. G. Jefcoate, usually called "Jeff," who was to become not only a close friend but one of the most loyal supporters of Paul's work.

But the furlough had its low moments as well as its high, for it marked the end of an era. Christopher and Jean were to be left in school in England. The separation which Paul had once vowed he would never let happen was now happening. It was the price a family must pay for the privilege of serving where human needs were greatest.

And yet, Paul tried to console himself, his own boyhood deprivation had not been without compensation. Close association with his mother, dominant, often uncompromising, might well have resulted either in accentuation of those qualities in himself or in open rebellion. The aunts with their gentle permissiveness, winning their way entirely by the discipline of love, had left him freer to develop in his own way, whether good or bad. His chief worry now was for Christopher. Used to a life of such untrammeled physical freedom, would he not find the restrictions of his English school and foster home intolerable?

But surprisingly it was Jean who was to find the adjustment more difficult. While Margaret went with Christopher to his school in Ramsgate, Paul, with the three youngest children accompanying him, took Jean to the station at Euston, where she was to take the train to Clarendon, a public girls' boarding school in North Wales. Even though she was to see the children later, Jean found it almost impossible to say good-by. Desperately fond of Pauline, she clung to the child as if she could not let her go. Even so it would be years before her parents comprehended the depth of her loneliness and sense of abandonment.

So Paul and Margaret left them, Chris a gangling youth of fourteen, his childish treble not yet broken, Jean a leggy tomboy of twelve, knowing that when they saw them again they would be almost man and woman.

Back in India, Paul needed to pay a business call at the home of the Marconis in Bombay. He took the family with him. As they approached the house through the garden they saw Gigi, now a nearly full grown leopard of nine months, chained to a post and sunning herself near the front steps. She had grown so big that Margaret, holding Pauline, was reluctant to go too close, and Mary and Estelle also hung back. Paul mounted the steps and rang the bell, and then turned back to stroke Gigi's head. The animal seemed as tame as ever. Paul had no idea that 'Tricia had seen this byplay at a distance and, before Margaret could call her back, had run up close behind him. Suddenly Paul was aware that the animal had tensed, her eyes half closed. Then she sprang past him, leaped on 'Tricia, bore her to the ground and lay over her, snarling, her teeth planted in the child's throat.

Not knowing what to do, Paul did the wrong thing. He seized the chain and tried to pull the animal away, which only made her sink her teeth more deeply. Carlo came bounding down the steps, shouting, "For heaven's sake, don't pull the chain!" He covered the intervening yards in two steps and gave the animal a hard blow on the snout, but even then the tenacious jaws did not loosen. Then Carlo pushed her cheek in, forcing the flesh painfully between her teeth, and finally Paul was able to pull the child free.

Margaret rushed up, horrified to see blood trickling from 'Tricia's throat. She was about to act the consoling mother when Paul gestured her back. With his usual equanimity he wiped away the blood, stood the child up, and took her by the hand. "Come on, Trish," he said cheerfully, "let's go into the house and get cleaned up. Gigi got to playing a bit too rough, didn't she?"

Tricia's obvious terror subsided. Her father's calm manner gave the impression that such things occasionally happened to most children, and there was nothing to be frightened about. Thanks, no doubt, to this matter of fact handling of the incident, it left no traumatic scars, except a few on her neck.

The Brands arrived back in Vellore on October 29th, earlier than they had planned, for, to his great satisfaction, Paul had been invited to attend the Seventh International Congress of Leprology to be held in Tokyo in November. His inclusion in the conference must indicate that at last the experts were beginning to acknowledge the relationship between surgery and rehabilitation and leprosy.

Though there was little more than a week between his arrival and the time of leaving for Japan, he plunged into a full schedule of surgery and teaching. He was lecturing to a class in orthopedics when an air letter came from the school doctor in England with the news that Jean had fallen and broken her arm. Paul anxiously scanned the description of the fracture, relieved to note that the school doctor had himself seen Mr. Drennan, an expert orthopedic surgeon, do an open reduction in the operating room in Rhyl Hospital. Being Paul Brand, he immediately utilized the incident as a teaching aid.

"How would you treat such a supra condylar fracture?" he asked. "Would you keep the elbow straight?"

"Oh, no." The students were all emphatic, since he had just recently drilled them well on fractures.

"Why?"

"Because," one explained, "there might be danger of a stiff elbow."

"Any other special dangers in this fracture?"

"Yes," proffered another. "It might even result in a Volkmann ischemic contracture if nobody noticed that the arm was swelling inside a tight splint, and this would cause the muscles to shrivel, leaving the arm a withered, atrophic little remnant, the fingers stiff and distorted, both hand and arm completely paralyzed."

Paul winced at this parroting of his own graphic teaching. Again he felt unbounded relief that Drennan, an excellent orthopedic surgeon, had been on the spot. Orthopedically

Jean's break, as the school doctor described it, was a tricky problem. With both a broken wrist and a broken elbow the wrist could not be set by traction against the elbow because the elbow was not stable, so the surgeon had done the best thing possible, put the arm in a Thomas extension splint. Still Paul was worried, though he did not express his fears to Margaret. The Edmunds, their doctor friends who were acting as Jean's foster parents, were in Canada. But he knew he could trust Drennan. He was obliged to leave for Tokyo without hearing further news.

Arriving in Tokyo, he immediately became immersed in the business of the International Congress. Most of the great leprologists of the world were present. Paul had suggested that there be a panel on surgery and rehabilitation, but the request had been turned down. He was told that he could sit in a panel on therapy and that he could speak in a panel on social work. Chairman of the Committee on Social Aspects was India's own Sri Jagadisan, loyal supporter of Paul's theories and himself an eloquent testimony of the efficacy of both surgery and rehabilitation in leprosy.

Paul's speech on the prevention of deformity was received with gratifying attention. "To be cured of active leprosy, but left with crippled hands and feet," Paul told the two hundred delegates from forty-three countries, "may be a victory over the bacillus, but it is a defeat for the man." To prevent such crippling was now their greatest challenge, and he showed graphically how this could be done. The film "Lifted Hands" was finished just in time for showing and was accepted for presentation. It was a tremendous success. He felt that he had actually gotten his message across.

But there were discouraging features. The World Health Organization held a committee meeting after the congress to discuss research needs. Accepting the principle that deformities were preventable and surgically correctible, they formulated good resolutions. However, one influential member objected to them. He had enjoyed Brand's presentation, he admitted, but claimed there was no proof of its accuracy. Some deformities could be corrected, yes. But he would have to see the work to be convinced of its wide application. He agreed to support a resolution calling for more investigation.

Later this same man, the medical director of the

Leonard Wood Memorial Leprosy Foundation, went to the Ryukyus and did a survey on deformities, publishing an article on his findings. He was surprised to find so much deformity among leprosy patients and insisted that the subject be studied further. Offering the sponsorship of the foundation and asking for matching funds from WHO and the International Society for Rehabilitation of the Disabled, he initiated an inquiry to be held at Vellore. So the temporary setback proved in time to be really a step forward.

In fact, this Dr. James Doull, with his sternly critical scientific outlook, proved in later years to be one of Paul's great friends and close allies. Paul always admired the way he could combine a great charm of manner with absolutely inflexible insistence on high standards in any scientific work.

Paul was able to do considerable research himself during his month in the Far East. Visiting Hay Ling Chou, "Island of Happy Healing" of the Mission to Lepers in Hong Kong, he studied the X rays which had been made of the hands of every patient who had ever come to the island. It was these studies, together with the bone studies made over many years by Dr. Gass, Dr. Paterson, and others at Vellore, which enabled the team to arrive at the figure of one per cent as being the proportion of leprosy cases suffering bone damage caused specifically by the bacilli.

In Hong Kong also he met Dr. Howard Rusk, noted American pioneer in the rehabilitation of the disabled. He told Dr. Rusk about Mary Verghese, and they discussed the possibility of a rehabilitation center at Vellore. This conversation was to have important consequences, not only for Mary but for thousands of India's disabled.

It was in Hong Kong that Paul received a letter from Dr. Howard Somervell. Neither he nor Margaret had been fully satisfied with the reports received concerning Jean's condition, and their concern had been deepened by a rumor that Drennan, her physician, was extremely ill. Finally Margaret had written their friend, Dr. Somervell, and asked him to go over to North Wales and see Jean if he possibly could and send Paul a report.

Paul was glad he was alone when the letter came, for never except in those awful hours in London when he thought he had leprosy, had he so plumbed the depths of misery. Drennan's sickness had been his last. He had gone back to see Jean after performing the operation, taken out the stitches, then three or four days later returned to flex the elbow under an anaesthetic. Doubtless he would have come again to check on her condition, but he had died. Though Jean herself had noticed that there was loss of sensation and she was unable to straighten her fingers, the house surgeon in the small hospital was satisfied that her fingers had range of movement and had no idea that she was suffering nerve damage. Now Howard Somervell reported that the arm was already becoming paralyzed. Though he did not say that there was danger of a Volkmann's contracture, Paul read between the lines. The thought of his little Jean, gay, agile, fearless, left with a withered useless remnant of an arm, ugly, shrunken, stiff in every finger, while he, the orthopedic surgeon, was taking care of other people's hands halfway around the world . . . it was almost more than he could bear! The knowledge that it couldn't have happened had he been there stung poignantly. He knew she had felt deserted when he had left her. What must she be feeling now!

He was back in Vellore when, just before Christmas, more news came. The Edmunds, back in England, had taken command of the situation and insisted that something be done. A surgeon from Liverpool had gone many miles to see Jean, taken her out of the splint and started intensive physiotherapy to try to save the muscles. He diagnosed a Volkmann's ischemic contracture. Then Mrs. Edmunds, a doctor herself, had taken Jean to London to Professor Herbert Seddon, whose report was more encouraging. He planned to do a nerve exploration just after Christmas. For the Brands it was a dark holiday season. For Paul one of its worst moments was looking at a family movie showing Jean swimming, one graceful arm raised, the other cutting a clean swath through the water. Never move that hand again! he thought with acute misery.

But the worst they feared did not happen. After the nerve exploration Seddon reported that the nerve condition was quite enough to account for the paralysis. After long and intensive physiotherapy both function and sensation gradually returned. But there were scars where the bone had penetrated the skin and a long and ugly scar resulting from the surgical exploration in the arm. The inner scars, though not permanent, were a long time healing. The girls at her school did not help. "I should think you'd want to keep that terrible scar covered," some of them remarked with youth's cruel tactlessness. Poor Jean wore long sleeved sweaters all through the hot weather.

But the episode merely intensified her loyalty to her parents, and it was she even more than Chris who rebelled against the stricter discipline of the new environment. One day when they were visiting in an English home someone remarked, "I think it's awful for your parents to allow you to climb trees the way they do." Jean looked at Chris. He nodded. Then silently but with extreme dignity they rose and walked out of the room.

20

One day Paul was standing beside a bed in the surgical ward watching one of his registrars examine a case with a couple of house surgeons standing by, when suddenly he was struck by an astonishing sense of familiarity with the scene. He stared at the registrar who, while asking a rather embarrassing question of the patient, had one eyebrow raised and, head tilted to one side, was peering out under his eyebrows with a little twisted half smile.

"However did you get that expression on your face?" he asked. "It's the exact image of my old professor in London."

The house surgeons laughed. "That's your face, sir," one of them said.

Paul was amazed and shocked. Was it possible that in those past years he had absorbed, not only the surgical teaching, but the little routine details of bedside manner right down to the position of the eyebrows and the twist of the lips and stance beside the bed?

"Then what am *I* passing on?" he thought with profound concern. "From where have I received it, and how far is it going? Because, although those eyebrows may be unimportant, I don't know whether they started with his teacher, or the man who taught *him*—perhaps they started with Hippocrates!"

He began to think back over some of his great teachers, trying to discover some of their characteristics in his own work, and he was glad to be able to recognize little shreds of Sir Thomas Lewis, Professor Pilcher, and others. And they in turn were inheritors of a long succession of other pioneers in Western medicine, reaching back through the centuries into the monasteries where men with little science but with a large sense of compassion developed skills and attitudes toward those who suffered. Just as he moved his eyebrows in imitation of his teachers, so many practicing medicine today might claim no religion yet were going through the motions and reflecting the attitudes of those who developed them with devotion, as a part of their service to God and their fellow men.

But the East also had its heritage of medical tradition, a culture and way of life developed through long centuries of coping with its floods, famines, pestilences, malnutrition, disease. The Western doctor coming to the East, smug in his scientific knowledge, made a grave mistake if he believed he was entering a void of medical education and science. Surgery was being practiced in India with some success before it was even thought of in the West. The indigenous societies of medicine, practicing arts handed down through the centuries from father to son, were by no means all quackery. There was much suffering in India, yes, but also much courage; a lot of death, but also a lot of birth; and with all the suffering and death, a patience and gentleness, a tradition of comradeship and loyalty between the strong and the weak. To be really a strength and help in a land like India, Paul had discovered, a doctor must understand and respect the patterns of culture which had evolved through its many generations of adjustment to its own peculiar problems.

For him this need became even more imperative during his third five-year term of mission service, marking the slow but certain breakthrough of his theories and techniques to the outside world. In 1959 the first trainees began coming to Vellore and Karigiri for intensive training in specialized techniques of reconstructive surgery, first workers from other leprosy centers in India and a doctor from England preparing for leprosy work in Korea. But by the following year requests were coming from many other countries.

By this time about five thousand reconstructions of hands and feet of leprosy patients had been carried out at Vellore and Karigiri. Paul, who had performed personally perhaps a half of them, was eager and ready to train these applicants— provided they came prepared to sleep under a tree or in a tent. It soon became a major problem to find housing for them. Building the necessary quarters for these postgraduate doctors and other single men residents received major priority among projects to be financed by funds from the jubilee year of 1960, marking the sixtieth anniversary of the founding of medical work by Dr. Ida. A new guest house at Karigiri was provided by the Mission to Lepers and the American Leprosy Missions.

In subsequent years this guest house was constantly full. Among the trainees were surgeons and physiotherapists from Venezuela, Argentine, Brazil, Spain, the Canary Islands, Turkey, Egypt, France, Equatorial Africa, Ghana, Nigeria, Cameroons, Philippines, Thailand, Burma, Ceylon, Singapore, Hong Kong, Japan, Korea, Formosa, Borneo, New Guinea, Switzerland, Belgium, and of course many from India and Nepal. Though Paul did much traveling, it was easier to train people in Vellore than for him to go abroad. Sometimes the language problems were difficult, especially with the South Americans and Spaniards, for he spoke no Spanish and many of them knew no English. French was sometimes a common medium, and his indifferent French was strained to the utmost. However, such difficulties were minor compared with the constant necessity of adjusting both teaching and surgical techniques to the needs and cultural environment of each individual country.

Some foreign visitors to Vellore came to share as well as learn. There was Dr. Hugh Johnson, an American plastic surgeon, who came for six months under a Fulbright teaching fellowship. In addition to a full teaching and surgical schedule at the hospital he motorcycled to Karigiri one day a week for surgery in leprosy deformities. Cheerfully adapting to Indian procedures, he exchanged his air-conditioned theater for an operating room which, though its temperature might run a hundred degrees, was open to the out of doors and shielded from the sun by a trellis of morning glories; shed his dignity along with his shoes for the loose pajamas and sleeveless shirt which were typical of Indian scrub attire; performed miracles on noses, eyelids, ears, lips, cheeks, palates. Under the tutelage of Mary Verghese or Ernest Fritschi or Paul himself, he learned the techniques of leprosy surgery and, fascinated and impressed, entitled his notes on the Brand operations "The Gospel of Hand Surgery according to Saint Paul."

One of Hugh Johnson's patients was Mary Verghese herself, whom the accident had left with one of the worst cheek depressions the American surgeon had ever seen. A devoted admirer of the courageous young paraplegic doctor, he found great satisfaction in restoring much of her former symmetry of features.

Mary had just returned from a year of rehabilitation in Australia, and she was fired with an urge to serve India's disabled, not just sufferers from leprosy, but the vast number of victims of polio, congenital defects, accidents, many of them paraplegics like herself, for whom almost nothing was being done. When she heard of Dr. Rusk and his Institute of Physical Medicine and Rehabilitation in New York, where students came for training from all over the world, she was seized with an audacious idea. Timidly she broached it to Paul.

"Dr. Rusk?" His eyes lighted with interest. "Yes. I met him in Hong Kong. Told him about you. If you want an appointment at his institute, by all means write him."

She caught her breath. "You—you really think I could—"

Paul grinned, but his eyes were understanding. "Mary," he said gently, "I think that if you believe this is something God wants you to do, nothing on earth is going to stop you."

She applied for the fellowship and got it. Spurred by her action, Dr. Carman, now the director, together with Paul and Dr. Chandy, whose departments would be most concerned, agreed that Vellore must have a new department of rehabilitation ready for her to direct on her return. The team gave her a farewell party in December of 1959, bidding her godspeed as she started on her long journey in a wheelchair halfway around the world.

"This may be a farewell to Mary Verghese," Paul said in his little speech, "but I prefer to call it a welcome to one of first Physical Medicine and Rehabilitation Centers in India. And because Mary has lost the ability to walk, but not her courage and devotion, who knows how many hundreds of others will be able to stand and walk and run on good strong limbs?"

Mary's departure was not the only change of personnel in

Paul's team during this period. When Dr. Gass went on furlough and Ernest Fritschi left for Madras to study for his diploma in orthopedics, later to pursue graduate work in England, Dr. Kamalam Job, one of Paul's early students who had specialized in pathology, was asked to be superintendent of Karigiri. A brilliant but devoutly humble man, he shrank from assuming the responsibility until, calling all the staff together, he assured himself of their confidence and support. Dr. Sakuntala Karat, a young woman graduate of Vellore and one of Paul's former pupils, took Ernest's place as specialized surgeon and teacher of the trainees. Dr. Selvapandian, another able young surgeon, was in charge, under Paul, of the combined departments of hand surgery and orthopedics. And Susie Koshi, wife of a staff doctor, took Chandra Manuel's place as manager of the New Life Center.

Of great help to Paul in his continued search for the right shoes for his leprosy patients was David Ward, youthful and vigorously enthusiastic physiotherapist at Karigiri. For years the two worked together, studying materials, thicknesses, pressures; especially pressures. It was easy enough to devise an apparatus for recording pressure for a patient stepping on the ground, but the ground was different from a shoe. Put a device inside a shoe, and the device itself was so thick that it made pressure. Drill holes in the shoe and put the device inside the sole, and the shoe was altered. Finding a substance thin enough and accurate enough to measure pressure without creating it or altering the shoe was another of Paul's long chases.

He started it on that furlough of 1958, consulting engineers, electricians, physiologists all over England. Finally the British Boot and Shoe Research Association told him that the Franklin Institute in Philadelphia had developed a thin pressure-sensitive transducer with a total thickness of only one millimeter. Writing post haste to the Institute, he secured some of these disks. But they had to be calibrated, and the current had to be amplified to be measured and recorded, and Paul was no electrician. The disks were of little use until John Bauman, a Mennonnite doctor from Western Reserve University, came to Vellore. A wizard at electronics, he hooked up the disks through a system of amplifiers and these again to an eight-channel cathode ray oscilloscope, a marvelous recording device recently purchased for the cardiology department. By attaching disks to the under side of a patient's foot, with every step he took they were able to get an accurate recording of pressure. It was a useful and fascinating study and added much to their skill in making shoes. Though Paul's was the original concept, it was Dr. Bauman and John Girling who did the work. Paul insisted that they be given prime credit in the article published on the project in the "British Journal of Bone and Joint Surgery," under the authorship of Bauman, Girling, and Brand.

But early in Paul's third term his work was interrupted by an event which affected the whole life of Vellore. He was working at the hospital on the afternoon when the news came, the telegram with the simple words, "Aunt Ida has gone."

It was May, 1960, hottest of all months in South India. Most of the senior staff had gone to the hills, yet the work of the hospital continued at full speed, its throng of patients undiminished, hundreds of doctors and nurses and students on duty with its daily routine.

Within minutes the news was everywhere. Paul could feel the sudden hush. Little groups of staff gathered here and there, but not to talk. There seemed nothing to say. Though they had expected this moment, for Dr. Ida had been in her ninetieth year and for a long time feeble, now that it had come there was an instinct to be together, to suffer as a family. They felt as brothers and sisters feel when a mother has passed away. Aunt Ida was the personal link that bound together every member of staff, every patient and student. The surgeon pausing in the middle of his operation felt exactly the same emotion as the girl who was polishing the sterilizer.

A few moments more, and the town had the news. Though few of its nearly two hundred thousand busy, jostling, roistering inhabitants knew her personally, there were few whose lives she had not touched. Men she had brought into the world stopped work and became silent. Women whose lives she had saved lifted corners of their *saris* to wipe their eyes. Stores were closed, shops shuttered, the bazaars deserted. Buses stopped running. As Paul walked along the street among the crowds hurrying to the hospital, he passed the *maidan* where some high school boys were playing football. He saw somebody run onto the *maidan* and gather the boys into a whispering group. The game stopped, and the boys quietly dispersed.

All that night a car traveled from Kodaikanal, bringing Dr.

Ida's body to Vellore. All night also loving hands were preparing an open carriage built on a trailer, making it lovely with drapes and fresh flowers. There was no public hall or church in Vellore that would begin to contain the crowds, so two services were held, one in the open court in front of the hospital, the other in the Church of South India's Central Church in the town. Shouldered by a group of doctors and visible to all who lined the streets, according to Indian custom, Dr. Ida began her last journey. Her face needed no artifice. The calm sweetness of love that had animated her in life continued unchanged in the deep peace of her last sleep.

As the procession began the two-mile walk to the cemetery by way of the church, nurses and students led the way singing. Doctors, technicians, and all hospital workers who could be spared followed. Then came the masses, crowds such as only India can produce—Vellore's leading citizens, shopkeepers, ricksha-pullers, artisans, laborers, Hindus, Muslims, sweepers, beggars—and not just from Vellore but from every town and village within traveling distance. Tears flowed. Hands, thousands of them, were lifted palm to palm or stretched out in an attempt to touch the carriage, as for sixty years they had reached to touch the hem of her dress. In the little cemetery itself the crowds almost caused a crisis, pouring through the gates, over the walls, even filling the trees. As Paul listened to the tributes, the ringing promises of scripture, most of them spoken not by preachers but by practitioners, he felt sadness transmuted into exaltation. This was an hour of triumph and thanksgiving, not of mourning.

"What a life!" he thought with reverent humility. "And what an ending to it! Oh, to be so completely loving!"

But it was not ended, of course. It was just beginning. Even as flowers showered into her grave, filling it to the brim, even as the doctors and nurses turned back to their duties in wards, laboratories, operating rooms, classrooms, clinics, eye camps, rural centers, Roadsides, one could feel the quickening of her spirit. In life she had had but one pair of skilled hands, one pair of swift, tireless feet, one loving heart. Now she had thousands.

21

This year of the passing of Dr. Ida marked a new era for Paul as well as for Vellore. From now on the shuttle was to flash faster and faster, the warp threads restrung to span all the major oceans and continents. He was away from home so much in subsequent months that his family almost disowned him.

"Is there company staying with you now?" one of the children was asked.

"No," the child replied, and then amended: "Oh, yes, there is. Daddy's there."

In July, Paul left Vellore for Geneva, where he had been invited by the World Health Organization to spend three weeks as a full-time consultant on leprosy and reconstructive surgery and rehabilitation, writing leaflets for use in the United Nations health program throughout the world. They decided to make a sort of vacation out of the trip, and Margaret went too. Added to her excitement over the holiday was the anticipation of seeing Christopher and Jean for the first time in two years, for they were going first to England. Somehow it did not occur to her how much they would have changed. Arriving with Paul in Victoria Station, she looked eagerly about for the same sized boy and girl they had left two years before. Presently she heard a deep voice at her elbow.

"Pardon me. Haven't we met some place before?"

She stared speechless, unable to establish the slightest connection between the tall, dignified young man and the reedy, awkward adolescent with the soprano voice. Paul's immediate reaction was to put his briefcase down on the platform and stand on it, so he could continue to talk down to his equally tall son.

In Jean the changes were less obvious but perhaps even more profound. With relief they noted that the injured arm gave every appearance of normal function. Though pathetically glad to see her parents, she had learned through bitter experience to do without them. The shell of aloofness behind which she had managed to hide her hurt and confusion was hard to break. Margaret could feel its resistance as her arms enfolded the still childish figure, a change even more significant than its gently budding adolescence. The two years when her child had needed a mother most, thought Margaret with a pang, and she had been half a world away! Would she ever be able to atone for their loss?

They purchased a car in England, and took both it and the children with them to the continent. They had a wonderful week of vacation traveling together in the Swiss mountains before settling in Geneva, where Paul spent his days in concentrated writing and consultation on the United Nations assignment. In late August he went to the United States to attend the Eighth World Congress of the International Society for the Welfare of the Disabled.

"You must come to America for this Congress," Mary Verghese had written him. "It's very important. I can't tell you why, but you must come."

Paul had intended to go anyway, since he had been invited to read a paper. One of the first persons he saw on arriving at the Waldorf Astoria Hotel, the meeting place of the congress, was Mary, sitting composedly in her wheelchair.

"Mary!" he exclaimed in delight, then, noting that she seemed to be alone, "How did you get here? Who brought you?"

"Nobody," she replied with calm competence. "I came alone. The people in the hospital were all busy, so I went out and hailed a taxi."

He chuckled appreciatively. "Mary, you're a wonder. Next thing you'll be telling me you're planning a trip to the top of the Empire State Building."

"I've already been," she replied. "Yesterday, just to prove I could manage alone today, I took a taxi and went on a tour of the United Nations building."

Human courage! marveled Paul. What couldn't it accomplish when wedded to a deep religious faith and a concern for other human beings!

"You probably know by now," said Mary, her dark eyes sparkling, "why I wrote you that you *must* come."

Paul made a face. He did know. He was to be a recipient of the Albert Lasker Award, one of medicine's highest honors, three of which were to be presented at this World Congress. While he despised all such personal plaudits, he was glad to endure it for the sake of the enormous impetus it would give the cause. For the first time in the history of the congress, leprosy was being recognized as one of the primary areas for work in world rehabilitation.

"Today we talk of rehabilitation for peace," said Dr. Howard Rusk, president of the world congress, welcoming the four-thousand rehabilitation workers from seventy nations. "Here is a great human tool more powerful even than the harnessed atom, because it brings new skills to produce, and new hope into the hearts of men.

"Much has been done, especially in the past decade, to develop rehabilitation programs for the paralyzed, the amputee, the cardiovascular and pulmonary cripple. But many of the needs of the disabled throughout the world are still unmet. For example, it is estimated that there are more working hands in the world disabled from Hansen's disease alone than by all the other diseases and disabilities known to medicine, including polio and nerve injuries."

The Lasker Award, donated by Albert Lasker, an American advertising man who donated all his fortune to promote the cause of health and rehabilitation, is given each year, but since the congress is held only once in three years, three awards are given together. The other two recipients in 1960 were the minister of health of Norway and Mary Switzer, director of the office of vocational rehabilitation of the U.S. Department of Health, Education, and Welfare whose friendship and support gained at that meeting Paul found of tremendous help in the years that followed.

The awards were presented at a huge banquet, with the three recipients on exhibition at a high table. Each received a silver statue representing the Winged Victory of Samothrace. Paul's was inscribed:

THE 1960 ALBERT LASKER AWARD
OF THE
INTERNATIONAL SOCIETY FOR THE WELFARE OF CRIPPLES
PRESENTED TO
PAUL W. BRAND, M. B., F.R.C.S.
FOR OUTSTANDING LEADERSHIP AND SERVICE IN THE
FIELD OF REHABILITATION

In that same month, August 1960, his work in leprosy was given another forward thrust by the publication of an article in the "Saturday Evening Post" by Steven M. Spencer, a writer who had visited Vellore on a tour of Christian medical missions in the preceding year. The article was titled, "Banishing the Horror of Leprosy."

But of even greater importance to the cause was a development which took place during the meeting in September of the World Commission on Research in Rehabilitation, which Paul attended as a leprosy consultant. At the instigation of Dr. Howard Rusk, a World Committee on Leprosy Rehabilitation was formed, uniting all the leprosy and rehabilitation organizations of the world in an attempt to study and solve their common problems. As a result of this committee's future research and recommendations Vellore and Karigiri were to become a pattern for similar centers of training in areas covering much of the world.

During subsequent weeks Paul gave lectures as a visiting professor at the University of Pittsburgh, where Dr. William L. White, who had been such a helpful and interested visitor at Vellore, was professor of plastic surgery. In October, Paul was invited to address a meeting of the American Society of Plastic and Reconstructive Surgery held in Los Angeles.

Three guest speakers had been invited to this meeting. One, Sir Archibald McIndoe, had died of a coronary before the program was printed. The other two were Sir Harold Gillies and Paul. Just as Paul was taking the plane from Denver to Los Angeles, he received news that Sir Harold Gillies also had died. "And then there was one," Paul thought, parroting the grim humor of the "Ten Little Indians."

As the plane crossed the Rocky Mountains it suddenly hit an air pocket, gave a sickening lurch, and plummeted.

"Well," thought Paul, "this makes it unanimous."

He was neither frightened nor especially disturbed. He had never considered length of life important, only quality. In his book, dying was not something to be made much of, or prolonged. Once he had been talking with another doctor who was avoiding butter for fear of a coronary, and Paul had observed that it might be rather a good way to die. Then why not a plane crash? Quick and easily accomplished. Paul had a private agreement with one or two of his doctor friends whom he trusted, that if he was dying from old age or some incurable disease, there would be no intravenous infusions or oxygen pumpings or similar life-prolonging devices. He could raise no enthusiasm for heart pacemakers, new kidneys, and such, designed to bolster the energies of a worn-out body for a few extra months or years. Jesus had not been concerned with how long people lived, only that they should live a full life, body, soul, and spirit.

But of course it was a relief when the plane leveled off, regained its momentum, and again mounted. Life was good, and he still had work to do. Besides, someone should speak to those plastic surgeons.

He did, showing a film and some slides with his speech, and the procedure went over with what he called a "tremendous bang." The surgeons were a keen group of experts, intensely inquisitive about new developments in their field, and they were thrilled with the challenge of leprosy. After the meeting, a group of leading plastic surgeons got together under the leadership of Dr. William White to discuss ways by which they could contribute their knowledge and skill. As a result, a program was developed in cooperation with the Vellore Christian Medical College which was to be of inestimable benefit to all concerned. The group organized itself into a Vellore Club, with the idea that each surgeon who agreed to the plan should take three months away from his work, visit Vellore in his turn, and thus maintain a continuity of plastic surgery, both teaching and practice, at the college and hospital.

The unusual success of the program in the years that followed was a result of the disciplined way in which it was planned and carried out. Only top men in the profession were sent, often the chiefs of plastic surgery in their hospitals. The three-month period was considered no holiday but a session of intensive work. Tours were encouraged at either end of the trip, but once a man arrived in Vellore all thought of holiday must be foregone. And the continuity should be maintained for at least two years.

When these men first volunteered to come they intended to pay all their own expenses. All were willing to sacrifice something for the cause. But as the program developed, their expenses were paid by arrangement with the office of vocational rehabilitation of the Department of Health, Education and

Welfare of the United States. The results were astonishing. Many advances were made in the Vellore operative techniques. A whole generation of postgraduate surgical trainees and undergraduate students were enriched by a great series of lectures and demonstrations from a remarkable group of leading experts.

The program did not terminate after the suggested two-year period. In January, 1965, it was still in operation with a dozen eminent plastic surgeons having contributed their service. Nor were the benefits by any means one-sided. Few American hospitals could begin to provide the variety of experience afforded a plastic surgeon facing the problems of India.

Before leaving California, Paul received some bad news. The Gandhi Memorial Leprosy Foundation, which had supported the New Life Center for several years, was to withdraw its support at the end of that calendar year. Though the administrators of the fund were still strongly sympathetic with Paul's work, they felt that their money should support projects benefiting a larger number of people. Two days later, still disheartened by this news, Paul was speaking in Mother Eaton's home church in Pasadena. After the meeting some representatives of the International Gospel League, to which Mother Eaton had belonged and which had for some years been helping to support Paul's mother's work, suggested to Paul that they would like to give something in Mother Eaton's memory.

"You may have to support our New Life Center," Paul remarked ruefully. "Our funds are being withdrawn."

Before he reached India he received a letter from Howard Lewis, the league's director, saying that the organization would assume support of the Center from January 1. A fitting memorial to the woman whose tiny savings had brought the small cluster of whitewashed huts into being! The new monthly donation was adequate to maintain twenty boys, finance the small hospital, pay two instructors in handcrafts, provide a cook, and relieve the worries of Susie Koshi, its dedicated director, who served without pay. There was not a day's lapse in funds for the work's support.

Back in Europe Paul made another contact which was to prove of great benefit to his leprosy work. Julia Sharp, the energetic secretary of Friends of Vellore in England, had arranged for him a trip to Stockholm, where he was the guest of

Rådda Barnen, the Swedish "Save the Children Fund," and also of the Swedish Red Cross and other charity organizations. At a small reception dinner where Paul described the opportunities for leprosy work, it was decided that the Swedish Red Cross should be the organization to participate in the Vellore program. His host, Mr. Olaf Stroh, who was not only keenly interested in rehabilitation but surprisingly well informed about Vellore, had apparently engineered this in advance.

Mr. Stroh persuaded his committee to give the Christian Medical College an outright grant of three hundred thousand *krone* for an operating room and housing for workers and trainees. Then he began implementing an idea which was to be known as the Swedish Red Cross Project, a program of domiciliary treatment and control of leprosy in the whole of a *taluk,* containing perhaps two hundred thousand people, combined with an attempt to bring rehabilitation to the patients in their own homes and also to provide industries and factories where disabled patients could find employment. The whole project was to be under the guidance of the Schieffelin Research Sanatorium in Karigiri. In years to come this project, together with staff members provided and financial assistance given to the work of the Karigiri hospital, was to be of inestimable value to the leprosy program at Vellore and later to be a model for a leprosy training center in Ethiopia. The friendship with Olaf Stroh, renewed on many future contacts, was by no means the smallest dividend Paul derived from that visit to Sweden.

But perhaps the most satisfying feature of the whole trip came after Paul's and Margaret's return to England, where, after Paul preached in his old church in St. John's Wood, Jean was baptized. Once more they left the children, not without qualms but with the assurance that the young fledglings had learned, if not to fly, at least to flutter about with tolerable confidence.

The trip had cost them participation in the most important celebration of Vellore's jubilee year. With the president of India, Dr. Rajendra Prasad, in attendance at the big August observance, the corner stones of two new buildings, a school of nursing and much needed men interns' quarters, had been laid. A living and ever growing memorial to its founder, the institution was constantly thrusting new tendrils into India's soil with all the vigor of a healthy banyan tree. Of its seven hundred thirty-five doctors, nurses, and technicians the great majority were India's own sons and daughters, working harmoniously with fifty overseas staff members from a half dozen countries. Its seven hundred ninety-five students—in medicine, nursing, pharmacy, pathology, radiology, public health, and other clinical laboratory services—represented the cream of India's youth. For every fifty medical students admitted, eleven hundred had applied. Its graduates were in demand in leading hospitals all over the country. In the year just ended its healing ministry had exceeded all previous records. In addition to its sixteen thousand in-patients and over two hundred and fifty thousand out-patients, over seventy-eight thousand had been treated at Roadside clinics and eye camps and nearly fifty-five thousand by the public health nursing unit. A huge growth to spring from the tiny seed planted by one woman in a little ten by twelve dispensary just sixty years before!

But Paul and Margaret did not miss all the celebrations of that jubilee year. A huge party was held in the assembly hall in honor of their return, especially in due recognition of Paul's recipience of the Lasker Award. Patients came from Karigiri, from the New Life Center, from Kavanur, the rural health center for leprosy patients. The staff and students presented an entertainment. The leprosy patients had prepared a program. Dramatic episodes depicted various events in Paul's life. He was laden with garlands, lauded with speeches couched in all the wordy extravagance of which Indian verbal genius is capable. Amid it all he sat in the front row, his hands at his head, embarrassed, overwhelmed, inexpressibly humble.

For Paul the crowning feature of that eventful year, 1960, was the Scientific Meeting on Rehabilitation in Leprosy, held in Vellore for ten days in November. It was sponsored by the World Health Organization, the Leonard Wood Memorial Foundation, the International Society for Rehabilitation of the Disabled, and the Vellore Christian Medical College. James Doull, Director of the Leonard Wood Foundation, was its organizer and chairman. The mere holding of the conference was a tremendous triumph for Paul and his team. For years they had been beating a big drum, proclaiming that certain things were so, while the experts had shaken their heads, asked cautious questions, commented skeptically, "That I'd have to see to believe." Now some of them had a chance to see.

The people invited fell into three groups: experts in leprosy, experts in surgery, and others who had actually combined surgery with work in leprosy. Many of the experts in surgery had never seen leprosy cases, and many of the leprosy experts had never seen any attempt at reconstruction. So it was a wonderfully impartial jury of professionals.

Each day a different subject was discussed: deformity patterns, eyes, hands, feet, lack of sensation. Many pre- and postoperative cases were shown. The detailed records compiled over the years were available for inspection and assessment. How thankful Paul was for the meticulous record keeping of Dr. Gusta Buultgens and the research assistants who had followed her! The surgeons from America and the United Kingdom confessed that they had never seen records of hand surgery kept in such detail. Every hand operated on through the years had had six photographs taken in standard positions before operation and another six after operation, and again a further six at each follow-up stage. Thus some hands had had as many as thirty-six photographs providing a dramatic documentation of the results of surgery or of physiotherapy, or in some cases of misuse and damage.

Shoes of various kinds were also exhibited. The outstanding feature of this session was the presentation of shoes designed for the same problems independently at three different centers. All incorporated the same principles: a rigid sole with a rocker bottom and soft insole.

For Paul one of the most pertinent discussions was on the classification of deformities. The question was asked, "How many leprosy patients are disabled by the disease?" Paul quoted a certain percentage.

"Too high," one leprologist objected. "Our figures show no more than twenty-five per cent."

Paul explained that at Vellore they regarded people as partially disabled if their hands and feet were anaesthetic."

The experts protested. "But you can't call that disability. Why, all sorts of leprosy patients have *that*."

Paul looked across at Guy Pulvertaft, one of England's leading hand surgeons. "Mr. Pulvertaft, I'd like to ask a question. Suppose there came to you in Derbyshire a working man who had had an accident in which the nerves of sensation in his hands had been divided, so that they were completely without feeling but still had normal motor power, at what percentage of disability would you grade him?"

Pulvertaft replied, "In England we grade anaesthetic hands with normal motor power as a hundred per cent disability."

There was an audible gasp from the leprosy experts. If he had said twenty-five per cent, they would have been surprised. Because they had lived all their lives among patients where anaesthesia was a normal condition, it had never occurred to them that this might be classified as disability. They had assumed that patients were unable to get jobs simply because of public prejudice. It was a startling and illuminating moment, a meeting of two different worlds. In their conclusions the group unanimously agreed that sensory loss should be considered a major disability.

Probably the strongest recommendation made by the conference was that leprosy research should no longer be carried out merely in institutions confined to leprosy and by leprosy specialists without the assistance of experts in other fields. It should be studied and treated along with other diseases in centers where a wide range of medical scientists would be available. The meeting was far more than a vindication of the Vellore team's achievements in research and surgery. It was a major victory in the long struggle to remove the age-old curse of leprosy and place it in the category of other crippling diseases, subject to the same scientific research, the same surgical techniques, the same possibilities of rehabilitation.

22

During this whole eventful year Paul's family had been sadly neglected.

"We'll have a wonderful Christmas," he promised the children by way of atonement, "the best one you ever had."

They decided to spend Christmas with Granny up on the Kolaryans. The trip itself was an adventure, the one-hundred-fifty mile ride in the Vanguard to Salem, then twenty miles farther across the plain to the foot of the mountains, using a borrowed jeep because the Vanguard was not built to clear the rocks in the road; finally the fifteen mile trip up the mountains. Granny had sent her little hill pony, her own favorite conveyance, also two small *dholies*, to ease the climb, especially the first steep miles of the ascent, but much of the way the older children preferred climbing on foot with their father. As they encountered the welcome cooler air at the three to four thousand foot height, eyes brightened, lungs expanded, and holiday excitement mounted. Finally came the arrival at Granny's little settlement, with rows of her schoolboys shouting and singing a welcome, waving banners of colored paper hoisted on long bamboo sticks.

Excitedly the children exhibited to Granny what was to be the central feature of this most wonderful Christmas of their lives, a fine plump turkey bought in Madras, stuffed and roasted on the plains and borne tenderly up the mountain, needing only a final heating. It was a fine turkey, Granny agreed. They would have it for the evening meal. At noon there would be rice and curry, a big *tamasha*, served out of doors to all the workers and their families. The children swallowed their disappointment at the delay, ate sparingly of the fiery rice and curry, and waited impatiently for the day's major feature.

Paul did not find the hours hard to fill. He was busier than on many days in the hospital, for Granny had a bevy of patients on hand for him to diagnose and treat. Karuninasan was again without proper shoes, this time not because they were put away for Sundays but because he had worn them through. Carefully Paul fashioned for him a pair of rocker shoes using material and implements at hand, a few bits of wood, his jackknife and a field sickle. He was never happier than when he was obliged to manufacture something out of next to nothing. The shoes finished and strapped firmly on the poor stumps of feet, Karuninasan was patiently instructed in their proper use. He must be especially careful when walking on uneven ground, not to let the foot turn, and he must *always* wear them. Karuninasan nodded vigorously. By now he was an apt pupil. Later he took Paul to see a fellow hillsman with an axe wound which he had kept clean and bandaged and which was healing beautifully. For Paul, if not for the children, the afternoon was all too short. But evening came, the oil lamps were lighted, and enticing odors drifted from the dark narrow back room of Granny's small house.

"Now," the children told each other with sighs of satisfaction, "it will really be Christmas."

But they had reckoned without Granny. First of course there must be the usual evening *jebbum*, prayer, with the teachers and their families. They came crowding into the little screened porch, faces beaming, and settled themselves on strips of matting. Always fervent and eloquent in *jebbum*, at Christmas Granny overflowed with her favorite "Praise the Lords!"

"*Stotherum, stotherum, stotherum!*"

The prayers went on and on, the flame in the small hurricane lantern flickering across the dark, intent faces. Then came Christmas carols, first in Tamil, then many more in English, all accompanied by a rhythmic clapping of hands. Pauline fell asleep, Patricia nodded, Estelle yawned openly. Margaret tried vainly to hush Mary's penetrating whispers. Paul had visions of the beautiful turkey slowly shriveling.

Suddenly the screen door was pushed open. Six rough village men in loincloths entered carrying a pole between them, a blanket knotted to the pole. Dropping it to the floor, they unknotted the blanket, and out rolled a woman, eyes staring, mouth open, lips dry and cracked.

"Back!" ordered Granny in a strident voice, pushing the men aside.

Before Paul could reach the woman to find out if she was living or dead, Granny had located the feeble pulse and diagnosed the ailment with uncanny accuracy.

"Typhoid. Dehydration." It was a statement, not a question. "Water!" she shouted to one of her helpers. "No, no, bring me some buttermilk. It's more nourishing."

A bowl of buttermilk was brought, with a spoon. Kneeling on the floor, Granny cradled the woman's head on her lap and, holding her face tenderly to one side, began spooning a few drops of fluid into her cheek, encouraging her with a constant flow of softly spoken Tamil to swallow it. Though the woman seemed completely unconscious, her throat did appear to move in little swallowing motions. If Granny increased the dosage to a whole spoonful, the woman would choke, so she just sat there, dribbling the liquid between the lips drop by drop, talking softly, apparently oblivious to all else.

"She'll keep at it all night," thought Paul.

He looked around the circle of lamplit faces, and had a queer sense of unreality. Turning to the children, he knew they felt the same way. The strangeness of the scene was reflected in their wide staring eyes: the rough tribesmen with their black torsos and long bare legs, the squatting figures huddled against the dark, the woman who to all appearances was dead. He caught Margaret's worried glance and returned to reality. Ideas began to click. Children . . . typhoid . . . Christmas . . . turkey . . . He touched Granny on the shoulder.

"Mother," he said very gently, "don't you think perhaps since this is Christmas we could have some Christmas turkey with the children and let someone else give this woman her fluid?"

She turned on him a look of absolute fury. "How *dare* you, Paul! How dare you talk about turkey when there's a woman here dying! Can't you see she's *dying*?" And back she went to dribbling the buttermilk down the woman's throat.

Paul looked at Margaret, Margaret looked at the children, and both nodded. Quietly she sidled out of the room with the children, took them into the little dining room, and there by the light of a tiny, smoky hurricane lantern and with almost no utensils they dismembered the turkey. After the children had eaten their little Christmas dinner, they crept off to bed.

Much later Paul was able to persuade Granny that perhaps there were some competent people in the group who could take her place for a bit, and she consented to eat a few scraps of turkey, then went straight back to the woman. Paul also persuaded her that with the children in the house it would be better to take her elsewhere, so a fire was built on the floor of a new schoolhouse not yet in use. The woman was laid beside the fire with someone constantly to tend her. In the morning she was alive and much better. Paul would have thought in terms of chloramphenicol and other special drugs for typhoid, which could not possibly have been secured in time. But Granny, with her tremendous concern and her instinct for the simple but right remedy, had saved a human life. The children's disappointment was the only casualty.

"Mummie, have we *had* Christmas?" one of them asked the next day.

Yet, looking back, they were to recognize it as a Christmas far more relevant to the original than the usual tinsel and gift-wrapped variety. In a setting almost as simple and poor as the stable of Bethlehem they had actually seen "love come down at Christmas," express itself in action. It was an experience they would never forget.

Less than two months after his return from the United States for the WHO conference in Vellore Paul was off again for the States, this time to keep an engagement as guest speaker for the American Society for Surgery of the Hand, meeting in Miami in January, 1961. It was an enjoyable episode, resulting in many new contacts, and, like the Los Angeles meeting with the plastic surgeons, was another major step in acquainting American medical personnel with the general concept of leprosy surgery and rehabilitation. To Paul the striking and almost incredible feature of the trip was the society's willingness to fly him halfway around the world and back merely to give a twenty minute address on "Mobility versus Stability in the Thumb." It meant that the speech cost them considerably more than one hundred dollars a minute!

His constant comings and goings were a source of worry and tension to everybody but himself. He refused to let his habitual equanimity be disturbed by late trains, faulty car mechanisms, Indian red tape, tight plane schedules. It was often Mrs. Furness, his secretary, whose blood pressure rose.

"Now, Mrs. Furness, what time must I be at the Madras airport?" Paul would inquire. Learning the hour, he would operate to the last possible moment, fill the car with passengers, and dictate to his secretary all the way to the airport.

Transportation for Paul was always a utility rather than a luxury item. Means of transit, whether plane or bullock cart, was for the purpose of getting where he needed to be as quickly as possible. He applied the same talent of ingenuity to his cars as to his operative equipment, using whatever means were at hand. The old gray Vanguard was frequently held together by bailing wire, string, or bandage plaster. It often came close to breaking the sound barrier between campus and hospital, aided in no small measure by the "Bombay" rubber bulb horn which, as is necessary on Indian roads, he squeezed and honked incessantly. His skillful surgical touch could wring from its simple mechanism inflections of wrath, disgust, polite insistence, or even a good rousing cheer.

Strangers such as the visiting plastic surgeons were almost as intrigued by his driving skills as by his operative techniques. His speed at the wheel was notorious. On one occasion Dr. Peter Randall of Philadelphia walked into the hospital lecture hall for a meeting of the surgical staff and student body to hear a visiting English surgeon speak on lymphatic obstruction. Paul's smug satisfaction over the meeting's punctual beginning was suddenly quashed by the discovery that he had forgotten to fetch the guest speaker from the college four miles away.

"You take over," he appealed to Dr. Randall. "Talk about something—anything—until I get back."

Lacking more constructive ideas, Dr. Randall began taking wagers on how long it would take Paul and his Vanguard to complete the eight-mile round trip through some of the most congested streets of Vellore. Knowing Paul, some of the audience made wild guesses, but to their startled amazement Paul beat them all. They were even more amazed that the guest was not stricken speechless.

The year introduced by the Miami trip brought to the Brands one particularly exciting link with the West. On her tour of India, Queen Elizabeth II was coming to Madras. The impending event aroused great excitement in Vellore since many of the staff were from Commonwealth countries. All of the British couples except the Brands received special invitations to the big reception. Paul and Margaret, more relieved than disturbed by the apparent oversight, derived great amusement from their British friends' concern over securing formal dress. Since most of the women wore *saris* to evening affairs, all were short of clothes except for a few who had just returned from furlough and had some items not too outdated. There was a tremendous flurry of trying on and borrowing of dress suits and dresses, as well as shoes, gloves, and other accessories.

Suddenly, just before the reception, an urgent note came to the Brands from the high commissioner's office in Madras. "Are you coming?"

Paul telephoned back. "No, we don't plan to come. We have had no invitation."

"No invitation! But you're to be presented to the Queen!"

"Well," replied Paul calmly, "we'll try to make it."

Any pleasure they might have felt at the honor was diluted, for Margaret at least, by shock. What were they going to wear! Everything they owned which might have been suitable had been loaned out. Various friends made suggestions and produced possible solutions. First Margaret tried on a short frock. "No, that's no good. Impossible!" Next she tried on a long dress belonging to Dr. Ruth Myers, American bacteriologist It was about ten years old and certainly outdated, but was the best she could find. Long gloves being unobtainable, she secured a pair of short ones.

"Well, that's me all fixed up," she told Paul. "Now what about you?"

He finally borrowed a pair of black trousers from one of the students and a rather fashionable Palm Beach frock coat from Ed Van Eck. Since Ed was much larger than Paul, tucks had to be taken in the sleeves, but even then it hung on him like an elephant's hide. The student being tall and thin, the trousers were too long and too tight. Margaret was busily turning them up as they rode to Madras, accompanied by the Gaults and John Webb. Halfway there the engine died. All attempts at resuscitation failed. They pushed the car to the side of the road and waited hopefully. Presently a long distance bus came along, and the driver, contrary to custom between scheduled stops, halted. He probably suspected their destination, for he offered to take them to Madras. He turned the bus into an express service and, knowing the roads would be closed if he did not reach the city by a certain time, he made record mileage.

When they arrived in Madras, the Brands went to the home of an Indian friend, Dr. Ernest Somasekhar. The doctor had heard of Paul's clothing predicament and had asked some of his patients for assistance.

"Come with me, Paul," he said as they entered the house, "and see if one of these will do for you."

He ushered them into a bedroom. Hanging from the mosquito net bars above the beds were twelve evening suits. Paul tried them on one after the other until he found one that fitted perfectly. A stiff-breasted shirt completed the outfit. He might have issued straight from a Bond Street tailor.

About a half dozen couples were to be presented. Before the ceremony they were carefully briefed. "You mustn't grab the Queen's hand, just gently hold her fingertips as you do a full curtsey. Your name will be given to her by the master of ceremonies. She may speak to you, she may not. If she does, answer and conclude each sentence with 'Your Majesty.' If she continues the conversation, you will thereafter address her as 'Madam.' And for the duke, you will say, 'Your Highness' and 'Sir.'"

The six couples were lined up at one end of the lawn where Her Majesty would first appear. Certain that she would bungle her part, Margaret envied Paul his inimitable calm. The fact that the Queen was late, delayed by many engagements, did not add to her assurance. But at last the moment came. The sovereign arrived and stood, looking very lovely, while the band played "God Save the Queen." Paul and Margaret were the second couple to be introduced. Paul was presented first, and immediately afterward the Queen extended her hand to Margaret. Taking it gently, as directed, by the fingertips, Margaret launched into the full bend curtsey. But something went wrong. She felt herself wobbling and would have fallen had she not grabbed the Queen's hand and regained her balance. This so disconcerted her that she completely forgot about "Your Majesty" and "Madam" and "Your Highness" and "Sir." Moreover, the royal couple were so delightfully informal and friendly that the ceremonious terms would have seemed like affectation. Ordinarily she did not end every phrase with "Madam" or "Sir" when speaking to her friends!

Paul had met the duke a couple of years before, when they had spoken briefly of leprosy work.

"Oh, yes, you're the hand man, aren't you?" the Duke greeted Paul, then inquired, "Tell me, are your patients really able now to get work?"

Amazed at the man's memory, Paul picked up the conversation where it had been left two years before.

They might have been talking with two old friends, thought Margaret as the royal couple moved on. She may have been guilty of grave discourtesy or even treason, but she had no regrets. She was proud of being British.

During the summer of that same year the family was all together again, for Christopher and Jean flew to India for their long vacation. Paul met them in Bombay, and Margaret took the four younger children to Madras to meet the plane. In spite of her efforts to prepare them, they were stricken speechless when out came a tall young man and a rather buxom young lady, descending the steps sedately and moving with dignity across the apron. All that day the younger children were as polite and restrained as with strangers. But that night Chips climbed up the outside of the house from his room to the terrace where the girls were sleeping. Creeping under their beds, he soon elicited squeals of terror, then shrieks of laughter. The ice was broken. They were all one family again.

Chips' teasing propensities had been encouraged through the years by his father's example, for Paul was an inveterate teaser. For instance, there was the Christmas turkey. It was a magnificent bird, the first they had had in India. It came live, giving opportunity for long anticipation, to all except Mary, who developed a tender attachment for it.

Near Christmas Estelle announced, "The turkey's going to be killed tomorrow."

"I know," said Mary.

"Are you going to have some?"

Mary regarded her with outraged dignity. "Would you eat your best friend?"

There were at least fourteen at the meal, counting guests. Paul seemed in an unnecessary hurry to get them in place. "Come along, come along and sit down. Pile in quickly, kids, can't you?"

When everybody was seated, he lifted the cover of the large meat dish, and out leaped the cat, streaking across the table, tipping over everybody's orange juice and water, the shrieks of laughter only adding to its consternation. And of course Mary, being her father's daughter, laughed hardest of all.

But as with the boy who cried "Wolf!", there came a time when Paul's teasing boomeranged. Vellore was planning for the visit of the Honorable Rajkumari Amrit Kaur, minister of health for the Republic of India, who had agreed to dedicate a new building.

"By the way," Paul announced, "Rajkumari is going to stay with us."

Margaret looked at him, first in dismay, then in mock horror. Some more of his leg pulling! They had been having a long succession of visitors, and with the dedication every one of their guest rooms was preempted.

"Really? And where is she going to sleep?"

"Oh, well," replied Paul airily, "there's plenty of room in our bed. I can move over."

The day before the guests were to arrive Paul asked in genuine dismay, "Where *is* she going to sleep?"

She really was coming!

23

Paul was in the middle of an operation at Karigiri when he was suddenly called to the telephone. "Emergency!" he was told. "They say you must come, no matter what you're doing."

It was Susie Koshi, manager of the New Life Center. "The workshop shed, it's on fire! It's all ablaze."

The telephone in the little office across the courtyard from the workshop registered sounds of excited voices, a muffled crash as the top beam of the workshop gave way, the crack of mud pillars bursting.

"Are the boys all right?" Paul demanded.

"Yes. Rajasakran got everybody out. It started in his work-room."

"Good. Then try to save the other huts by pouring water and soaking the thatch, I'll be there as soon as I can. Tell the boys to be careful of their hands."

He hung up, rescrubbed, and returned to his operation. Since there was no one to take over, he completed it, then rushed to cover the fourteen miles to the college campus. Though the loss of the New Life Center would be a severe blow to the rehabilitation program, it was the boys he was worried about. Under the stress of excitement and fear, what damage might not be done to insensitive, fire-fighting hands!

Through the haze of smoke he saw that most of the white-washed huts were still standing. Relief was tinged with amazement. Those thatched roofs were inflammable as tinder. How had they kept the fire from spreading! The workshop was a smoking ruin, but all the other buildings were intact. As he came into the central courtyard the boys crowded around him, faces blackened and woebegone.

"It was my fault," Rajasakran admitted, almost in tears. The fire had started in one of the workrooms where plastic sheets for making microscope covers were being softened in an open oil bath over a kerosene stove. He had accidentally tipped the oil bath, and the contents had caught fire, rapidly spreading through the other inflammable material in the shed. At once he had gotten everybody out of the building and had tried to save the lathe, which he knew was the most valuable piece of equipment.

"Good boy," Paul said.

His first act was to examine the hands and feet of every one of the boys. Though all had worked feverishly, not one hand or foot had been damaged. None showed a single blister. Then calmly and reasonably Paul tried to show the boys, especially the heartbroken Rajasakran, that it was not the terrible disaster they imagined.

"There is only one thing that is really valuable in this New Life Center," he told them, "and that is the new lives themselves. It is the hands and feet that are precious. It is the courage and the faith that are all-important. Every one of you has demonstrated his courage. You have worked hard and yet in the state of emergency you have shown me that you have learned to value your hands and to protect them from fire and excessive stress. Every one of you is wiser and better able to meet an emergency than you were one hour ago." He reminded them of other blessings. There had been no breeze. There had been a shower recently, otherwise there would have been insufficient water. And perhaps it had taught them all a much needed lesson, how careful they must be in this type of work with plastics. Then he took them into the little chapel, and together they sang a hymn of thanksgiving, "Praise him, praise him!"

"It was like that story in the Bible," one of the boys wrote to Sadagopan, now employed in a leprosy sanatorium. "All I could think of was our Lord Jesus standing in the boat with his disciples in the middle of the storm and saying, 'Peace, be still.' "

Paul was more dismayed than he seemed. The workshop had

been fashioned bit by bit, with tender painstaking labor, much of it by his own hands. Some of the most satisfying hours of his life had been spent there. And it was the heart of one of his most beloved projects. He wrote to Howard Lewis about the loss, and the group in Pasadena immediately offered to replace it. The new workshop which took shape in the following months was much more substantial and fireproof, providing far more suitable housing for the expensive machinery which the increasing competence of the patients demanded. The plastic microscope covers were only one of the many new crafts which were furnishing the patients both rehabilitation and profitable employment. Besides the original jigsaw puzzles and wooden toys, they were now making many plastic articles, jars for pathology specimens, license and name plates and picture frames, as well as simple wooden furniture. The new building was finished in time for Mr. Jefcoate ("Jeff"), Paul's enthusiastic supporter from the Friends of Vellore in England, to share in its opening ceremonies on his visit to Vellore the following winter.

Paul deplored his increasing work load which deprived him of close personal contact with the New Life Center. In July 1961 he assumed added responsibilities as principal of the Medical College. He took the job with many misgivings, for he knew the difficulties of combining it with his leprosy research and teaching. And, though he had the help of able assistants, he soon found that he had underestimated the task.

Even in the minor problems of administration he encountered frustration. One of his first projects was an attempt to synchronize all clocks, those of the hospital with those of the college four miles away. The plan was to communicate the time by telephone twice a day. It lasted about a week. And the synchronization of several hundred human beings into a society of harmony and self-discipline was even more baffling. In general rules became less stringent; there was a definite move toward freedom of discussion and increased trust between students and faculty. Knowing Paul, students understood that he expected them to apply the Christian principle of concern for others in their campus and hospital relationships, and generally they cooperated. He found the clerical details of his job more irksome than its problems of discipline.

But there were some administrative details that Paul never

found irksome. These were usually connected with Vellore's constant building projects. Since 1954, when John Carman had become director of the Medical College and Hospital, Paul had worked with him closely on plans for most of the buildings, acting in fact as deputy director from 1956 until his appointment as principal. Both men were keenly interested in building and full of original ideas. Though they were not always in agreement, by hammering out their arguments and complementing and supplementing each other's ideas, they usually came up with far better plans than either could have devised alone.

In the autumn of 1954 both of them went to Beirut, accompanied by Dr. Jacob Chandy, head of neurology, and Sir Samuel Ranganathan, the Vellore council chairman. This expedition, financed by the Rockefeller Foundation, gave opportunity to study the planning of the buildings at American University and greatly influenced the plans for the new outpatient dispensary at Vellore. During Dr. Carman's furlough in 1956-57 Paul was largely responsible for the construction of this building. He worked with Jack Carman on most of the building projects during those years of the fifties and early sixties, the school of nursing, the men interns' quarters, the rural hospital, the physical medicine block, and many others.

It was astonishing how a knowledge of building had contributed through the years to his work in leprosy. For instance, there was the Cheshire Home in Katpadi. Cheshire had been a wartime ace, the only Englishman who flew with the team dropping the bomb on Hiroshima. After this his whole life had changed. He would give the rest of his life to saving, rather than destroying human beings. He decided to found homes for incurables and cripples. After establishing ten of them in England, he had come to India and opened similar havens in Bombay, Calcutta, and Kodaikanal. Here Dr. Ida had met him. There must be one in Vellore for Paul's leprosy patients! As usual, she had gotten her way. A Cheshire Home for leprosy patients, mostly those recommended by the hospital, had been established at Katpadi. Paul was asked to help plan it and, after its completion, to open it. To his intense interest, plans for a new Cheshire Home were being shown and discussed, and he was asked to examine them. The crowd gathered for the dedication were either amazed or amused to see the eminent doctor down on the floor on his hands and knees, like a child enthralled with a new toy, poring delightedly over the blueprints.

During the year of his principalship, Paul's interest in building extended to other projects as well. Occasionally there appeared on his daily calendar in his hospital office an item such as "Building committee, 5:30 p. m., home." Naturally his secretary assumed that he would need various official files and plans made ready for the meeting. He should have looked in on the "committee!" He would have seen the principal, dressed in an ancient and tattered, but beloved, pair of shorts and an old shirt, puddling about in his garden with several ecstatically happy children passing bricks down an assembly line to where a small playhouse was in process of construction.

The children having become bored with usual types of building, Paul had decided to teach them bricklaying and had bought several cartloads of bricks. At these five thirty "committee" meetings and often on Saturday afternoons the cry would be broadcast, "Come and help build!" All the children on the college compound would assemble and be assigned different duties. Their favorite area of activity, of course, was mixing the mortar. Paul's methods being educational as well as recreational, the children were thoroughly trained in the art of making corners and laying bricks.

One afternoon the principal of the Teachers' Training College came to ask Paul to give a Republic Day lecture at his college. It was an official but unannounced visit. Arriving at the house, he saw a coolie tramping about in ragged old shorts up to his knees in mud, surrounded by a horde of noisy, happy children.

"Hello," Paul greeted him. "Anything I can do for you?"

The man hesitated. "I was just wondering if Dr. Brand lives here."

"Yes. This is the Brand place."

"Would he be in this afternoon?"

"He's here," replied Paul, then at the man's look of bewilderment, "I am Dr. Brand. May I help you?"

At first the principal looked as if he had come to the wrong house and did not know what to say. Then, appreciating the humor of the situation, he smiled and explained his errand.

It was during this year of Paul's principalship that Margaret, preparing a pair of Paul's trousers for washing by the *dhobi*, noticed an official looking letter in one of the pockets. Asserting the prerogatives of an interested wife, she took it out and read it.

"It is the good pleasure of Her Majesty Queen Elizabeth II to confer upon you the honor of Commander of the British Empire . . ." Gasping, she hastily absorbed other phrases: "For promotion of good relations between the Republic of India and Great Britain," and so on and so forth.

The C.B.E.! One of the most coveted decorations bestowed by the crown, just below knighthood! And Paul hadn't even mentioned it!

"Paul, did you know this was in your pocket?" she asked at the earliest opportunity.

"Oh, yes," he replied. It might have been an invitation to a friend's dinner party. "I knew it."

"Did you answer it?"

"Yes."

"What did you say?"

He grinned. "Well, it's not my business to interfere with the Queen's good pleasure, is it?"

Though investitures were held four times a year in England, none of Paul's scheduled trips coincided with one of the dates, and the high commissioner did not often come to Madras from New Delhi. In order to be validated the honor must be conferred within a year of its pronouncement. Months passed, and the time was near expiration. On hearing that the high commissioner was not coming to Madras, Paul wrote and asked the deputy high commissioner in Madras if it would be convenient for him to call at the government office on a certain day and pick up the documents and the insignia of the order.

"Yes, do," came back the reply. "Bring your wife and come to lunch."

A happy arrangement, Paul thought. No formality, no fanfare. And he would not even need to make a special trip, for on the specified day he would be passing through Madras on his way from a meeting at Vellore's sister medical college in Ludhiana, North India.

Stopping between planes in Delhi, Paul spent a night in a second-rate hotel. Noting that his traveling suit was rumpled, and remembering his appointment in Madras, he tried, not too successfully, to put a bit of crease in the trousers. A good thing that the presentation was to be an informal affair!

Margaret was afflicted with a sudden attack of dengue, so Alison Webb met Paul at the Madras airport. She had driven from Vellore in the Vanguard with Estelle. The plane was late, and they drove directly to the government house. To their surprise they saw flags flying inside the colonnades, and the compound was full of flashy cars.

"What's this?" muttered Paul. "Have we come at the wrong time?"

It was Alison whose female intuition enlightened him. "Don't you see? It's all for *you*!"

Paul parked the battered old Vanguard among the shining limousines. He was suddenly conscious of his crumpled suit, unimproved for having been slept in on the plane. But then, he reminded himself, he was lucky to be wearing a suit! He often traveled without one. Catching glimpses of colorful *saris* and smart frocks flitting about the verandahs, Alison, with her simple summer dress and windblown hair, shrank back into the car.

"I can't go in there," she said. "Look! They're all dressed up to the nines!"

"Nonsense," returned Paul cheerfully. "If they insist on making a fuss over us, they'll just have to take us as we are."

But as they approached the front door even he was a bit disconcerted, for all the elite of Madras were there, the mayor and his wife, guests of the British Embassy, many of his own professional friends. Entering, they found the whole throng lined up for the investiture. Alison tried to hide her dishevelment behind some of the faultlessly dressed ladies, but twelve-year-old Estelle stood straight and composed in her simple cotton frock, as dignified as a young princess. Paul was proud of her.

To his intense embarrassment, a wide red carpet was rolled out, and he was told exactly where to await the entrance of the deputy high commissioner, then where to stand for the ceremony. Surreptitiously he tried to straighten his suit and tie. There was a burst of martial music, whereupon the official came down the stairs wearing all the regalia of his office, plus formal morning suit and tails. He took his place with solemn dignity. Paul was just about to start forward toward the spot

marked for him on the red carpet when his friend Dr. Somasekhar appeared at his side.

"Pardon me, Paul," the good doctor murmured in his ear,
then quietly (shades of the Delhi hotel!) removed a bedbug
from his lapel.

The deputy high commissioner was most kind. Making a
complimentary little speech and reading the citation, he
presented the insignia of the high honor: a parchment containing a statement of the citation and signed by the Queen and
the Prince, together with a gold cross bearing the facsimile
of King George and Queen Mary, attached to a ribbon to be
worn about the neck, all ornately boxed in a red leather case.
Then followed a very formal and splendid dinner, with the
deputy high commissioner, the mayor of Madras, and many
other dignified officials in attendance.

Dinner, red carpet, rumpled suit, morning dress and tails,
gorgeous frocks and *saris*, cotton dresses, citation, gold cross,
bedbug. . . . It was truly an occasion to live in one's memory.

And equally memorable for Paul was the dedication on January 5, 1963, of the new physical medicine and rehabilitation
building, one of the first institutions of its kind in all India.
The presence of Dr. Sarvapalli Radhakrishnan, President of
India, who opened the building, was testimony to the importance of the event, certainly the crowning achievement in
Vellore's fifteen years of pioneering in Paul's two major concerns, orthopedics and leprosy rehabilitation.

Like most of Vellore's constantly growing ministry, it was a
cooperative enterprise, financed by groups representing three
different nations. The basement unit, containing a modern
splint shop, was provided by the British Leprosy Relief Association. Paul had started this unit some ten years back with
only three workers. The new unit was to include fourteen
workers. During its first year in the new building it was to
contribute twenty-seven artificial limbs, four hundred and
thirty braces, and fifteen hundred and thirty-one surgical shoes
and other appliances. Its development was one of Paul's long
dreams come to fulfillment.

But the building was far more the fulfillment of Mary
Verghese's dream. Without the accident which had made
her a paraplegic it would have been years before the much
needed department could have become reality. When she

returned to Vellore from her years of postgraduate study in New York's Institute of Physical Medicine and Rehabilitation, she was qualified tentatively to head the new department. She would be fully qualified when, after two years of experience, she would return to the United States to take and pass her oral board examinations, becoming a diplomate of the American Board of Physical Medicine and Rehabilitation. The first floor of the new building, financed by the Polio Research Fund of England, with its splendid facilities for physiotherapy, occupational therapy, and vocational guidance, became the heart of a program not only for healing the disabled but for training workers in the healing skills of rehabilitation.

"We trust," Dr. Carman expressed the purpose of the new program, "it will provide facilities to set up an international training center for surgeons, physiotherapists, and others to aid in the worldwide campaign for rehabilitation and treatment of leprosy patients and in the more general application of the principles of rehabilitation for all our patients."

The second floor, to be known as the Swiss Ward, was a gift from *Emmaus Suisse*, a movement of "the poor helping the poor," started by Abbé Pierre. Anxious to help people poorer than they, the members of this group had developed a keen concern for leprosy patients. In fact, they had desired that the ward bearing their name should be used entirely for leprosy.

"No," Dr. Carman had replied to their request, "that would defeat our whole purpose. The greatest contribution we can make to the cause of leprosy in this day of changing attitudes is to make provision for its treatment unsegregated from other diseases." The Swiss group understood and agreed willingly.

In harmony with this new approach which Paul had for years been striving to implement, the Swedish Red Cross which, after his visit to Sweden in 1960 had introduced clinics in villages around Vellore, primarily for the diagnosis and treatment of leprosy, was now designating them *skin* clinics, for the benefit of all patients suffering from skin ailments, thus placing leprosy in the same category as other skin diseases. So gradually the old taboos and prejudices were being broken down.

During his third term Paul was engaged in another project of rehabilitation which was supplementing all these new undertakings. For years he had lamented the inability of the deformed and crippled of India, both leprosy patients and others, to obtain employment. Most automatically became beggars or were dependent on their families. Though the Indian people, steeped in traditions of family loyalty, cheerfully accepted this responsibility for their aged and infirm and disabled, the patients themselves were often doomed to meaningless existence. For years Paul pondered the problem. The answer, of course, was employment. Not sheltered workshops and factories, as in the West; they were too expensive for India. Nor was the New Life Center a solution, since it was really only a handicraft project. Good though it was, the output and business profit of the program would never convince industrialists of the value of employing the handicapped.

"What we need is a factory," Paul said to John Webb, "employing only the disabled, run on proper business lines and showing a profit, a showpiece center where we can invite industrialists, prove to them that handicapped labor can compete on equal terms with industry in general. But *how!*"

He talked to others, to Robert Bruce, manager of the English Electric Factory in Madras, with an English couple named Muirhead in Bangalore, he a lawyer, she an active promoter of charities. All were kindred spirits. Making themselves a committee, they formed Abilities Trust, with the four men as trustees and Esther Muirhead as secretary, and set about trying to find ways and means of starting a factory, contacting various engineers and exploring possibilities for processing different types of products. As a final step the committee approached Paul's friend Mr. Stroh and the Swedish Red Cross about the possibility of their providing capital. They were enthusiastic.

The plan became reality. A factory was built. Within a short time it was in full production, with more than fifty disabled persons employed, over half of them leprosy patients, the remainder amputees, polio paraplegics, and sufferers from other disabilities. Manufacturing typewriter parts, it became a pilot project which performed the double service of providing employment for the disabled and serving as an example to industrialists. The Swedish Red Cross also started a matchbox factory in cooperation with Swedish Match Companies in India, a village project employing many disabled people working in their homes. Because of interest in the Abilities Trust project, the Swiss Mission from the Evangelical Church established another factory in Katpadi, employing some disabled workers in the making of tools. So there sprang up a complex of rehabilitation projects about Vellore, ranging from crafts training at the New Life Center and the construction of matchboxes in cottage industries to highly skilled toolmaking.

"Not bad," commented Paul to one of his colleagues on the committee. "Our Abilities Trust has really achieved its object without spending more than the postage on the letters we've written!"

But international developments in leprosy work were even more exciting. The World Committee on Leprosy Rehabilitation had determined that the greatest need was for training centers, to serve other parts of the world as Vellore and Karigiri were equipped for serving India and Southeast Asia. In 1963 Stanley Brown toured Africa for the committee and visited Addis Ababa in Ethiopia. He recommended it as a site for such a center for all Africa.

Here the Princess Zenebene Worq, established with the help of a grant from the American Leprosy Missions and later taken over by the government Ministry of Health, was under the direction of Dr. Ernest Price, an able colleague with whom Paul had worked on his first African trip. Situated in a highly endemic area, with three thousand leprosy cases around the hospital, it offered unlimited possibilities for training and for demonstration of a balanced leprosy and rehabilitation program under the sponsorship of the International Society for the Rehabilitation of the Disabled. Visiting Addis Ababa, Paul came away fired with enthusiasm and determined that somehow the money must be raised for a training center in Ethiopia.

As the end of his third missionary term drew to a close, he knew that he was approaching a crossroads. There were decisive choices that must soon be made. Where could he be of greatest service in the coming years? In Vellore? Others would soon be capable of taking over his work there, Ernest Fritschi in reconstructive surgery, Kamalam Job as head of pathology at Vellore and superintendent of Karigiri, and that fine husband-wife team of Benty and Sakuntala Karat, specialist physician and specialist surgeon, who were returning to Karigiri, where they had received their early training years before. In England? Certainly he should be there for the sake of the children. Traveling around the world, sharing his techniques wherever he was most needed? Family, surgery, leprosy . . . next to God, his three great loyalties! Up to now he had been able to serve all three. Must he now turn his back on one of them? And if so, which one?

Whatever the decision, the family would still be rooted deep in India. Four of his cousins were here as missionaries: John Harris, who was also working in leprosy and had spent some time at Karigiri; Ruth and Monica Harris, who ran their own small medical center in a town near Granny's mountains; Nancy Robbins, who was at Dohnavur. And then of course there was Granny herself.

At eighty-four Evelyn Brand was still living on the Kolaryans, but she was already making plans to move to the Pachas, third of the five mountain ranges to which she and Jesse had dreamed of taking the Gospel.

Though she was tough and stringy as a green withe, due to a creeping paralysis her limbs were almost totally disabled. Disdaining crutches but tolerating a pair of braces, she managed to walk slowly and awkwardly with the aid of two ill-mated bamboo sticks. But that did not keep her from traveling. On the back of her little pony, an Indian boy leading, she journeyed constantly, covering hundreds of miles, camping out in all weathers, sleeping on wood, on stone, on bare ground, living the simple life of simple people, loving them and beloved by them.

There had been a time when Paul had worried about her, had tried to persuade her to live nearer to medical help, but that time was past. He knew now that she had thought things through in detail and that death, in whatever unpleasant form it might come, was a squarely faced issue. She would far rather keep on with her work until the last moment, than to be under the best medical care in the world. God had led her all her life. She was on the hills at his command and had absolute faith that she would be given strength to carry on until he sent somebody to take up her work. She would never allow a word of praise. If she accomplished anything, it was only by God's grace.

No, Paul had no obligation to his mother except to follow the same leading of love which had been her sole guide.

24

It was wrong, Paul had told himself at fifteen, seeing what the loss of his father had done to his mother, to become so emotionally involved, to love anyone to the point of being dependent. He would never let this happen to him.

But when Margaret fell seriously ill in England soon after their arrival on furlough, he knew as never before that he *had* let it happen, and gladly. No life could be richly complete without such love and dependence, even though the cost might be pain.

During her illness he became a different person, concerned only for her welfare and happiness. He cared for her like a nurse. He went into the kitchen and cooked, spurred the reluctant children to perform household chores, did the washing, prepared beautiful trays for the sickroom. He bought her pots of chrysanthemums. When she had a birthday in June, he helped Alison Webb plan a party for her, inviting among others all the occupants of the house in Kew, Brands, Fritschis, and Webbs, thirty people in all, an affair faultless in detail from flowers to quantities of strawberries and cream, insisting on making most of the preparations himself and doing the washing up afterward.

Margaret slowly recovered from the period of extreme pain and lethargy, the probable result of her bout with dengue in India. The progressive muscular atrophy which they had feared did not develop. In June she was well enough to accompany the family on a camping trip through Europe, one stop being at Valbonne, in the south of France, a picturesque monastery taken over by a French Protestant order for the treatment of leprosy.

The Vauxhall Victor estate car was taxed to its limit of capacity with eight Brands, plus two of Christopher's school friends, as well as the weight of a trailer loaded with tents and camping equipment and baggage. Christopher's two friends soon recovered from their dazed unbelief that there could be so many girls in one family and were indistinguishable from the Brand clan. Three weeks of camping in eight sites scattered through France and Switzerland improved their French and snorkel swimming techniques, satiated their appetite for peaches, grapes, and plums, and furnished pertinent object lessons in international friendship.

It was a summer to be treasured, for with Paul's departure westward in September of 1963, it would be nearly a year and the equivalent of travel twice around the world before he would see his children again. For by now he had received appointment as fulltime director of orthopedics on the permanent staff of the Mission to Lepers, while at the same time he retained his relationship with Vellore as professor of orthopedic surgery and his advisory post as member of the World Health Organization expert panel on leprosy. He was prepared for the present to live a life divided, like all Gaul, into three parts, one in England, one in India, a third in whatever part of the world his services might be needed.

To his joy, Margaret accompanied him on the initial laps of this trip, its first destination being the International Congress of Leprology in Rio de Janeiro. In all the history of these quadrennial conferences this was the first to devote a session to surgery and rehabilitation, and not only one session but two. Paul participated in two panels, one on reconstructive surgery, the other on physical medicine and rehabilitation. Margaret, he believed, presented the best paper of the whole congress on her work in eyes.

Dr. Kamalam Job, then studying pathology under Sir Roy Cameron in London, was also with the team at Rio, and his paper, "Reaction in Leprosy," resulting from his studies at Vellore, received international acclaim. Paul was intensely proud of the poise and distinction with which this early student and long associate represented Vellore and the Mission to Lepers.

He was proud also of some of his short-term trainees such as Dr. José Árvelo. Dr. Arvelo, who had been an outstanding student when he had come to Vellore for rehabilitation study, had persuaded the Pan American Health Organization to sponsor a training seminar and establish a center, and he had started a tremendous program of leprosy rehabilitation at Caracas, Venezuela, swiftly bridging the gap between a complete lack of rehabilitation techniques and use of the most advanced patterns. As a result the World Committee on

Leprosy Rehabilitation hoped that this project in Venezuela, initiated by the P.A.H.O., might become the training center for the whole of South America.

Paul and Margaret were together during this tour of South America, later of the southern and eastern United States, where their trip was crammed with meetings, sometimes, as in New York City, six or seven speaking engagements in one day. Here for the first time Paul realized how closely his and Margaret's work synchronized. The presentations were really effective and enjoyable when they were on the platform together. He would start talking informally about hands, feet, or noses, and then move on to eyes. "Well, there's no sense in my talking about eyes," he would break off, turning to Margaret, "because here's the expert." Then Margaret would take over for awhile until she got bored, whereupon she would sit down and Paul would continue the presentation.

The long journey would have been intensely wearisome except for visits in the homes of the plastic surgeons and others who had worked with him in Vellore, stopovers with old staff members, and surprise meetings with former students now on postgraduate assignments. The first of November, Paul and Margaret had a few days together in Montreal, the last in many months, after which she went home to the children in England and he traveled west for more months of an intensive tour which would take him finally back to India.

A typical schedule, such as he followed in Canada, might include the following: He would arrive by plane sometime in the morning, to be met often by the press at the airport, then go straight to a radio or television station for interviews. There would follow a luncheon at the local medical college. In the afternoon he would probably lecture to medical students or to a seminar of doctors, then perhaps at teatime to a women's meeting, and that evening at a church service. The next day he would visit the hospital, perform ward rounds or an operation, perhaps go to lunch with a committee of the Friends of Vellore or speak at a Rotary Club. That evening there would be another church meeting. The third day he would travel again. Two days and two days and two days, one series after the other, ad infinitum. Seventy-four take-offs and landings. Only two days in the whole four months were completely free, and those had to be jealously guarded by friends, one in Philadelphia, one in Melbourne, Australia.

To Paul the most striking feature of the trip was its contrast with those of his previous furlough. Then he had been struggling to find ways of arousing public interest, to stimulate the imagination of his listeners. Now he found to his embarrassment that he was often preceded by exaggerated ideas of his and others' achievements. The questions of reporters often implied that they believed the leprosy problem was all solved!

Not that he didn't on occasion encounter apathy! Once was in Los Angeles where he was scheduled on a certain popular emcee's late, late show for a five- to ten-minute interview. Paul was the second guest on the program, and when he entered he could see that the emcee was already bored. There he sat with a huge cup of coffee which looked big enough to hold a liter. After taking a long draught, he looked Paul over with a minimum display of interest, and consulted his list. His eyebrows quirked.

"Oh? So you're leprosy, are you?"

"Yes," replied Paul.

"Well—" the emcee obviously didn't know quite how to start—"I suppose that means you treat lepers." Stifling his yawns, he continued, "Now why do they need someone like you to help them?"

"I guess you don't realize their condition," said Paul with undramatic quietness. "When people have had leprosy, even when they are cured, they have problems that hardly anybody really understands. Their deformities often put them out of a job, and even from a home and family; and some of them don't even have a cat."

The emcee blinked. "Did you say—a *cat*?"

"Yes," replied Paul. "Isn't that awful?"

The emcee looked down at his coffee cup. He picked it up and took a long drink. "All right. I'll buy it. Why is it so terrible that they haven't got a cat?"

"You wouldn't have been surprised," replied Paul, still in the same quiet voice, "if I had said that a blind man needs a dog to see with. A leprosy patient lacks skin sensation and nobody realizes what it means when you can't feel pain. You need to surround yourself with new defenses. In Indian villages the rats quickly learn that it is quite safe to take a bite from insensitive hands or feet, when a man is asleep. So a cat beside your bed takes the place of pain sensation."

The emcee set down his cup. Every trace of boredom had

vanished. "This is really terrible," he said. "Why don't we know about things like that? Maybe we can do something." He buried his face in his hands. When he looked up, his eyes were keen with interest. "I say, tell me more about your work."

So began an interview which, instead of lasting ten minutes, continued for more than half an hour.

California was the scene of another far more difficult episode. Dr. Robert Chase, chief of surgery at Stanford University and one of the plastic surgeons who had spent three months at Vellore, had arranged with the university chaplain for Paul to speak at a Stanford Sunday morning service. People from many surrounding churches had been invited. The date was November 24, just two days after the assassination of President Kennedy. On Saturday the chaplain called, much distressed. What should he do about the Sunday service? Paul also had been worried. He said at once that he thought it should be a memorial service and that his part should be canceled. The chaplain did not agree. There was to be a memorial service later on, and he thought that if some appropriate references to the calamity were made, the sermon could go on as before. Paul asked for some time to think it over. Later he called back and asked the chaplain to make the decision; he emphasized that he would be glad to take no part in the service. However, he felt that he could not merely speak briefly about Vellore. It could be either Vellore or a sermon, but he could not divide the two.

"Go ahead," the chaplain decided. "Use the time as you think best."

Sunday morning brought the additional shock of Oswald's death. Most of the audience had seen the event, live, on their television sets. Emotions were again cut raw. Arriving at the chapel, Paul found it big as a cathedral, ordinarily half filled but this morning packed to the doors. There were at least three thousand people, students, many faculty members including the university president, all the latter robed for a processional. Paul suddenly felt like a stranger in a house of mourning, the one foreigner in a situation that was preeminently national. And yet here he was, the speaker! What enormous effrontery! It was as if a passing tourist had offered to light the funeral pyre of Mahatma Gandhi.

To make matters worse, in the middle of the service after the preliminary solemnities, the chaplain got up, obviously nervous, and began making apologies to the congregation. This presentation had been arranged long ago, he explained, and he had not felt able to cancel it. When Paul mounted the steps of the high pulpit, he wished miserably that he had insisted on canceling the appointment.

But as he stood looking down into the sea of upturned faces, hurt, bewildered, questioning, something happened to him. This great mass of people were like sheep who had lost their shepherd. They were waiting to be led. Perhaps they needed what only an outsider like himself could give. Never had he prayed so earnestly for guidance. He read to them from I Corinthians 12, about the body of Christ, and gave out his text: "If one member suffers, all suffer together."

"It does not seem appropriate," he began, "that a person from overseas should be leading you in this service. And yet I wish I could make you understand how all over the world, in churches, in chapels, in halls of assembly, in homes, everywhere, people are grieving with you in your loss. Sometimes it is in these moments of deep distress that we are drawn closer together as Christians, as human beings, and are made to feel our oneness."

He told them about the beautiful octagonal stone chapel at the Vellore Medical College, open on all sides to blooming flowers, to a vista of mountains and changing skies; how at this very moment, for India was many hours away and the chapel service was held at six thirty in the evening, students were gathered on mats on the polished stone floor, sharing in the sorrow of their Christian friends halfway around the world. He told about the day Dr. Ida had died, an American living in a far country, how within a few hours of the news of her passing the whole life of Vellore had come to a standstill, shops had closed, buses stopped running, sports ended, and everybody had started moving toward the hospital until the roads were thronged and the gates jammed, in an amazing spontaneous demonstration of affection for a little old lady who had spent most of her ninety years in loving, healing, serving them. And because of her love and concern, even though she was a foreigner, they regarded her as one of themselves—no, more than that, loved and revered and almost worshiped her.

"This fellow feeling in times of suffering," Paul continued, "is really a sign of corporate life. If a person doesn't feel his hand or foot when it is injured, we speak of that foot or hand as dead. It's the pain that makes us realize that the hand or foot belongs to us."

Easy then to move to the plight of leprosy patients, whose loss of corporate pain and sensitivity was one of the tragic features of the disease; easy to tie up his story of leprosy and the suffering mood of the day into the theme of the oneness of the Body of Christ, the church of God all over the world!

But to Paul the important discovery was not only the success of his message. It was that within a few sentences of starting his theme he felt in the huge audience a tremendous uprush of warmth and affection and solidarity. It was heartwarming afterward to hear the expressions of gratitude and affection. Never in his memory had he received such a response to a sermon. It was as if he had started out being a stranger in the house and had finished by becoming one of the family.

He flew on westward, visiting leprosy work or telling about it in a variety of places: Australia, New Guinea, Sarawak, Thailand. Australia presented as grueling a schedule as most of the American cities. In Sydney alone he gave ten radio and five television interviews.

"They seemed to think I was some sort of celebrity," he wrote Margaret with genuine amazement.

One of the greatest joys of this Southeast Asian tour was the constant reunions with trainees who had been at Vellore and Karigiri, seeing them in their national habitats, struggling to establish new methods of leprosy treatment. It was exciting to go through these foreign areas replete with strange faces and languages, then suddenly to see well known features which he had faced time after time across the operating table, hear a familiar voice which had joined week after week in the give and take of the hand clinics. It had been equally true, equally exciting, on his previous visits to Hong Kong, the Philippines, Ceylon, Africa.

In Sarawak there were Dr. Kreshowski, a Polish refugee with a Scottish medical degree, now working in the British colonial service, who had taken his hand surgery training at Vellore; and Generawa Binmok, a native of Sarawak, who had trained in physiotherapy at Karigiri. Both were doing an excellent job.

In Thailand Dr. Praphon and Dr. Ake Thard Tong, who had each been in Vellore for a year, were working in a leprosy hospital which, when Paul had visited it six years before, had exuded an atmosphere of decay and perpetual death, no operating room, no facilities for any sort of rehabilitation. Since then the King of Thailand had provided money to build an operating theater and a rehabilitation ward, with commencing industries, and, though the unit was in its infancy, at least cases were being restored to physical normality. Paul exulted in the sight of these boys of his "doing their stuff." In Manoram there was a fine team of missionary doctors and nurses starting work with leprosy patients.

But the trip to New Guinea was the high point of the tour. The government had asked him to visit the country to make recommendations about leprosy rehabilitation work, and the Mission to Lepers was anxious to start activities there. Paul found himself in Port Moresby, with about five days to cover the whole territory of Papua and report on its leprosy situation.

It was a thrilling, incredibly beautiful, often hair-raising experience. The country was startlingly wild and rugged, its mountains seeming to leap out of the ground in jagged peaks. Since there was no road to most of the places he wanted to visit, the government placed a small, one-engined Cessna plane at his disposal, and he made the tour in company with Dr. Roderique, the Ceylonese local leprosy officer, Dr. Clezy, an Australian surgeon who was to come to Vellore for training as soon as plans for the work were developed, and a young Australian pilot, who nonchalantly took off from a small airport at Mount Hagen, coaxing the laboring plane up over the huge crags, then diving down the other side of them, landing the party on one after the other of tiny little airstrips in different parts of the highlands. These airstrips seemed to be shaved off flat from the tops of the mountain ridges.

It was soon obvious that the pilot must not only know the terrain like a map craftsman but also be an expert in recognizing up and down air drafts, even before he encountered them. Otherwise he would smash his plane on a mountain peak. On one trip, to cross a mountain range, he was heading for a little patch of clear sky on a ridge when the clouds lowered and blocked the tiny opening. In a gorge at the time, the pilot had to make a one hundred and eighty degree turn to retrace his way. By this time the gorge had become so narrow that

Paul was sure they were going to scrape the tops off the trees. In fact, after they landed he actually looked at the wheels of the plane to see if any leaves had become lodged there. Having once crashed in a one-engine plane and sworn he would never travel in one again, Paul and his habitual equanimity received some severe jolts. However, before the trips were finished he had developed considerable confidence in the young pilot, especially after an exceptionally hair-raising episode.

There was one very short airstrip where there was said to be a continuous updraft of air coming up the side of the mountain to the very edge of the strip.

"If you aim for it in the ordinary way," the pilot gently prepared them for the coming ordeal, "just as you get to it you get lifted and overshoot the runway. Therefore you have to aim as if you were going to hit the mountain, and then just before you would have hit it, this updraft takes you and lifts you onto the runway."

Remembering previous nerve-racking experiences when the pilot's wizardry in judging air currents had been fully proven, Paul and his companions tried to believe him. But, heading straight toward a rocky slope into which the plane would apparently crash the next moment, it was a bit difficult. Sure enough, however, the updraft lived up to its name. With a few blessed yards to spare it lifted them gracefully over the rim of mountain and deposited them on the tiny runway in a smoothly beautiful landing.

It was worth all the nerve strain. The study revealed conditions of tremendous challenge. In remote tribes they visited there were many members who had never been outside their own tribal territory. In some areas no man had ever traveled farther than five miles from his home. Disease patterns were extraordinary. In certain sections there was a ten per cent incidence of leprosy, but not a single case of tuberculosis. Foot deformity was shockingly prevalent among leprosy sufferers because they had no way of getting about other than on bare feet, and walking with anaesthetic feet up and down the rough jagged mountain sides was literally tearing their flesh and bones to pieces. They were walking their legs right into the ground! Paul saw cases of people walking about with missing feet, putting the whole impact of their weight on the ends of their tibial bones. Though the difficulty of getting such people to wear shoes might be almost insurmountable, the country presented unsurpassed opportunities for work in leprosy, especially the area of deformity prevention.

The trip was abundantly worthwhile. In an advisory capacity Paul was able to assist in developing the program already initiated by the government of New Guinea, which Dr. Clezy had been chosen to organize. They were able to find two mission hospitals, both Lutheran, which had very good facilities for operating, and the government agreed that these should be made the headquarters for the new program of surgery in leprosy. A close integration was recommended between the government program and the Mission to Lepers and other mission programs, involving cooperation between mission physiotherapists and the work of the government surgeon. During the next few months Dr. Clezy would prepare for his new responsibilities by becoming one of Paul's trainees at Vellore. Wonderful to discover that an impulse generated by a little team of workers in Vellore had helped spark a chain reaction of human concern which was stimulating a fresh appraisal of the problem on all continents, even on remote islands of the sea!

And so . . . passage to India again. As the plane bore him through the final arc of his globe-spanning trip, Paul contemplated his future.

The next year promised to be exciting: six months in Vellore, six in England, with frequent shuttlings on missions to other parts of the world. Would this continue to be the pattern of his life? Except for the separations from his family, it could be satisfying. The training centers in Africa and Venezuela would be only the beginning. He could spend years helping to organize both these and other such centers, and still vast areas of the world would be untouched.

But there were other possibilities. There was the need to develop better techniques of surgery. Or—how he would love to devote himself completely to research! Suppose he could help find some means of restoring pain! It was no more impossible than man's other scientific miracles. And how infinitely more important to the Sadagopans of the world than repairing their hands and feet!

Equally challenging was the thought of sharing his spiritual resources with others. How far he himself had traveled in his concept of God, from the bearded, majestic Figure with halo and scepter to the God of dynamic involvement in every battle of man's spirit, the God of D. N. A., the wonderful spiral nucleus that holds the code of every new living creature, and which, more significant even than the brain which it builds, must bear the imprint of the mind of God! Perhaps he could help others bridge the gap between science and religion, find Loving Purpose at the source of the whirling electrons and the spiral nuclei.

Life was too challenging. It offered too many choices. What a pity that a man had only one life to spend, one pair of feet, two hands, ten fingers!

Back in Vellore Paul was operating on a paralyzed hand. He had the forearm open and was testing muscle after muscle to make sure the tensions were just right. Each time a muscle was pulled a finger would move, bending or straightening at one joint and then another.

"Our new transplants must fit into the pattern of the whole hand," he told his assistants. "They must not dominate it, nor must they be slack."

At last the job was finished; the final stitches were being placed. Paul turned to the watching students. "What you have seen is only the beginning," he told them. "My work takes one hour or two, but now the real job begins. These muscles have been moved around, and this boy's brain must now learn where they are and what they can do in their new situation. This is where the whole team swings into action, physiotherapists, occupational therapists, all the people who are going to help this lad feel that the struggle of reeducation is worth the effort. Of all the people on the team, the patient is the most important."

The sleeping boy stirred a little and seemed about to waken. The assistants and nurses were busily applying dressings and plaster. They knew that once Paul was on his favorite theme, they would get no more help from him.

"You saw how slow and clumsy were the finger movements I produced by pulling on those muscles. Have you ever watched the fingers of a pianist? I still get excited every time I see that kind of coordination of mind and muscle. Every time a finger strikes a note, there has been controlled movement of a dozen muscles, supported by the balanced tension of scores of others. And the music you hear is the music of the mind interpreted by ten fingers in harmony. Now"—he turned to the physiotherapy trainee with matter of fact abruptness—"your job is to get those fingers linked up to the mind."

Minutes later, relaxed over a mug of coffee, mask under his chin, Paul felt a deep sense of frustration. It was wrong that the surgeon should always get the limelight. He could be only as good as the whole group. And how little he or any other member of the team was really able to accomplish! All the millions of leprosy patients in the world still needing help, all the unsolved problems! And life for himself already two-thirds over!

His gloves were off now. In a gesture expressive of his frustration he lifted his hand, its creases lined with little flecks of talcum powder, and impatiently flexed its fingers. Then he looked at them intently. Which one of them had performed that operation? The index finger, perhaps, or the thumb? He laughed aloud. Of course not. They were just instruments, tools of his mind. He could ask only one thing of them, that they be responsive, sensitive, obedient to his will. Just as God asked of him . . .

"That's what I am," he thought with sudden clarity, "just a finger. Or perhaps a thumb."

Frustration? Hardly! What more could any man ask of life than the knowledge that he was a finger or thumb among other fingers, and that the hand was the hand of God?

Epilogue

NEW HORIZONS

When we left Paul and his family in 1965, he was employed by the British Leprosy Mission, with his headquarters in England. The Mission had purchased a house for them in Ealing on Colebrook Avenue. As a major part of his work he was spending parts of each year at Vellore, at Caracas, Venezuela, and at Addis Ababa, Ethiopia, sharing his techniques of surgery and rehabilitation on three continents.

Paul wanted a medical career based in the United Kingdom, but he wanted one that would permit him to continue his leprosy work and provide time for travel. It was not difficult to secure a post, for he had all his qualifications, including his F.R.C.S. In fact, he had been offered two significant positions, one at the Royal National Orthopedic Hospital, where Professor Seddon was anxious for Paul to become his successor after a few years. But the highly secured English system of medicine required a certain number of sessions each week, which limited opportunity for overseas activity. It seemed he would have to devote himself solely to orthopedics or continue his full-time work with the Leprosy Mission, involving teaching and perhaps writing, but with little creative activity aside from the trips overseas.

In addition to Paul's travel and absence from the family under the Leprosy Mission, the new life in London was professionally unsatisfying for Margaret. By English medical standards she was regarded merely as a qualified doctor, not as the experienced ophthalmologist she had become at Vellore. She had never been able to take time away from Vellore or the family, either to sit for examinations or to take the special courses in ophthalmology offered only in England, where a period of residency was required. So now all she could secure in her specialty was outpatient work at ophthalmology clinics, where she seldom saw the same patient twice and there was little opportunity to develop personal relationships or to use her specialized skills.

Then suddenly another door opened. In 1965 Paul was on an extended tour of lectures in the United States and his usual teaching sessions in Venezuela. He came to Carville, Louisiana, site of the United States Public Health Hospital, the only institution for the treatment of leprosy in North America, where he gave talks on his techniques of leprosy rehabilitation at Karigiri, emphasizing how surgical reconstruction, hand and foot therapy, and the program for making shoes had all been integrated. After the lectures the director, Dr. Edgar Johnwick, approached him, face alight with enthusiasm.

"We've never had a pattern of rehabilitation like this at Carville. I am amazed at the progress made in India compared with that in this country. Surely our patients should have the same opportunities as those in India!"

Before Paul left, it was suggested by the Chief of Rehabilitation, Dr. Roy Phalzgraft, that Paul join the staff at Carville. He was intrigued. What an exciting challenge! But—exchange his own country for another? Of course it wouldn't be the first time. And what was his country? India, where he was born—England where he grew to manhood, or all the others where he worked for weeks at a time? Already he was a citizen of the world. Yet, the possibility raised a tremendous number of questions.

"Would I qualify for work here?" he asked Dr. Johnwick. Before even considering the offer, Paul had to know if he could do surgery and treat patients in America without taking further examinations. He was not about to go back and study medicine all over again. Another question: Would there be a responsible position for Margaret, an opportunity for her to practice her unique skills in ophthalmology? A third problem? Would he be permitted sufficient leaves of absence to continue his important work overseas?

These questions were easily answered. Dr. Johnwick immediately got on the phone to Washington, and before the day was over he had solved all the problems. Margaret could be offered a position, and both Paul and she could be granted permission to practice by the Public Health Service. Time for overseas visits could be arranged. Johnwick then took Paul to his home, where discussions continued. He had purchased an ocean-going boat, which was moored on Lake Pontchartrain near New Orleans, and both he and his wife Hazel had taken Coast Guard pilotage courses that qualified them for coastal navigation in the Gulf of Mexico. Shades of the past, thought Paul! He had gone to India with plans for building a boat to sail up and down the Palar River, and now he was being offered a job by an enthusiastic yachtsman who invited him to go sailing along the mouth of the Mississippi and into the Gulf. Another inducement!

Paul met other staff members eager for him to come—Oscar Harris, the chaplain, and his wife Juanita; the Brubakers, Merlin and Polly, former missionaries with children about the ages of the young Brands, who had just bought a horse. What fun, they suggested, for all the children to have horses to ride over Carville's large open fields and levee of the Mississippi right outside the front door!

Paul sat down and talked to his family on tape for a half hour, breaking the news of this amazing opportunity to continue with leprosy work, surgery, and research, yet with a base where the family could be together. With the increased salary he could offer the children a choice. They could remain in England and complete their courses, with holidays in Louisiana, or they could come to the States and go to school. What did they think?

"I'll know in a couple of months," he told Edgar Johnwick, then went on his way to complete his tour.

The tape arrived in England, and the family sat around and listened to it . . . once . . . twice . . . and again. There were varying reactions. Christopher was immediately enthusiastic. He had finished school and was quite uncertain about what to do. He was continuing his study but not really enjoying it, and the thought of going to America and starting over again gave him a sense of freedom and new perspective.

Jean was distressed. Another separation from the family after all she had suffered alone with her broken arm and paralyzed hand? Leave the new home she was so excited about helping to furnish? She had just started nurses' training at St. Thomas's Hospital, one of the world's best, founded by Florence Nightingale, and she loved it. Everything had seemed perfect. But now . . . Mary, who also was contemplating nursing, was ambivalent. The new country might offer real challenge. The younger children were excited by the prospect of adventure.

But all understood the significance of the offer to their parents. It would mean continued medical work in leprosy for both of them in orthopedics and ophthalmology, a veritable Godsend. All, even Jean, agreed that it must be accepted. The answer went back across the ocean— *Yes.*

Edgar Johnwick wanted Paul to come at once, that summer, but his conscience prevented him from agreeing. It was not the first time the troublesome voice of duty had occasioned a delay. While still in India, the year before assuming work with the Leprosy Mission, he had been told that the post of Professor and Chairman of Orthopedics was open at his old medical college, University College Hospital in London, and he had been encouraged by the staff to apply for it. What a temptation it had been, to go back as a professor in his own college! But to leave India suddenly would have been an evasion of responsibility. His work at Vellore had not been finished. He had sent a refusal, adding hopefully, "But if the position is still open in another year, I will be glad to apply." It had not been open. Yet he was sure he had done the right thing. And what had seemed at the time to be personal loss had created new and significant opportunities for service.

Now again conscience made him delay. He had important commitments. He must give the Leprosy Mission proper notice. They settled on January 1, 1966, for the big transfer. And again the delay had what seemed at the time unfortunate results, for during the second half of 1965 Edgar Johnwick suffered a heart attack and died. Though Paul was assured the invitation to come still applied, he felt an irreparable loss.

Christopher did not wait for January. As soon as the decision was made he packed his bags and left for the States, where he enrolled at Louisiana State University's northwestern branch at Alexandria, only three hours from Carville. He selected marine biology for a major, combining his interest in biological studies with his love for the sea. Jean decided to remain in England and continue her nursing studies. The rest of the family came to America on schedule, Paul arriving in Carville by January 1, the others following him during the month.

Between the time of Johnwick's death and Paul's delayed arrival, the acting director at the hospital had developed a different administrative setup from that planned by Johnwick. He wanted the Departments of Surgery and Rehabilitation to remain separate rather than combined under Paul's direction. As Chief of Rehabilitation, Paul was responsible for all its aspects: physical and occupational therapy, vocational guidance, social work. But he was only a consultant in surgery. Though he was usually called in on cases involving major or difficult operations on hands, surgery was not his prime responsibility, and the older surgeon in charge was sensitive to the fact that Paul had far more knowledge and expertise in hand surgery. A difficult situation! Paul solved the problem by taking only a minimal involvement in surgery and trying to make it clear to his colleague that he was there only as a consultant, not to diminish the work of anyone else.

Problems, yes, but as with his previous delay, this unexpected change in his responsibilities offered an even greater opportunity. He had had too much surgery in India, operating almost day and night, and when not operating, teaching. Now he could take time to read literature on the biomechanics of the hand and foot, to put all the things he had learned on a more specific basis, and to find out why the things that worked did work and how those that didn't work might be changed. So again what seemed to be loss resulted in unexpected blessing—another proof, as so many times in his life, that if he followed the dictates of conscience, he could always depend on God's leading.

Margaret's situation was entirely different. Carville had never before had a full time ophthalmologist. A Professor of Ophthalmology, Dr. Jimmy Allen, had come once a week from New Orleans, and, since she did not have board qualification in ophthalmology, Margaret welcomed his support as she started her new work. From the beginning it became tremendously significant. As in India, she found that great numbers of the patients developed eye complications that were not recognized until difficult to treat. She saw every patient in the institution at intervals and was able to detect and begin treatment on early lesions. She concentrated all her skill and intense concern on the most severe cases. Many patients, some of whom had been in the hospital for years, were blind or almost blind. Many had lost one eye and had only tenuous residual sight in the other. She worked with them day after day, healing ulcers, trying to prevent the onset of glaucoma and iritis and all the multitude of complications affecting the eyes of leprosy patients.

As years have passed, she has become recognized as one of the world's leading authorities on problems of the eye in leprosy, teaching numerous students in seminars at Carville. Many of these students come for training on their way to the mission field or other work in foreign countries. She has written many publications to aid in further understanding of the eye in leprosy. Often she goes to international congresses to make presentations on this very important subject, which she has made uniquely her own.

But most important and satisfying has been her relationship with the patients. She has the biggest and busiest clinic of any doctor in the institution. She combines regular and careful examinations with personal interest and encouragement that endear her to patients in a special way. "I am sure," one person commented, "she is the most beloved physician as well as the busiest in the hospital." And not the least of her contributions has been her involvement in the chapel program through speaking, planning, singing in the choir, and playing the violin.

"I think," Paul reports with gratitude, "it has been a wonderful thing for her that God has guided us to this place, where she has a ministry that she never could have had anything comparable to in England, perhaps not even in India."

To Margaret, as well as to Paul, have come new spiritual insights from the work at Carville. And often it has been one of the patients from whom she has received even more inspiration than she was able to give. For instance, there was Julian.

He was an elderly patient. Like most other leprosy sufferers, he had loss of sensation. One leg had been amputated. He had lost the sight of one eye, and vision in the other one was becoming increasingly defective. Because of the lack of sensation in his eye, he did not blink enough, and the dry cornea threatened to reduce his vision even further. His hearing was fair with a hearing aid until the battery began to run down. He was very sensitive to such loss because he was dependent on his remaining sight and hearing to communicate and read, which was his greatest recreation. When unable to hear or see, he developed hallucinations that people were trying to harm him. Unfortunately, after surgery on his eyelids to alleviate the dryness, he developed some post-operative swelling and for a day or two was unable to use what little sight he had. His hearing aid had begun to lose its power. His lines of communication were closing.

"Don't worry," Margaret tried to tell him. "We will fix your hearing aid."

He knew someone was speaking, but could neither hear nor see. In a desperate voice he shouted over and over, "I cannot see, I cannot see, my battery is dead. Poor Julian! Poor Julian!"

It was such an odd statement that for a moment she felt like smiling. Then she sobered, thinking, "How dependent our spiritual sight is on our spiritual 'battery.' I know mine is. I'm sure that if I allowed the Spirit to keep my 'battery' charged the way it should be, my insight into people's real needs and problems, how to reach them and help them, would be more acute."

There was another patient who, like many at Carville, had come from Puerto Rico. At arrival his condition was very poor. His hands and feet were grossly infected. He had lost all skin sensation, had no sense of pain, heat, cold. Both eyes were badly inflamed, a condition likely to result in blindness. During his first two years at Carville his small amount of vision dropped markedly because he had developed complicated cataracts. Unfortunately, in order to treat the massive infections of hands and feet, he had been given an antibiotic that was toxic to his auditory nerve and he became quite deaf. Also, he was rapidly growing blind. There was so much damage to his nose that his sense of smell also was nearly gone. Only his sense of taste remained. He was treated with clofazamine, one of the modern drugs for Hansen's disease, and his general condition was improving. But without sensation, sight, hearing, and smell, he was dying inside. He just lay in bed curled in the fetal position, his only contact with the outside world the taste of food put in his mouth.

But the time came when his disease was sufficiently under control so that Dr. Jimmy Allen, the consultant, and Margaret felt it was safe to operate on his cataracts. But how could they communicate with him to get the necessary "informed consent"? There was no way. Though he had a perfectly active brain, they could not get through to it. Finally they were able to work through the Puerto Rican police, who contacted a relative, and permission was secured. When the day came to take him to the surgery, he did not resist. It was as if he knew that something was being done to help him, willing for it, whatever it might be. He was quiet, cooperative. They operated, and he regained about 40 percent of his vision. He awoke, came alive once more. Though he could not feel, hear, or smell, he could *see!* He began going regularly to chapel where, though he could do nothing more than watch, he was once more a part of a fellowship, a part of the world. He knew that he was with people who cared about him.

"How like us!" thought Margaret. "God so often sees what we really need, what He wants to do in our lives, yet we are too insensitive to recognize our need, to let Him do it. So we don't give our 'informed consent,' and He can't do it without our consent. He is just looking for us to say, 'Here I am, Lord. If you want to do something with me, do it, because I know that You care.'"

So, like Paul, Margaret found Carville a school for spiritual growth as well as a new and challenging opportunity for professional service.

Paul's visits overseas began almost as soon as he was established at Carville. It was embarrassing to walk out so soon after he had arrived, but it had been made clear to him that he should regard overseas consultations as a part of his job. The U.S. Public Health Service was anxious that its world outreach be recognized, and to this end any publicity about helping leprosy-work in countries in Africa and Asia was helpful. So Paul was able to go in his official capacity, "on duty," although it was usually the American Leprosy Missions that paid the travel fare.

The project that Paul and Stanley Browne had helped start in Ethiopia had finally become established. Many Missions and Foundations in Europe and the U.S.A. had contributed, and staff had been recruited; buildings had been added to the old Princess Zenebeworq Hospital, and now patients were under treatment, and students coming from many African countries. The project was called ALERT (the All-Africa Leprosy and Rehabilitation Training center). The name emphasized the importance of rehabilitation in the concept of the center, and Paul felt that he must make sure that the surgery and physiotherapy got off to a good start. He was able to recruit Dr. Luther Fisher, an orthopedic surgeon trained in hand surgery, who had just come out of the army. Luther had been looking for an opportunity to serve in Christian medical mission work overseas, so was ideal for the job. He, Martha his wife, and their five children had settled in Addis Ababa. Now Paul went off to spend time with them to help them adjust, and to learn about the special problems of surgery in leprosy.

That was the easy part. It had become second nature to Paul to adapt hands and feet to the limitations of having no sensation. It was fun to go over it all with a willing young surgeon and have it filtered through a fresh and well-trained mind. Paul always said that teaching was a learning experience for him. He loved to have his ideas challenged, modified, or even reversed as the result of that kind of interaction.

The difficult part was fitting it all into the framework of a new culture and environment in Ethiopia. The stigma of leprosy was more severe there than in India. Transportation was more difficult. Roads were almost non-existent in some of the areas where leprosy was most prevalent, so patients had to walk many miles, barefoot, for treatment. They arrived with fresh ulcers on their feet, and infections that made surgery impossible until they had had time in hospital to heal their wounds. For obvious reasons patients must be treated in or near their homes, hence medical and surgical teams had to make regular trips into the country. Land Rover ambulances with four-wheel drive were sent from Europe and were driven over some of the roughest country Paul had ever experienced.

On some of these trips Paul found his concerns turning in a new direction. This was no sudden change, but an emphasis or perhaps just a new awareness of what he had known most of his life. His work had been in helping individual people and bringing health to the sick and strength to the crippled. All the time he had seen signs, first in India and now in Ethiopia, that the root cause of many diseases was poverty and malnutrition. He had also observed that the earth, which sustains all of life, was being depleted: its water polluted, its forests retreating, and its deserts advancing until the lives he had tried to save would join the multitudes dying for lack of food and water.

A fresh awareness began on one of the Land Rover trips in Shoa Province at the start of the rainy season, at an elevation of 11,000 feet.

The rolling hills of the Ethiopian Highlands were intersected by deep canyons and ravines, cut by rivers that ran into the Blue Nile. The sturdy Land Rover often had to follow a winding roadless course up and down the margins of these ravines. On one occasion, having seen a group of patients in a village on the south bank of a canyon, the Ethiopian doctor looked across and waved to a small group of patients within shouting distance who were gathered on the north side. "We'll be with you soon," he yelled. "Soon" meant two hours: one hour following the canyon upstream to a point where it could be forded, and then another hour downstream on the other side. There were no bridges, and the canyon was too deep and its walls too steep to be traversed.

Waiting for the patient's records to be checked, Paul wandered off with an Ethiopian friend, Ato Abebe, who served as translator. In talking with a peasant farmer working on his field of growing tef (a fine grain that was a staple in that part of Ethiopia), he noticed that the field was covered with large boulders, and the tef was growing up between the stones. There was no way the field could be tilled or harvested without working one's way between and around these great stones. It started to rain, so Paul and Ato Abebe walked back toward the shelter. The path led along the side of the canyon, between the field of tef and the chasm. Ato Abebe pulled Paul away from the edge, warning that the path might break away in the rain and plunge him sixty feet into the stream. Even as they walked, he saw it happen. A crack developed just about a foot from the edge and a great clod of soil slipped a little, then fell away, breaking into fragments on its way down into the stream.

"That happens all the time," Ato Abebe commented. "Our Ethiopian soil is going down into Egypt every time it rains."

Feeling strangely disturbed, Paul turned back to talk to the farmer, who was still working in the rain. He spoke to Ato Abebe. "Ask him why he does not roll these boulders off his field, and use them to build a wall at the edge of the canyon. He would be left with a clear field where he could till and harvest more easily, and he would stop the loss of the soil into the canyon." It seemed such an obvious solution that Paul's voice may have carried a note of contempt that the farmer had been stupid enough not to think of it before. Ato Abebe knew the answer to Paul's question, but he let the farmer say it first. "This way at least I have a field to cultivate,'"he said sadly but without bitterness. "My family has been growing tef here for generations, and we are allowed to do it because the field looks worthless with all these rocks. If we made it look good, the Amharas from Addis Ababa would soon be here with papers drawn up by lawyers to say that the field really belonged to one of them. They would threaten to evict me, and then say that I would be allowed to continue farming, but that I must give half of the crop to them, as payment of rent. I prefer to keep the rocks on the field to make it look bad—that way I can keep my land." Ato Abebe was an Amharic himself, but he nodded his head to confirm the truth of what the peasant tribesman had said.

Paul went back to Addis Ababa determined to find out more about the loss of soil, and about the hardships of the peasants of Ethiopia. The next week he went to visit Bud Prince, an American who was the representative of A.I.D., the official channel of assistance from the U.S.A. Bud had lived in Addis Ababa for many years, and knew most things that occurred. He was cheerful and helpful but not optimistic. He said, "You have stumbled onto the tragic reality of Ethiopia. It used to be a country of forests in which the trees held the soil and kept up the water table. In the last few generations most of the forests have gone. Now the soil is running down the slopes into the rivers and into the Blue Nile, to Egypt and the sea. The only people who could have stopped this process were the emperor and his chosen cabinet, and perhaps the church. They are all Amharas, and collectively they own all the land. They make all the laws, and they do not want to lose control or see other tribes become owners of farmland."

Paul nodded, "But couldn't we convince them that the country is being ruined by the loss of soil and that the workers and peasants will never be interested in conserving their land if they have no stake in the future?" Bud smiled and shook his head. "We've tried. The Ford Foundation and the Rockefeller Foundation have been here, and they have had experts study the whole economy and the farming methods. They have offered big plans backed by financial aid to stop erosion, improve agriculture, and to build up food supply and exports. We in A.I.D. would have joined them in this, but there was one condition that we all had Bo insist on: No progress could be made unless there was land reform, so that farmers could have a real interest in improving their own land."

"What did the government say about that?"

Bud sighed and paused. "I believe the emperor really wanted to go along with this program, but he could not carry his cabinet ministers with him, or even the church, which owns a lot of land. None of them wanted to see other tribesmen owning their own farms. So the Foundations packed up and went home." Paul had gone to Ethiopia primarily to establish the All Africa Leprosy and Rehabilitation Center. He was not there to advise farmers or to plant trees. He knew that foreigners who tried to intervene in politics were often told that it was none of their business, and were asked to leave. But he found himself lying awake at night and seeing the crack in the soil, and the great clod of earth falling away into the stream. He felt he *had* to do something.

Paul had come to know some important people in the capital city, including the Minister of Agriculture. He also knew and admired the emperor, Haile Selassie II, who had been very helpful in the establishment of the leprosy project, and who had taken the trouble to come just a few months before and declare it officially open. The emperor's grandchildren used to go to Clarendon, the same school in England that Jean and Mary and the other Brand children attended, and they knew each other. When he first met the emperor, Paul had mentioned the grandchildren by name and had been rewarded with a smile of recognition and welcome from the diminutive but very regal Emperor. Perhaps now Paul could use these contacts to find out whether land reform could come to Ethiopia. The emperor was a Christian, and head of the Ethiopian Orthodox Church, one of the oldest Christian churches in the world. Surely the Church would want to help the poor peasants to obtain justice.

He went at last to Onni Niscannen, the Executive Director of the ALERT project, to ask his advice. Onni was from Sweden and had been in Ethiopia most of his life. He had worked with many organizations supported by Swedish charities. He had been an athlete, and had gained popularity as a trainer and coach to the Ethiopian Olympic teams. He had helped Abebe Bekele, the Ethiopian marathon runner, who was to win two successive Olympic gold medals for Ethiopia. Onni knew the emperor well, and was willing to talk with him. However, he was clear that the approach should be slow. "We are here for leprosy work, and any idea that we introduce should start from there. There is a Swedish Baptist Mission working with leprosy patients, and they have developed a farm under the direction of a Swedish farmer who is experienced in working with poor soil conditions. He and his wife—and now their son—are doing a wonderful job in rehabilitation by farming. Their farm workers used to be beggars in Addis Ababa. The emperor has donated hundreds of acres of good farm land to the mission. There is a scheme for providing a plot of land for each worker once he is trained. I must take you there and let you see something good that is happening right now."

They climbed into a little single engined Cessna airplane, operated by the Missionary Aviation Fellowship, and flew over some mountains, then down to a sloping area of farmland just on the edge of an escarpment that overlooked the plains below. The pilot flew low over a grass airstrip, to drive away some buffalo grazing there, then circled and brought the plane down to a bumpy landing.

The Swedish farmers met Paul and Omni, and took them on a tour around the farm. Paul's depression vanished, for a while at least, as he saw what could be done by a couple of dedicated Christian farmers, supported by a kindly emperor. Scores of leprosy patients, once beggars in Addis Ababa, were working in a long line, harvesting tef. Each carried a sickle, and sang strange Ethiopian melodies as they worked in rhythm, cutting and stacking grain in field after field. The land had been contoured to prevent rain from running down the slope. Also, trees and bushes had been planted at intervals to form wind breaks and to support banks to hold the soil. It was a wonderful example of how farming should be done in the Highlands of Ethiopia.

Paul could not forget his own professional responsibility, and he had to point out to the farmers that some of the leprosy patients had wounds on their hands, caused by the way they were holding their sickles. Their hands would sometimes slip down gradually from the handle and come to rest on the back of the blade. Not feeling any sensation or pain, they would not realize that each stroke of the sickle was cutting into their hand, until the sight of blood usually alerted them to change their grip back onto the handle again.

It did not take long to show them how to fix a thick rim on the end of the handle so that the hand could not slip off onto the blade. That one simple adaptation probably saved dozens of fingers from destruction during that harvest.

Paul had gotten so used to thinking in terms of stress on hands that it sometimes amazed him that others would miss such an obvious danger. Then he remembered that it was only days ago he had become aware of the need for conservation of the soil in Ethiopia, while to the Swedish farmers it had been obvious from the start.

Paul talked to them about his own concern and about the possibilities for change. They agreed about the need, but felt that it would not come by political action, but only by pilot projects like their own. They hoped other missions would come and that bigger demonstration projects would make an impact on the thinking of the government and the landowners.

Meanwhile the ALERT project was making friends in new ways. It happened that in those early years Luther and Paul were the only qualified orthopedic surgeons practicing in Ethiopia. The queen in the royal family, Princess Teneneworq, had been so impressed with the new ALERT hospital that when one of her young grandchildren fell and cut a tendon in her hand, she told the mother, her daughter, to take the child to ALERT. "But that is a leprosy hospital!" exclaimed the princess. "Leprosy or not, it has some good surgeons, and they will take care of the hand." The Princesses did not question the word of the royal matriarch, so Paul had the privilege of operating on the hand of the littlest princess. All went well, and the news soon got around that the emperor's own grandchildren were attending the Leprosy Hospital at ALERT. Before long the children of cabinet ministers and well-known industrialists were walking up the same path to get orthopedic help for their deformities and injuries.

Paul was delighted. The actual numbers of nonleprosy patients he treated was not enough to crowd out any leprosy patients, but the effect on the stigma of leprosy was enormous. People who heard and saw leading citizens attending ALERT could not go on believing that leprosy was an "untouchable" disease anymore.

Before Paul could take advantage of his new standing with the royal family and bring up some of his new concerns about trees and land, his time was up. He had to go back to Louisiana to pick up the threads of his new job.

In the rehabilitation research at Carville, Paul encountered the usual frustrations over lack of money. It was difficult to obtain necessary funding for this new program from the existing hospital budget. Then came one of the really wonderful and climactic coincidences of his life. He had a phone call from Mary Switzer, Commissioner of Vocational Rehabilitation in the U.S. Department of Health, Education, and Welfare in Washington.

"We hear you've come to the United States, and that's just what our country has been waiting for!" she greeted him. "It gives us an opportunity to apply in America what you have been working on in India. Can we help in any way?"

As a result of their conversation she decided to come to Carville, certainly one of the most important government officials who had ever visited the hospital, and she brought with her a retinue of advisers. Paul had become friends with this remarkable woman when both had been honored as recipients of the Lasker Award in 1960, and she had been fascinated by his work with leprosy. Even then he had admired her dynamic, perceptive, compassionate qualities as well as her unusual administrative ability. Now he discovered that their meeting and mutual understanding had been a portentous experience.

After her tour of the institution she met with the director and other administrators and delivered what amounted to an ultimatum: "This institution is a relic of the past," she told them. "We are still looking on leprosy as a custodial responsibility. We don't put enough emphasis on research. We're lagging behind India in this respect."

Mary Switzer was a woman with phenomenal leadership ability. It is fitting that the building now housing the offices of the U.S. Department of Health and Human Services, one of the largest in Washington, is named the Mary Switzer building. She had been developing vocational rehabilitation as a major branch of the Department of Health, Education and Welfare, and she convinced Congress that it pays to rehabilitate the handicapped to make them independent. She included a new proposal for leprosy rehabilitation in the program and told Paul, "If you will start really serious rehabilitation research, we will fund you from Washington."

An unexpected and exciting challenge! Paul and his colleagues set to work. They developed a research program with many different emphases: health education; the forces applying to insensitive feet and hands; the breakdown of insensitive tissues; the patterns of muscle strength in the absence of sensation. One of their major objectives was to develop a system to serve as a substitute for pain, which might warn patients when their hands or feet were in danger.

The program was ambitious. They hired nine new staff members, including a health technician, another physical therapist, and a shoemaker. The Department of Electrical Engineering at Louisiana State University accepted a contract under the program. Their assignment was to develop tiny pressure-sensing devices, called transducers, which would respond to different degrees of pressure by giving different audible signals. These transducers were to be attached to fingertips and to the soles of the feet so that the way in which people used their hands and feet would be reflected by a tone heard through signals carried by fine wires up the patient's arm or legs to a hearing aid. The sound of a high tone would signal that too much force was being used on a certain part of the body. These little devices were meant to imitate the function of normal pain nerves.

The research team also developed a pressure-sensing sock equipped with tiny capsules that contained a blue dye, designed to break at a pressure greater than that normally experienced by a person walking. If a shoe fitted badly or there was some prominent bone that took more pressure than the rest of the foot, that part of the sock would turn blue and reveal the location of the danger. Then the design of the shoe could be changed to compensate for this pressure. The socks were made by the patients, providing not only protective therapy but profitable employment.

The simple, cheap socks were more successful than the tiny transducers, which proved both expensive and unreliable. It was impossible, Paul found to his regret but also to his ever-increasing reverence for the marvels of the human body, to imitate the beauty and wonder of the normal nervous system. Each little artificial nerve ending cost 450 dollars, and tended to break down in the rough-and-tumble of work at a carpenter's bench. It was hard for patients to know just which finger was giving the pain signal, so they were slow to respond effectively to relieve their stress. Because in the normal body some parts can quite safely accept pressures that are much too great for other parts, another problem was to determine the level of force or temperature at which danger should be signaled. Also, parts of the body that have been recently bruised or burned are more vulnerable to further damage at lower pressures than are normal tissues. A normal pain system takes note of this, and normal people feel pain at a lower level of pressure or temperature after they have recently been slightly injured. When the tissues are healed, the threshold of pain returns to normal, too. These amazing adaptations of the human body could not be imitated by machines, especially when the devices had to be small enough to fit on fingertips without making a projection there that would get in the way of work the hand had to accomplish.

The biggest problem proved to be the fact that patients got accustomed to the sound of noises in their hearing-aids, and did not take any notice of the message being sent. They would proceed to do what they wanted to do even when a noise in their ear said "Stop! This may harm your finger!"

Looking depressed, one of the engineers came to Paul. "We shall never succeed, however good our sensors are. We are trying to imitate pain, and it is obvious that pain does not protect unless it HURTS. It is no use just telling a person that there is danger in what they are doing if you know that they want to do it. They simply are not interested in knowing how much pressure they are putting on their fingers, or on their feet. If you want us to imitate pain, we have to hurt. Surely there must be a way to hurt these folk enough to make them care!"

Although Paul had come to the same conclusion, he had not come to the point of taking action. Now he asked the professor of electrical engineering, Dr. Tims, how he thought it could be done. "I have a graduate student," he said "and he would like to make a special project out of this. He thinks he can make a little shocking coil, based on a battery. We could fix it so that when a signal comes to the coil, a pair of electrodes would spark a high voltage, at low current. If the electrodes were affixed to moist skin, they would give a harmless but quite painful shock. Of course, it would have to be on skin that could feel pain." He told me that the whole device could be made about the size of a thumb.

"Okay, let's try it," Paul replied. "People with leprosy always have normal sensation in one or two places in the body that are protected from cold, and the obvious one for this would be the armpit. We could strap the coil into the axilla, and use an electric shock in place of the tone in the hearing aid; or we could use the tone for early warning, and the shock as the actual pain."

So they tested it. It worked. A few patients tried it, and they proved that it did hurt, and that it only caused pain when they were using a great force on their hands. It seemed that it really might be a very good idea. Until one day when Paul was watching patients in the manual arts department, a young patient was trying to undo a rusty bolt on a motorcycle engine that he was repairing. He seemed to be having trouble of some sort. Paul saw him reach under his shirt to his armpit and switch off his shocking coil, then put all his force on the wrench, loosening the nut on the bolt, after which he reached under his shirt and switched his shocking coil on again.

Paul turned and left the room. He called the engineers and gave his verdict, but they already knew the weakness of the system. Paul just had to put it into words. "We have failed," he said, "We shall never succeed in imitating pain until we can have a system in which the switch is out of reach. We cannot force people to accept a painful jolt unless they want it, and it seems that nobody wants pain. We may as well quit spending time and money on a system that will not be effective."

It was a depressing conclusion, but it allowed the engineers freedom to concentrate on systems that would educate patients, and show them how to avoid trouble. They made pressure-sensing gloves and socks that would change color when too much force was used. These were helpful in an educational sense, but never became the real protection that pain is.

They also began to develop more protective devices to serve as physical barriers against damage. These included special shoes that were rather like the shoes that had been used in India. These at Carville were better than those from India because the engineers were able to make better and more detailed analyses of the actual pressures experienced by feet during walking, and how people change the way they walk when they cannot feel. The partnership between engineers and shoemakers turned out to be one of the most productive parts of the whole research enterprise.

The new opportunities for research led also to a far better understanding of the best muscles to use in transplant surgery. It had always bothered Paul that the choice of a strong muscle to replace a paralyzed one was a sort of guesswork. There are so many factors in a muscle that make it unique for the job for which it is intended. Some muscles contract only about a half-inch to control their joints, others three or four inches. Some can pull with great force, others are geared more to bending a little finger. Paul set up a workshop to study the action of muscles and make mechanical analyses. Now, while operating, he knows the mechanical capability of every muscle and can actually choose the right one for the movement desired, test it at the time of surgery, and achieve a better balanced hand for the patient.

The study of nerves led to another remarkable coincidence. During his first journey to the United States, he had searched for someone who could explain to him the pathology of the nerves in leprosy, but had found only one person able to throw some light on the problem, Dr. Derek Denny-Browne, the eminent Boston neurologist. At this point, Paul needed a specialist in neurology with a background in nerve pathology who could set up research on the causes and patterns of paralysis. Finally, he advertised for one. There was not much response because leprosy was considered such a strange and exotic disease, but who should see the advertisement but Dr. Denny-Browne, then nearing retirement! He had among his pupils a brilliant young man, Tom Sabin, just at the end of his residency and already a specialist.

"Look at this!" he said to Tom. "I know that fellow Brand. He came to see me twenty years ago. He's an orthopedic surgeon who not only knows his job but *thinks*—and if he's wanting the help of a neurologist, here's a wonderful opportunity. You'd better apply."

So Tom Sabin came, and during these wonderfully productive years of working with Paul, he made the studies that demonstrated irrefutably that the germs of leprosy cause damage to the nervous system in relation to body temperature, causing lack of sensation in the cool parts of the body—such as the hands, feet, ears, nose— leaving the warmer parts, such as the fleshy sections of the cheek, undamaged. Paul had long believed this was so, had published an article about his suspicions years before, but had had no actual proof. Now, by carefully mapping all the sensory patterns of the lepromatous patients, they indeed found that there was a close correlation between the thermographs (the heat photographs of the body), and the sensitivity. The cool parts became insensitive, the warm parts did not.

One curious case gave further corroboration. This patient's hands were insensitive, and had been so for years, yet were beautifully preserved. In fact, his whole body was almost completely insensitive from head to foot except for the warm areas like the armpits. But he pointed out a little spot on the palm of one hand near the base of the fifth finger, which had normal feeling. Checking the patient again and again, they repeatedly found normal sensation in the middle of an otherwise insensitive hand. Then they took an infrared photograph and found that the little area was hot!

"Why are you all so interested in my old birthmark?" asked the patient.

"Birthmark?"

"Yes, I was born with a purple birthmark, and they treated it with carbon dioxide snow, but I can still feel it pulsating."

So . . . it was explained. This vascular abnormality, called a cirsoid, had brought a lot of extra blood to that small area and kept it warm, and he had never developed active leprosy in that spot. (A little fortuitous demonstration of their discovery that leprosy bacilli don't like warm parts of the body!) This knowledge was used by Dr. Kirscheimer, Chief of Pathology Research, and led to his choosing the armadillo as the best animal for the study of the bacteriology of leprosy. Because the armadillo has a temperature about eight degrees below that of humans, it forms an ideal environment for leprosy bacilli. It is now recognized worldwide as the best source of live Mycobacterium leprae.

From this new location in the West where leprosy is not prevalent, Paul's advances in treatment and surgery have been applied to ailments other than leprosy. People with paralysis and insensitivity caused by gunshot injuries, stab wounds, diabetes, radicular neuropathy, and spina bifida began coming for help. As years passed, the staff at Carville became known throughout the country as teachers and consultants for these ailments, especially diabetes. The staff also gained expertise as therapists for the elderly who, lying in bed or sitting in wheelchairs, tend to be unaware of developing pressure sores and ulcerations.

"It probably costs more than a billion dollars a year," Paul believes, "this problem of elderly patients who do not move enough. They take pain remedies to keep them quiet and comfortable, so they do not feel the urge to move normally and change their position. Sooner or later they develop bedsores or pressure ulcers. It's an enormous problem".

Paul's contribution to treatment of the elderly and of diabetics has stimulated medical attention all over the country. Patients who previously might have required amputation of injured or infected feet may now be fitted with special shoes to save their limbs. Many diabetes specialists and orthopedic surgeons believed, as doctors of leprosy formerly believed, that the feet of diabetics break down as a result of the disease, or just as a result of poor blood supply. They have needed to recognize that even if the blood supply is poor, most diabetic feet will last quite well if the absence of pain sensation is recognized as the main problem. In each case Paul and his staff outline very simple measures to make sure that a patient wears properly fitting shoes, that the pressure inside the shoes can be checked as the patient walks, that he does not walk too far or too fast, and, if the feet are already damaged, that rocker shoes are provided. Now, when Paul is asked to speak at seminars or write articles or chapters for textbooks, the commonest requests are in the field of diabetes and of feet.

Feet! Like hands, they have become for Paul in these recent years a "magnificent obsession." He loves to feel that in his ministry he has become an advocate for feet. "Hands speak for themselves," he says, "but feet are usually hidden in socks or shoes. Painful feet cry and nobody hears, because their owner is ashamed to show them to others. Insensitive feet suffer damage but have forgotten how to cry. They all need an advocate. As I study these feet," he says, "often they are stinking, ulcerated, distorted, wounded, repellent. But I feel somehow God has given me the special grace of loving feet. I have a T-shirt that has two big footprints across the chest and big bold wording, 'Feet Need Love, Too.' And they do."

He finds it a joy to minister to an elderly person who has deformed and painful feet. It is usually a woman who is confined to a room because she cannot walk, and feels inadequate and ashamed. Paul takes a sheet of a new moldable material made of polyethelene foam, heats it until soft, and then presses the patient's foot into it. After about three minutes when the material has cooled and set, he lifts the foot away, cuts away the excess foam, and puts the new insole into a shoe that has been made with extra depth to accommodate it. Because the molded soft insole supports every part of the sole evenly, the patient can usually stand and walk without pain. The result is overwhelmingly surprise, delight, and gratitude, because independence and dignity have been restored.

Paul speaks often of the time when Christ washed the disciples' feet. Recently in Dallas at a meeting of the Christian Medical Society he was giving lectures on medicine, evangelism, and how God can use people in medical work. The Society gave him an award very different from the many plaques, medals, statues he has received. It was a block of wood topped by a little earthenware basin containing a towel. It bore his name and the words "Servant of the Year."

"It made me very happy," he commented, "but I must emphasize that it is no sacrifice for me to serve feet. I want to praise God for this special grace that has been given to me. I love feet. I go to my foot clinic and I caress these feet and help to heal them and put them in shoes they can wear. It's a source of real joy to me."

Always Paul has been impressed with the function of pain in the body. Now more and more he realizes what a blessing pain is to the human race. "I find in the United States," he writes, "a great fear of pain. Perhaps television advertising has emphasized this with all the companies competing to market their pain-relieving drugs. Their message is that pain is a terrible thing; an enemy. In this mass of advertising nobody ever says that pain is a good thing, that you shouldn't immediately suppress it but listen to it, because it's your body talking to you, trying to help you understand how to live better. Instead of just taking aspirin for nervous tension headaches, one should first pause and ask, 'Why do I have the nervous tension that gives me the headaches?' Instead of taking Alka-Seltzer for stomach ache, I should stop and wonder, 'What have I eaten to give me a pain? I must remember not to eat those things again. Or maybe I should not eat so much so fast.' Coughing, too, is a blessing. It may be telling you of something down there that needs to come out; or perhaps that you are inhaling an irritant. So you shouldn't simply suppress your cough, but listen first to what it is telling you and try to minimize the things that cause it."

This philosophy has been a recurrent theme in his writings and in the increasing number of lectures he has been called to give around the country.

What of the more intimate family life of the Brands during these years? What of those delightful, unpredictable children? As might be expected, they have been pursuing courses as original and adventurous as climbing trees and scaling parapets in India. The tightly meshed web of family has stretched to encompass far places and a diversity of careers, but the filaments are as strongly intertwined as when all were under one roof at the bungalow in Vellore.

Christopher, after graduating with good grades from Louisiana State University, was planning a career in marine biology when he learned that although he was a British subject, as a student in the United States on a resident visa he was still subject to the draft. Opposed to the Vietnam War, but not wanting to evade his responsibilities by running away from the draft, he enlisted voluntarily. As a volunteer he had more choice in the type of work he would do, and hopefully, could avoid the armed combat he opposed. He was sent to Thailand and worked in Food Quality Control, where, perhaps because of his interest in marine biology, he became an inspector of fisheries.

After completing his term of service, he returned to Louisiana

State University for a master's program in food science with emphasis on sources of food from the sea. Upon graduating, he joined the Environmental Research Laboratories, an organization in Tucson that specializes in the use of solar energy and in growing food in deserts and other environmentally hostile regions. His first assignment in the Sonora desert of Mexico was a lonely existence made bearable only by his love of music and reading.

He was thankful in 1981 for transfer to a mariculture farm on the north shore of Oahu. This new and exciting life included wind surfing and congenial friends, especially a girl named Kelly, who shared his enthusiasms. When E. R. L. assigned him to Singapore to prepare a new farm, he immediately asked Kelly to marry him in the ten days before his departure. Paul, off on his annual spring visit to India, was unable to attend the wedding, but Margaret, Patricia, and Estelle were there and saw the happy couple off to Singapore on their "working" honeymoon.

Since that time, Christopher has become an expert in the science of growth of shrimp and other seafood. He and Kelly have worked mostly in the tropical areas where warm water speeds growth. They have a lovely daughter named Evelyn in honor of Granny Brand, whose life has influenced everyone in the family.

Jean, while lovingly agreeing with the family's decision to move to America, had remained in London. After finishing nurses' training, she felt more and more called to do full-time Christian work. She spent three satisfying years as a student in the London Bible College, earning a Bachelor of Divinity degree and improving her talents in speaking, teaching, and developing her lovely singing voice and skill with guitar. Then she felt called to go to India as a missionary—not as a nurse, but as a Bible teacher.

The trip to India was an exciting adventure in itself. With three other young people she offered to drive a Land Rover ambulance overland from England to Nepal! The vehicle was registered in her name, and she became the chief driver. It was an eventful journey through Belgium, France, Italy, Yugoslavia, Iran, Afghanistan, and on to India. In Iran there was an accident: the Land Rover turned over, requiring extensive repairs in Tehran. For two months Jean remained there with the vehicle, acquiring wonderful friends and many noteworthy experiences. Finally arriving in India, she delivered the Land Rover, and moved to Bombay.

There she worked in a community church for six years, helping it develop creatively, and living very simply in a tiny one-room apartment. Then, feeling that the church was strong enough under its indigenous leadership, she returned to England, first to Southampton, later to Teddington, and joined one of the house-church community fellowships comparable to the church in Bombay, India. Initially she earned her living by nursing, but found the duty hours somewhat inflexible, often conflicting with commitments to her church service. Drawing upon her natural flair for color and design, she became an interior decorator. Now she has her own little business, and works on her own time schedule.

"It's interesting," Paul comments, "that Jean has in a sense struggled with her own self-image in the role of spiritual ministry that has traditionally been filled by men. Though she is equipped by her degree and training to become a minister of a church, the organization in which she is working takes the view that women have a different ministry. Now her church has asked her to write a book on the role of women in the church. When I visit her, I am impressed by the love and appreciation people have of her spiritual values." Jean's book was published in England by Triangle Books, and is titled *A Woman's Privilege*. In it she works her way through the Bible, pointing out how very special and yet how very different, as compared to men, is the role that women have played in the kingdom of God. She sees men as usually more suited to leadership roles, and women as those who create the atmosphere in which both men and women work best in the service of the Lord. The book has opened the way to many speaking engagements and to a growing ministry in counseling and in Bible teaching.

Mary, the gay, the lively, the irrepressible—what of her? She came with the family to Louisiana, and entered Louisiana State University School of Medicine in New Orleans for nurses' training. There she met Jim Jost, a quiet, thoughtful, medical student—a fit complement to the bubbling and impetuous Mary. They fell in love and were married. Mary insisted that the wedding be held at Carville in the patients' chapel, where the family were active worshipers and workers. Like all the Brand children she felt that the battle against leprosy as well as the warm fellowship with leprosy patients was a family endeavor, and she wanted the patients to share in her happiness.

After her graduation Mary secured a position in New Orleans and helped support Jim through his final year of medicine. Then, for his internship and residency program they moved to Minneapolis, "into the cold, cold north," as Paul described it. When Jim began a private practice, they settled in St. Cloud, Minnesota, where he practices general surgery. They now have four children: Daniel, Rachel, Stephanie, and Alexandria, and a lovely home that is often a center for holiday gatherings of the Brand family.

"Mary is as full of beans and crazy as ever," Paul says, "and is bringing up the children in much the same way the Brands were brought up, with plenty of scope for originality." Mary produced the first of the grandchildren, a boy called Daniel, in November 1972, which was about the time Paul was feeling low about his failure to make a workable pain system, and about the poor outlook for people who had no normal sensitivity to pain. True to his orthopedic training, Paul had to check out his first grandchild to make sure Daniel had normal hands and feet and spine. Daniel checked out A-1. There was one test Paul had to include: He waited till Mary was out of the way, then took a pin. He did not want to really hurt the little fellow, but had to know if he had a normal pain system.

It was normal! Paul looked with delight as young Daniel pulled his hand away, and looked angrily at the pin. Then he looked at his finger, then at his grandfather and back again to the pin. He was learning fast. He was learning about pins; about grandfathers, too! Paul had spent hundreds of thousands of dollars to employ expert engineers to design and make a pain system that would offer just one pain sensor for each finger, but had failed to make it work. Here was this baby, born of a mother who knew no engineering, yet equipped with thousands of pain sensors in each finger; each sensor was geared to a threshold just right for the tissue it was to protect, and all of them effective and with built-in mechanisms for supply of energy and nutrition, designed to last for eighty to a hundred years without need of maintenance; and the switch was out of reach!

Paul felt a sense of failure as a bio-engineer. But as he handed Daniel back to his mother, he had a feeling of awe and wonder at the perfection of the engineering design of even the smallest human being, and a new reverence for the Creator of all mankind. He had been thankful for pain sensation before, but perhaps never with such intense appreciation as now.

Estelle. How often it's the gentle, quiet ones who have the most interesting and unique experiences! At Louisiana State University she earned both a bachelor's and a master's degree in education. Living at home, she made many friends. Some of the young men were anxious to be more than friendly, but she was never sure enough of her feelings to say "yes." In the chapel choir at Carville are both staff and patients. Sylvester Pauelua from Hawaii, one of the choir members, had suffered a mild form of leprosy for many years. He had some insensitivity in hands and feet, but not to the extent of severe deformity. His face was unmarked by the disease, he was strong and in good health, and the leprosy was becoming negative. Singing in the choir together, Estelle and Sylvester became good friends.

The friendship did not end when he returned to Hawaii. Letters kept coming. They kept praying. It was not altogether a surprise when two years later she announced simply, "We want to get married."

Her only concern was that any children they might have could possibly develop leprosy. Paul could not give them any firm assurance, although the probability was extremely low. The family loved Sylvester, and gave their approval.

Estelle took a teaching position in Honolulu, and they decided to have the wedding service in Hawaii. The two families made a happy arrangement. The Paeluas would provide everything for the wedding and reception; the Brands would bring their family to Hawaii. No small task, with Jean in India, Patricia and Pauline in England, Mary in Minnesota, and Christopher in Mexico! Paul calculated that it took 150,000 miles of air travel to bring just the immediate family, including children and grandchildren! But it was worth it—a rare holiday and reunion for the family, as well as a joyous occasion. The Paeluas and their church family roasted a five-hundred-pound pig in the traditional Hawaiian manner, and served it as part of a feast along with octopus and other traditional Hawaiian festive foods.

After a year or so in Honolulu, Estelle and Sylvester moved to a plot of land on the "Big Island" of Hawaii, which Sylvester had owned several years. There was no electricity, piped water, sewers or other amenities of civilization. To start a fruit plantation, they had to clear the land before planting the guava and other trees. With the help of local church members, they also built their own house.

Once, Paul and Margaret had telephone calls from Mary and Estelle on the same day. Both wanted to share with their parents an exciting new development.

"Our swimming pool is in," reported Mary, "and we're using it for the first time!"

"At last," announced Estelle with equal excitement, "we were able to install a real kitchen sink, and we're using it for the first time!"

Afterward Paul and Margaret could not decide which of the two children was more excited. One thing was clear—the compensations of simple living on the good earth are fully comparable to the advantages of a more affluent lifestyle. Since that time the first little house has given place to a larger one, also homemade with the help of a professional carpenter from the church. This one is built on poles in true Hawaiian style, and is to be wired for electricity.

There were other important additions. Before Christmas of 1981 Margaret went to assist at the arrival of her namesake, Margaret Ipolani Pauelua. Three years after that came young Stephen, as tough and strong as his sister was dainty and sweet. With the demands of a growing family, Estelle continued teaching, driving into Hilo each day to teach a church preschool class. Sylvester also plies his craft as a trained draftsman. It's a simple life, yes, but one with the basic joys of love and fellowship and close relationships in their little Hawaiian church.

Patricia was nearly twelve when the family moved to America, moving from a girls' school with strict discipline to a less structured coeducational setting. What changes the new school brought! A very pretty girl, she was the immediate focus of male attention. She was having a marvelous time and was on top of the world. However, after a year or two she came to her parents in a thoughtful mood.

"You know," she said soberly, "I'm having a good time and it's a lot of fun, but I want to make something worthwhile of my life, and I really need to study. Could I go back to boarding school, to Clarendon in Wales?"

They were amazed but delighted at this evidence of maturity. She returned to Wales, graduated with excellent grades, and later entered University Medical College, in London, her parents' old school. After obtaining a research degree in the physiology and anatomy of the nervous system, she went on to finish her medical course and to complete an internship in London. Later, in residency training in American hospitals, she chose anesthesiology as her specialty. At the University of Washington in Seattle, a center that has pioneered in local and regional anesthesia and in the management of pain, she studied the way pain can be relieved by blocking certain nerves with longlasting local injections so that people with intractable or incurable cancer or other diseases may be able to lead pain-free lives.

Having completed her residency program, Patricia was ready to begin looking around for a position that would keep her in the

Northwest, near to the mountains and the skiing, and the waters of Puget Sound. She joined a group of anesthesiologists in Seattle, and settled down to work.

However, others had also been looking around, and liked what they saw of the young woman doctor who cared for the patients who slept on the operating tables. In the face of some stiff competition, Dr. Michael Peters carried off the prize, and not long afterwards the whole family gathered together again to welcome a new member of the clan. Patricia and Michael were married in the garden of their beautiful new home on the edge of the cliffs of West Seattle, overlooking Puget Sound.

As Paul stood with the minister, giving the challenge to the young couple, he could look out over the water and see the snowcapped Olympic mountains in the distance. As time was bringing this new experience to the family, the towering mountains symbolized the unchanging love of God.

Marine biology, theology, nursing, teaching, medicine! What other career could be left for the youngest of these versatile and adventurous offspring? *Pauline*, the baby, always felt a bit left out. She was so young when the family left India that she has few memories of it. When she was still playing with dolls or climbing trees the others were flying off into distant places and activities. But her time would come.

After moving with the family to America and attending school there, she followed Patricia back to England and graduated so brilliantly from Clarendon that she could choose any higher university training or profession. Again following Patricia, she applied to medical schools and was accepted at more than one, including Newcastle, where John Webb was settled and delighted at the prospect of being her surrogate father. But Pauline identified her real love as literature, history, and drama. Finally she came back to the states and entered Wheaton College, where she majored in English literature and won a writing award.

After graduation Pauline moved back to England, and found an interesting job working with Program Production at B.B.C. Television in London. Like Jean, she also found deep spiritual satisfaction in the same organization of community charismatic churches that are based on house groups. Here in this unstructured fellowship both young women found a spiritual home, a vital, personal, satisfying fellowship. In Pauline's case, however, this stage was to last only a few years. A handsome young Wheaton graduate, Mark Nelson, whom Pauline had known only superficially while at college, appeared on the scene in London.

He was spending a year in London in the course of a Ph.D. he was completing in philosophy at the University of Notre Dame. Feeling lonely in the great city, he turned to his Wheaton address book and found that Pauline Brand was also in London.

As the friendship became closer, Pauline knew that a crisis was on its way. Mark was clearly bent on marriage and life together on some college campus in the U.S.A. His rivals for Pauline's heart may have included a man in the shadows, still uncommitted, but also included London and England with which Pauline had fallen deeply in love.

The year drew to a close, and Pauline drove Mark to London Airport where he was to catch his plane back to the U.S.A. During this last trip Mark again asked Pauline if she was ready to become engaged, but the answer was still "no." Finally, with baggage checked, came the last farewell at the security barrier through which only one could pass.

Amidst the hurly-burly and noise, in a voice almost too soft to hear, she said, "Ask me again, Mark!" This time the answer, loud and clear, was "YES." They had time only for a swift dance of farewell around the astonished security staff, then they parted, to meet again much later in America just weeks before the wedding in the town of Farmville, Virginia. The reception was held at Hampden Sydney College, where Mark was now a lecturer.

After becoming a journalist on the staff of the local newspaper, and then a part-time teacher at the local state college, Pauline has settled, for a time at least, on freelance writing. This is because she needs to give priority to the demands of a new member of the family, Eleanor Clair Nelson, who arrived on the scene in April 1988 and immediately took charge of everybody within the sound of her voice. The eighth grandchild has proved to be a magnet for both grandparents, and, in their unbiased opinion, is really a very beautiful child.

So the web has been stretching, expanding—each strand still tightly bound to the center of family love and concern, down among the lush plains and bayous of Louisiana, a country in climate and environs very much like their beloved India.

The Public Health Service Hospital at Carville occupies a beautiful riverside plantation of some four hundred acres, about seventy-six miles up the Mississippi from New Orleans. The number of leprosy sufferers in this part of the country has been growing since the arrival of the first slaves from America. In the 1890s Carville became a center for these sufferers who had been segregated under appalling conditions in the city. The center has been gradually transformed through the years until now, under government ownership and supervision, it is one of the most modern and well-equipped hospitals of its kind in the world. Renamed "The National Hansen's Disease Center," it is important on a worldwide basis in the fight against leprosy.

Paul and Margaret were as much at home on the hospital station in Carville as they had been in the bungalow on Dr. Ida's college campus. Their house overlooking the Mississippi on the plantation property was old but commodious, one-story, like most Indian bungalows, but large enough to accommodate all the children should they come home at once. Over the attic is a little room with windows facing out on the river, an ideal watchtower for observing the colorful panorama of river life. Bird-watching, too, was a favorite pastime. Their beautiful oak and pecan trees abound in as many exotic species as the neems and pipals and banyans of India. Here, it is the mockingbirds that sound their melodious early morning tocsins.

Though Paul never did realize his dream of sailing in the Gulf, the family soon began to take full advantage of the surrounding waters. Soon after arriving, Paul built a canoe. Its wood frame was covered with a skin of heavy vinyl fabric, and the family, especially Christopher and Paul, spent many enjoyable days camping, navigating rivers, exploring remote bayous, and bird-watching. More than once they managed to sink the craft, but with the usual family scorn of danger or disaster they got it up, and started again.

Carville was no remote backwater. About halfway between New Orleans and Baton Rouge, it offered limitless opportunities for wider activities. And for Paul and Margaret it was a focus of worldwide involvement. Trainees come from many foreign countries where there is far more leprosy but poor educational facilities. Some come just for the various short courses that are held through the year, but others come to spend six months or more and to work in a department to learn much more. Margaret, being one of the very few ophthalmologists in the world who specializes in ocular leprosy, frequently has a trainee working with her. She has become adept at communicating with a mixture of signs and pointing, as her trainees may well be expert doctors but far-from-fluent in English.

With memories of India, she is always willing to teach diagnosis and treatment of eye conditions to paramedical personnel, nurses or therapists, who come from countries where there are no doctors able to see the eye complications of leprosy patients.

Nothing makes her so happy as an opportunity to visit Brazil or Turkey or some other country where one of her previous nurse-ophthalmology trainees is working. Several of these young women have managed to absorb Margaret's enthusiasm as well as her technical instruction. They have succeeded in identifying large numbers of cases that show early signs of eye damage, and putting them on treatment that will save the eyes. Trainees have also managed to identify cases having immediately serious problems needing the attention of a specialist, and have been able to interest a local ophthalmologist and convince him or her that these special cases are of such scientific interest that they should be seen—even if there is no way the patient can pay a fee.

Paul goes early each spring to attend the meeting of the governing board of Karigiri, of which he is chairman. After a succession of different types of governing organizations, the leprosy research and training center is now an independent charity, supported principally by the same two missions as formerly: the Leprosy Mission International based in London, and American Leprosy Mission, Inc. Paul usually spends a few weeks at Karigiri and Vellore during these annual visits. He feels the need to keep up with changing personnel and policies, and is in demand for lectures and chapel addresses at both institutions. For the past few years Margaret has also been returning to India at the same time, to conduct the annual course in ocular leprosy for doctors. Her travel for this course is funded by the Christoffel Blinden Mission.

It is always a joy for Paul and Margaret to see the progress made by the institution under the superintendency of Dr. Ernest Fritschi, one of Paul's first assistants. With an F.R.C.S. from England and practical experience in Indonesia and Ethiopia, Ernest has brought to Karigiri skillful leadership and strong Christian concern. The place has become internationally famous. Undoubtedly it is today one of the best field research centers and training places for leprosy workers in the world.

Ernest has wrought remarkable changes in the place. When the site was selected, it was a totally barren area with ground sloping up toward the rocky eminence of Elephant Hill. There was not a single tree, just little thorny scrub and dry stringy grass that the goats kept eaten down to the ground. The first superintendent, Dr. Herbert Gass, began planting trees, but Ernest started a forest! Registering Karigiri as an ecology project with the Indian government, Ernest planted hundreds of trees and arranged for a tank cart drawn by bullocks to keep them watered until their roots were deep enough to tap the subsoil. The transformation is unbelievable. Like Paul, Ernest is an ardent ecologist.

"It isn't just that the vegetable and animal species were created for the benefit of the human race," Paul says, "but that it's all one, a great concept in which all of creation has a mutual interdependence. Unless we have concern for the soil and water and plants and animals that we so ruthlessly exploit today, it will mean irreparable loss. We are turning both Africa and America into deserts. Louisiana, where I live now, has beautiful rich soil that has all come from Iowa and Ohio and Kansas and other states. Agribusiness is interested only in quick profits, and loves wide treeless plains that can be tilled by giant machines, leaving soil vulnerable to rain and wind. We are creating water famine for the future by emptying deep sources faster than they can be renewed, and then contaminating what is left with toxic wastes."

Because of these convictions, Paul finds his return visits to India a bittersweet experience. He loves to see the mountains of his birthplace where ancient farming practices still are carried out, with terraced fields to save the soil. This land has been farmed for thousands of years, but still has topsoil remaining. The West with all its technology, he thinks, can do little for the Indian farmer except help him get better strains of grain to improve his yield. He is saddened to see the plains of India, where population pressures are too much for the land, where trees are being cut for firewood, and the water table is falling every year. But when he comes back to Karigiri, and sees the forest where once there was barren ground, he knows that even one man can make a difference.

On one of these annual visits Paul took the first step toward a new phase of life that was to bring rich spiritual fulfillment. His friend John Webb, then director of the Christian Medical College and Hospital, had a request.

"Would you give a series of talks to students and staff, perhaps eight or so lectures on your favorite topic—medicine and religion, or if you prefer, science and faith?"

It was a challenge. Paul chose for the series a revision of the series of lectures that he had been in the habit of giving as an elective course to final-year medical students. He had called these lecture-sermons, "Doctors' God." They stressed medical ethics and covered aspects of the human body as related to the Christian's function as a member of the body of Christ—the bones, skin, blood, hands, feet, nerves, muscles. He had first outlined one of them, on "the hands of Christ," years before at the Christmas party for the leprosy patients who reside in the hostel called Number 10.

The lectures that year were given in a new auditorium at the Vellore Christian Medical College, a memorial to Dr. Ida, its founder, and they were taped.

"They should be in a book," was the enthusiastic response.

Paul brought the tapes back with him to Carville and dutifully tried to transcribe them. But—a book? He could talk so much more coherently and effectively than he could write! Evenings were his only time to work on the project, and by then he was so tired that his mind could not formulate ideas. But he tried. He even submitted a manuscript to a publishing company. "Not enough material for a book," was the reaction. "Perhaps you could turn it into some magazine articles."

Then came a fortunate development. Philip Yancey, a young author, editor of the magazine *Campus Life*, was gathering material for a book called *Where Is God When It Hurts?* and was traveling around the country interviewing people who had suffered pain and loss. He was putting all these interviews together to write about human suffering for those who believe in a God of love. Paul had previously written several pamphlets for the Christian Medical Fellowship, one of which, *Escape from Pain*, outlined Paul's idea that pain is good and a great gift from God. Having read this, Yancey came to Carville and spent several days talking with Paul and interviewing patients to discover the harm that comes to people who cannot feel pain. He found himself in agreement with Paul, and the two men found they had much in common. On impulse, Paul decided to show him his own manuscript and ask his opinion.

"May I take it with me?" he asked.

Returning later, he said to Paul's surprise, that not only could the material be made into a book, but there might even be enough for two books. He would feel it a great joy and privilege if he could do some research and add some ideas, and he would try to loosen up some of the rather closely woven style of writing. Could they write the book together?

The writing of the first book with Philip Yancey was a totally new experience for Paul. He had become used to being the leader in any project he undertook. As a surgeon he led the team in the operating room. In research the others carried out his ideas. As teacher or preacher, he was up front while others listened. Now, with Philip the writer, Paul was the learner. He learned that some of his paragraphs were too long. He was too wordy. He had to find more anecdotes to lighten the flow of his argument. When he had none, Philip was not put off. "Come on, Dr. Brand! You can't tell me that after thirty years as a surgeon you have no experiences to illustrate the point you are making! Or perhaps if you have no experiences, you should not make the point at all. It is only valid if it has been proved in real life." So Paul had to go back and think and remember. He also drew Margaret into the project because her memory was often better than his. Sure enough, there were plenty of people who came to life again after years of forgetfulness, and their stories did indeed make the chapters much more readable.

The manuscript shuttled back and forth between Carville and Chicago, and sometimes Paul and Philip were able to get together to thrash out some points and review progress. Paul was surprised at how much Philip was able to contribute even in the areas of biology and anatomy, where he was not the professional. Many of the interesting and little-known facts about the human body that appeared in the book came from Philip's reading in the library, rather than from Paul's stock of knowledge. It was Philip who realized that the nonmedical reader would appreciate these little-known facts.

So the first book, containing about half of Paul's original material, was finished. It was titled *Fearfully and Wonderfully Made* and was published in 1980. It became an award winner and top seller. Then they set to work on completing the project by bringing out the second book, titled *In His Image*. Both books eventually were brought out as paperbacks, and are often sold as a pair, which was how they were first planned.

This writing has proved a great blessing to Paul. It has forced him to clarify his thinking and put into concrete form his basic philosophy of life. And the response from readers has been a revelation. Hundreds have indicated that the book has brought them a new understanding of their worth and function in God's world.

Many of the responses have been from people who, for one reason or another, have despised themselves, who were in some way crippled or deformed—perhaps an obese girl or a paralyzed boy. And many have discovered the beauty of God's work even in a paralyzed leg or a disfigured face, recognizing that there is a marvelous harmony and beauty in all the millions of cells that form their bodies. Paul's writing has shown them that they also are essential elements in the body of Christ.

In their student days in London both Paul and Margaret had been influenced by the Christian Union, part of the wider organization known as the IVF, the Inter-Varsity Fellowship of Evangelical Unions. This was composed of small groups of Christian students in each university and college around the country. As they had moved up into their hospital studies, they attended the medical branch of this organization, the Christian Medical Fellowship, made up of doctors and medical students. During the period of intellectual stress, while young Christian students were being taught theories that seemed to conflict with their faith, it became really important to meet together and think through the relationship between their medical knowledge and their Christian faith. Paul served for a time on the Executive Committee of the IVF and appreciated the great men and women who were its leaders. In later years, in India, he was to serve the Indian students in much the same way he had been helped in his early years.

Now, fifty years after those student days, Paul was drawn again into the organization that had been a help to him. In the intervening years Christian Medical Fellowships and Societies had been formed in many countries all over the world, then had formed an Association that would link them together and organize international gatherings and congresses for mutual help. The president of this International Christian Medical Dental Association was a physician world renowned for his work in leprosy, Dr. Stanley Browne, who had been a missionary in Africa for much of his life, and who had helped Paul in the search for a suitable site for the ALERT training center in Ethiopia.

An International Congress had been planned for 1986 in Cancun, Mexico, and Paul and Margaret decided to attend. Just weeks before the Congress an urgent letter came for Paul carrying the sad news of Dr. Stanley Browne's sudden death, and asking Paul if he would be willing to stand for election as president in Stanley's place. Not only that, but would Paul please accept the committee's request to give the keynote address that Dr. Browne would have given at the start of the Congress!

This new responsibility for Paul did not involve any administration, but it did put him in a position of spiritual leadership among

Christian physicians at a critical time. Medicine and surgery were making huge strides into new areas of control of the process of life and health. Organ transplantation, genetic engineering, in-vitro fertilization of the human ovum, intensive care units that could keep biological life going long after the brain was dead—these and other life-support systems raised ethical questions that all doctors were concerned about. It was important that Christian doctors should be in a position to know where to draw the line when some new scientific advance seemed to call on them to act in a way contrary to their faith. They wanted to know the biblical point of view, but the Bible and the Church had no clear teaching on some techniques that were both too new and too complex to have been studied adequately. Suddenly Paul found himself being pushed forward into being a spokesman on issues that he himself had not thought enough about.

The plus side of this new responsibility was that it brought Paul into contact with groups of Christian doctors all over the world. He would sometimes go to a country such as Japan for a surgical conference, or to New Zealand for a tour sponsored by the Leprosy Mission. While there he would be able to meet with doctors or students in each major city, see their work, and pray with them. Sometimes he would speak at a broader gathering of doctors and hospital workers and challenge them all with the claims of Christ and with the need to serve. It was a special joy when, from time to time, he would be able to meet a doctor who had been his student at Vellore, and who was now putting into practice the things he had learned from Paul years before.

It was becoming clear to Paul at Carville that his own broadening ministry was now pulling him away from his daily work too much. It was time to retire from direct medical care, and devote himself to the writing and teaching that God was blessing in a new way. It was hard to say goodbye to the staff and patients who had become part of his life, but it was even harder for Margaret to do the same with her patients. Paul had been involved in research and teaching more than in direct day-to-day care of patients. Margaret was with her patients all the time, and they loved her and had come to depend on her in some unique way. She always had a listening ear for their troubles and concerns, even when these had nothing to do with their eyes. They would think up a reason to go to the eye clinic. ("This eye has been itching lately.") But it was obvious that the real reason for the visit was that somebody had been unkind or that a word of encouragement was needed, and nobody could give that as well as Dr. Margaret.

So there were tears at the farewell party that the patients gave, and many of the tears were from the blind and those with few friends. They clung to Margaret, and her tears mingled with theirs as she knew that without them there would be a big gap in her own life as well.

Patricia and Mike, in Seattle, had found a little cottage that they thought would be ideal for the parents. It was close to their home, and it had a lovely view over Puget Sound.

So it was packing time at Carville. The cottage would not contain even half of the goods that had accumulated over the years at Carville. Finally, after garage sales and give-aways, the moving van set off, and Paul and Margaret climbed into their little car to drive three thousand miles to the Pacific Northwest—to new friends, a new church, and new responsibilities.

An anticlimax to an active, vigorous, productive career? Hardly! For all his life, Paul believes, God has been leading him, preparing him for his final phase of activity that may well be the most creative and productive of all.

A winding-down of the biological, physical phase of his life, perhaps, yes. Biological growth, as he often says, comes to an early climax. But there is another dimension of life (call it wisdom?) that involves the integration of knowledge and history and experience and can come only in later life.

"I believe," says Paul, "that people in their fifties and sixties and even seventies are better able to give a balanced leadership than some of the younger people who would be inclined to rush off on a new idea without the realization of what past experience has contributed."

For example: Just recently Paul was assisting a brilliant young surgeon to perform an operation on a leprosy patient's face. It was a long and tiring procedure. The young doctor was operating on his own, with Paul merely in the background, helping, suggesting. But there were several times when Paul could foresee problems and answer questions of judgment impossible for even a very skillful person without the benefit of experience.

Physical . . . mental . . . and then finally, peak and climax of all life's phases, the spiritual. Perhaps only in later years can this part of life come to full fruition. As Paul says, whereas the physical goes up and down, the spiritual should go up and up. So at last, as he commented about his incomparable mother, Granny Brand, when she had reached her nineties: "The spiritual becomes the only significant part of being. At that stage it just shrugs off the temporal, the housing, the physical cloak, and is then wholly spirit, ready to rejoin its Maker."

"It's wonderful to me," he continues, "that God is able to lead a person, in a sense without one's conscious planning or volition, through years that, while one is active and vigorous and bubbling with ideas, may well be as much preparation as achievement."

For nearly seventy years he has experienced this divine leading, but only now does he feel able to discern its pattern. He remembers the agony when in his early twenties he thought he was following the will of God, turning down medicine and going into building trade education; then, feeling this a mistaken calling, following what had seemed God's guidance in entering the Missionary Training Colony. Then came the later impulse to study medicine. Surely that was of the Holy Spirit, in spite of raised eyebrows from family and snide remarks from others. "What is Paul doing now? Is he going to spend his whole life being trained? Why did he spend four years in the building trade if he was going to finish up a doctor? What next?"

Then India, with no special purpose in view, certainly no suspicion that he would be working with the problem of leprosy! All of these impulses at the time he had not fully understood, yet all revealed themselves as necessary designs in the pattern of his life. Even the building training had been vital for effectively rehabilitating his leprosy patients by teaching them the use of tools or for studying the mechanics of muscles during these years of research. Strangely enough, many people unacquainted with him personally would refer to him now as a medical bioengineer because of his work and writings in the field of engineering as related to hands and feet, pressures, muscles and their internal forces. Truly God has worked in mysterious ways, leading him when he was least aware of guidance.

One of Paul's greatest gifts, equal to his medical skill and scientific proficiency, is his ability to communicate.

"Religion," he believes, "is communication. The agelong effort of the Holy Spirit is to communicate, and it can be done only by person to person, one person sharing the presence of the Holy Spirit with others."

For sheer enjoyment Paul's favorite activity these days is teaching and preaching. He no longer feels he has to worry about pleasing people; whatever name he has made for himself or failed to make, is already done, so now it is a matter of trying to please his Lord—and (why not?) enjoying himself! The enjoyment comes across. It probably adds punch to what he is saying.

At a recent convention of Evangelical Medical Missions, held in the new Billy Graham Auditorium at Wheaton College, Paul was giving the morning Bible studies. His subject one day was "Fruit Bearing," and he was trying to reconcile the diverse objectives of those who think medical missionaries should have the spreading of the gospel as their main goal and those who feel that, as doctors, they should concentrate on medicine. Suddenly he brought out from under the podium a large bunch of luscious purple grapes and held them up.

"What do you think about when you see grapes like this?" he asked. "I think how nice they would be to eat. I am sure the disciples thought that when Jesus was talking about the vine and the grapes. . . . In fact these look so good I think I'll eat some right now." And Paul proceeded to start eating several grapes with loud sounds of gustatory pleasure emerging from the microphone. He also began to spit out the pits in all directions. In the riot of laughter there must have been some who felt the whole charade was a bit demeaning to the solemn occasion and to the clean auditorium now dotted with grape pits.

Suddenly Paul became serious. He asked the crowded audience, "If you stand back and look at what I have just been doing, what is its significance, in the widest, cosmic sense? I have just been planting a vineyard in the Billy Graham Auditorium. Unfortunately, the birds of the air—pardon me, I mean the janitors—will probably sweep away most of those seeds, but perhaps one or two will lodge in a crack and germinate. In any case, if I come back next year, I am going to look in the garbage pile and see if I can find my new crop of grapes. I ate the grapes because they are delicious. But the real biological purpose of grapes is to spread the seed. Now, as Christian doctors we are to be delicious; our lives and our work should commend themselves so that people come to us because they want what we have to share with them. In so doing the seed of the gospel is being spread and planted. That is our real purpose."

On another occasion when Paul had to preach he marched up the center isle of the church in his bare feet and announced his text,

"How beautiful upon the mountains are the feet of him that beareth good tidings." After announcing that he really wanted to talk about bearing the good news of the gospel, he said: "But I first want to talk about beautiful feet. My feet are beautiful, and I like for you to see them. They are beautiful because I walked barefoot a great deal in my childhood and continue to today, whenever I can, and I have never worn constricting shoes with pointed toes."

He went on to express his anger at the fashion shoe industry in the West and at the barbaric way women are almost forced to wear shoes with high heels and pointed toes. By the time they reach old age, most women in the United States have developed bunions, corns, and other foot problems. "If women want liberation they should begin with a battle for liberation from shoe fashions. This is a proper subject for a church service, because it is an insult to God's creation when we distort and cripple beautiful mobile strong feet. We do honor God when we care for our bodies and keep them healthy. They are then better to carry good tidings."

So we find Paul a happy man, with a wonderful wife, walking barefoot along paths that may not always be conventional but are always fresh and exciting; eating grapes and spitting out seeds; enjoying the wilderness, the mountains and the sea; feeling a part of all life and an advocate for its preservation; retiring soon from structured employment and finding perfect freedom in the service of the One who is the true God and our eternal life.